BIG BOOK OF BART SIMPSON

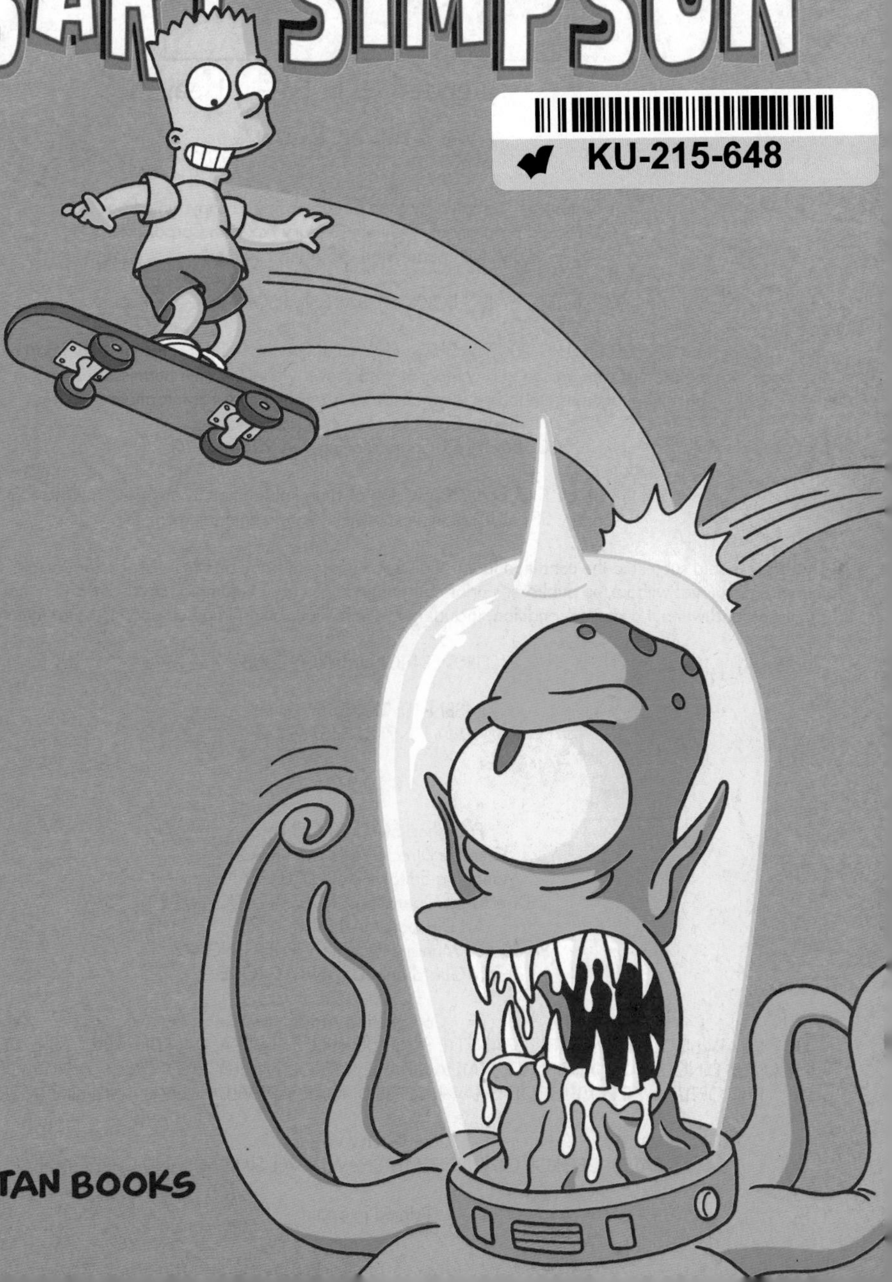

TITAN BOOKS

Dedicated to Burpo:

How you ended up in Kitty Heaven
we'll never know.

BIG BOOK OF BART SIMPSON

Published in the UK by Titan Books, a division of Titan Publishing Group, 144 Southwark St.,
London, SE1 0UP, under licence from Bongo Entertainment, Inc.

FIRST EDITION: MARCH 2008

ISBN-10: 1 84576 944 9
ISBN-13: 9781845769444

4 6 8 10 9 7 5 3

Publisher: MATT GROENING
Creative Director: BILL MORRISON
Managing Editor: TERRY DELEGEANE
Director of Operations: ROBERT ZAUGH
Art Director: NATHAN KANE
Production Manager: CHRISTOPHER UNGAR
Legal Guardian: SUSAN A. GRODE

Contributing Artists:
IGOR BARANKO, KAREN BATES, JEANETTE BOSE, JOHN COSTANZA, DAN DECARLO, MIKE DECARLO,
FRANCIS DINGLASAN, JASON HO, NATHAN KANE, CAROLYN KELLY, SCOTT MCRAE, BILL MORRISON,
PHIL ORTIZ, MIKE ROTE, SCOTT SHAW!, CHRIS UNGAR, ART VILLANUEVA, AND MIKE WORLEY

Contributing Writers:
JAMES BATES, GEORGE GLADIR, SCOTT SHAW!, GAIL SIMONE, AND CHRIS YAMBAR

Printed in Spain

TABLE OF CONTENTS

5 BIG FAT TROUBLE IN LITTLE SPRINGFIELD

16 GRRRL-WHIRL

23 CLOSE ENCOUNTERS OF THE NERD KIND

34 BART'S DAY AT THE ZOO

44 TALENT HUNT

49 MAXIMUM BART

54 FUTILITY BELT

63 TERROR ON TRIOCULON PART 1

69 TERROR ON TRIOCULON PART 2

74 TERROR ON TRIOCULON PART 3

80 BATTLE OF THE BOY BANDS

85 SKY-HIGH BART

92 WHO WANTS TO WIN A
POCKETFUL OF
QUARTERS?

107 QUANTUM COLA

113 BULLY FOR YOU

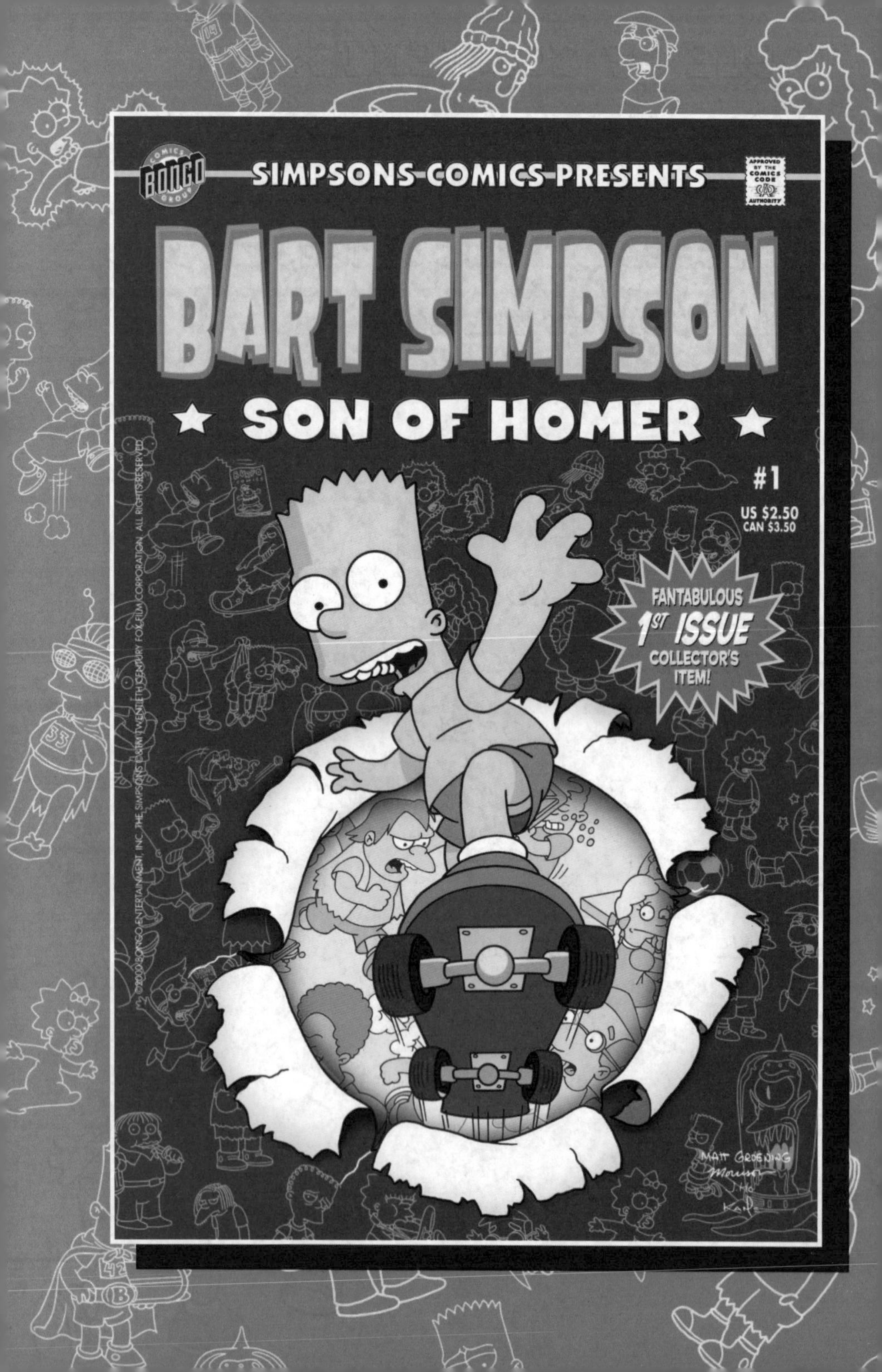
BONGO COMICS GROUP
SIMPSONS COMICS PRESENTS
APPROVED BY THE COMICS CODE AUTHORITY
BART SIMPSON
★ SON OF HOMER ★
#1
US $2.50
CAN $3.50
FANTABULOUS 1ST ISSUE COLLECTOR'S ITEM!
©2000 BONGO ENTERTAINMENT, INC. THE SIMPSONS ©&™ TWENTIETH CENTURY FOX FILM CORPORATION. ALL RIGHTS RESERVED.
MATT GROENING

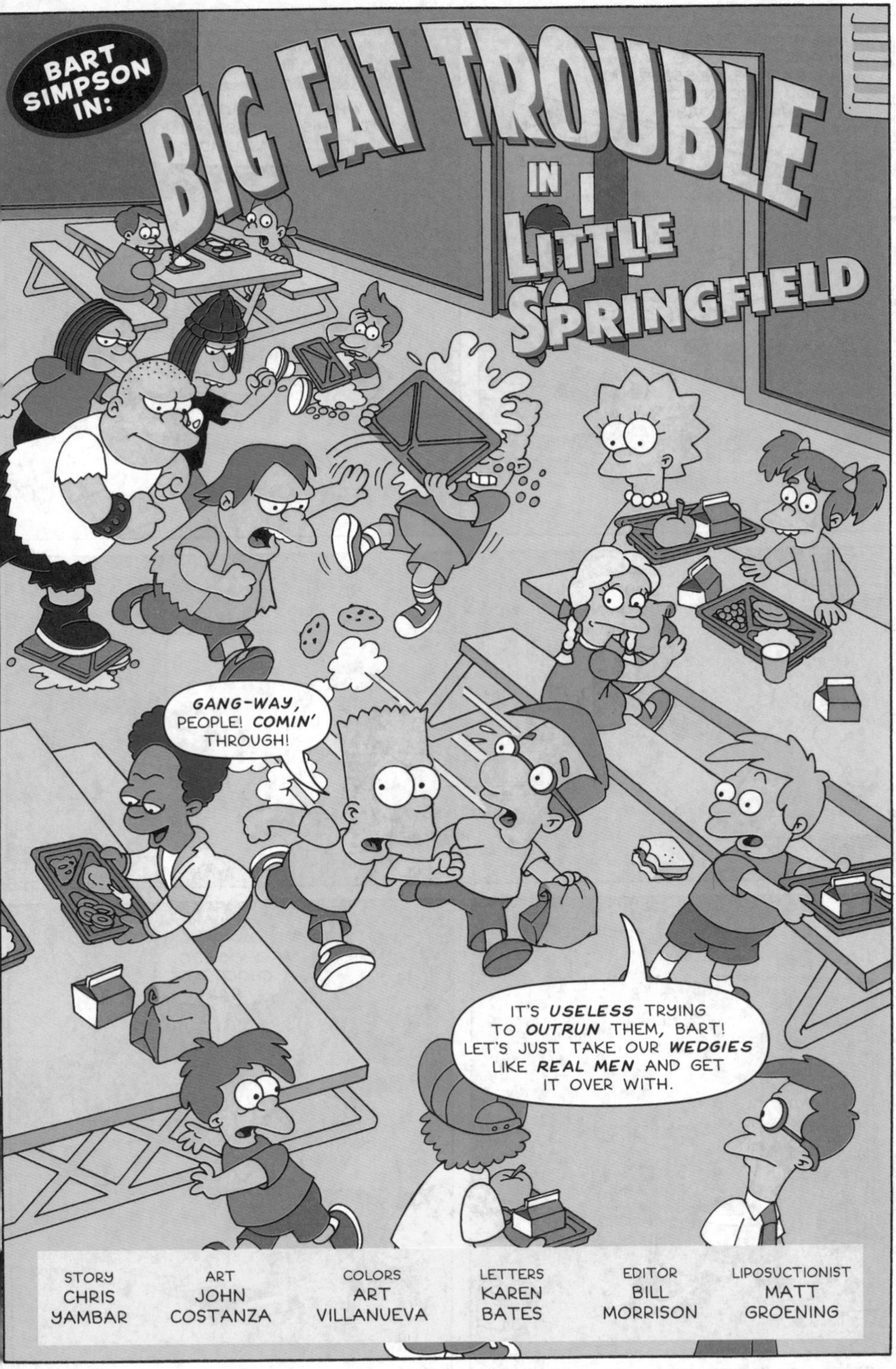
BART SIMPSON IN:
BIG FAT TROUBLE IN LITTLE SPRINGFIELD
GANG-WAY, PEOPLE! COMIN' THROUGH!
IT'S USELESS TRYING TO OUTRUN THEM, BART! LET'S JUST TAKE OUR WEDGIES LIKE REAL MEN AND GET IT OVER WITH.
STORY CHRIS YAMBAR
ART JOHN COSTANZA
COLORS ART VILLANUEVA
LETTERS KAREN BATES
EDITOR BILL MORRISON
LIPOSUCTIONIST MATT GROENING

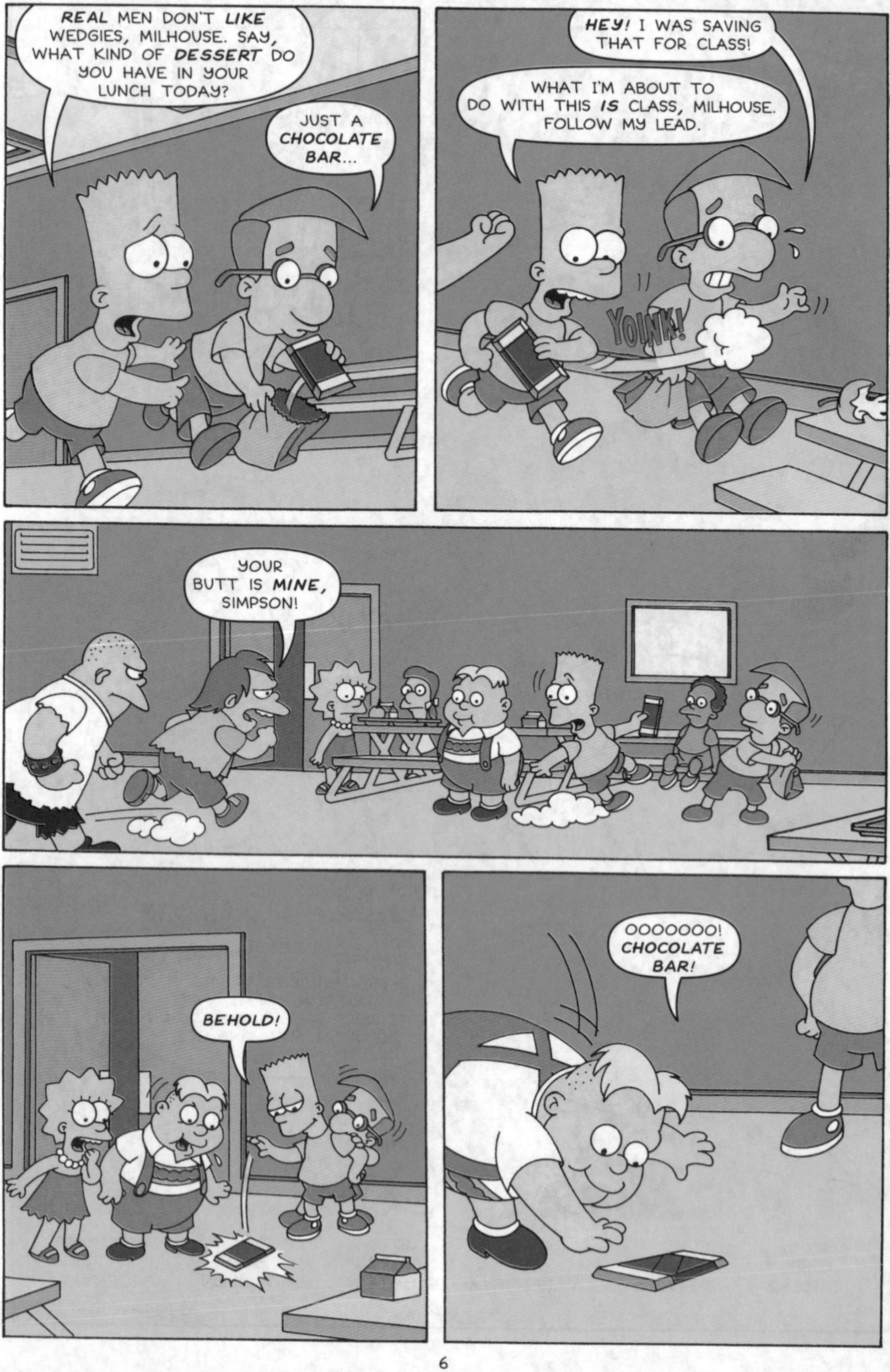
REAL MEN DON'T LIKE WEDGIES, MILHOUSE. SAY, WHAT KIND OF DESSERT DO YOU HAVE IN YOUR LUNCH TODAY?
JUST A CHOCOLATE BAR...
HEY! I WAS SAVING THAT FOR CLASS!
WHAT I'M ABOUT TO DO WITH THIS IS CLASS, MILHOUSE. FOLLOW MY LEAD.
YOINK!
YOUR BUTT IS MINE, SIMPSON!
BEHOLD!
OOOOOOO! CHOCOLATE BAR!

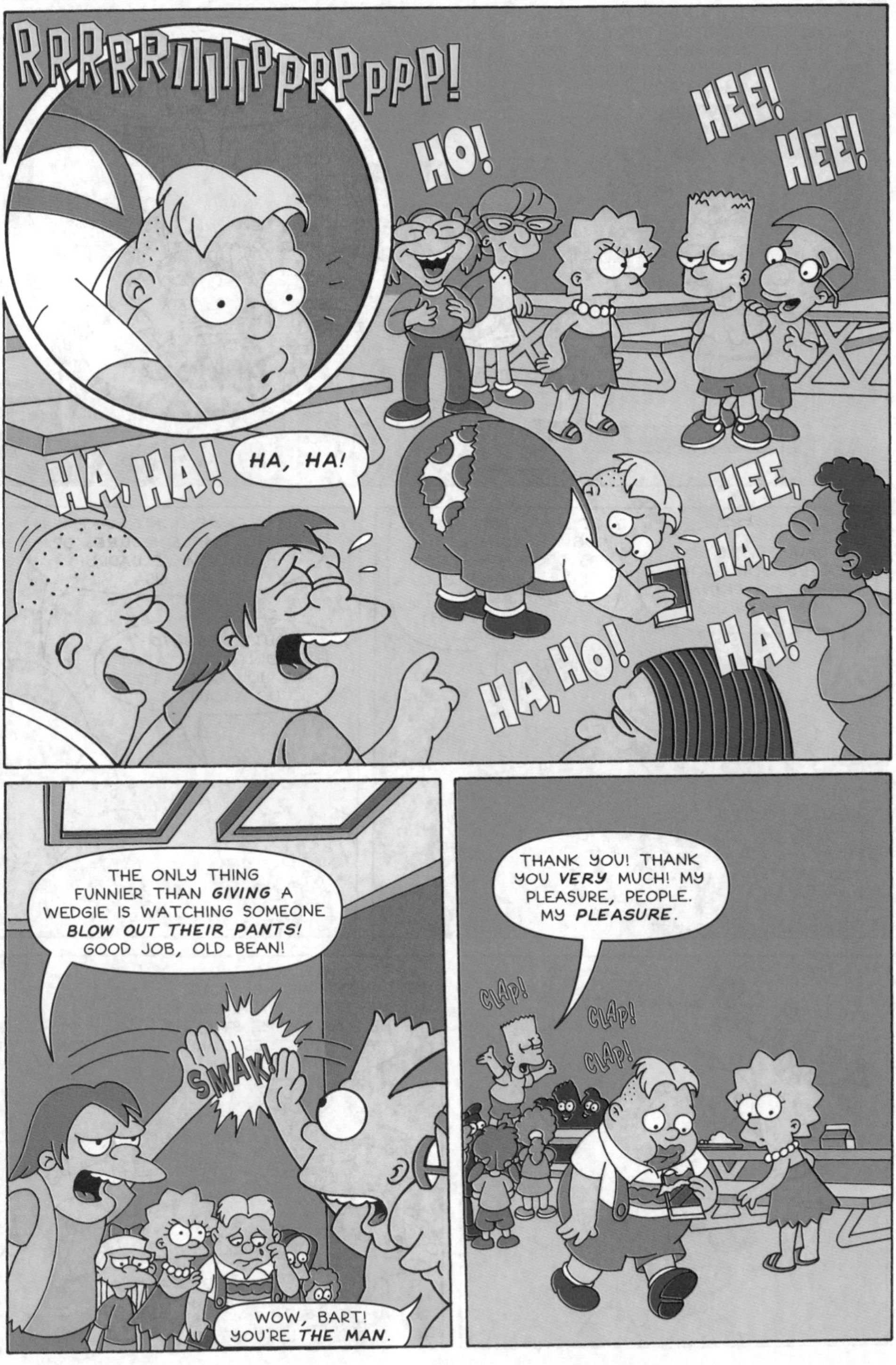

RRRRRIIIIIPPPPPPP!
HO!
HEE! HEE!
HA, HA!
HA, HA!
HEE, HA, HA!
HA, HO!
THE ONLY THING FUNNIER THAN *GIVING* A WEDGIE IS WATCHING SOMEONE ***BLOW OUT THEIR PANTS!*** GOOD JOB, OLD BEAN!
SMAK!
WOW, BART! YOU'RE ***THE MAN***.
THANK YOU! THANK YOU ***VERY*** MUCH! MY PLEASURE, PEOPLE. MY ***PLEASURE***.
CLAP!
CLAP!
CLAP!

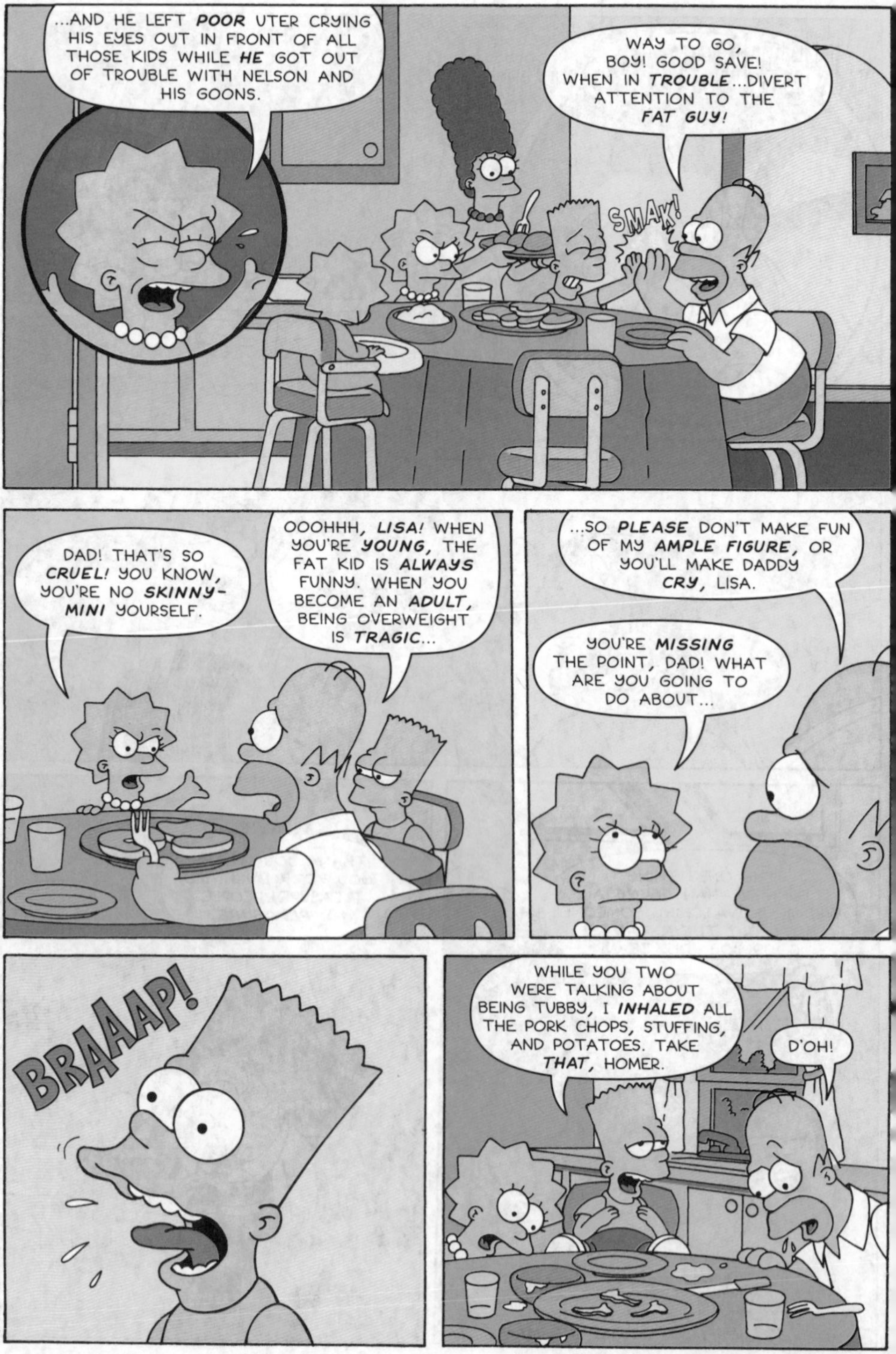
...AND HE LEFT POOR UTER CRYING HIS EYES OUT IN FRONT OF ALL THOSE KIDS WHILE HE GOT OUT OF TROUBLE WITH NELSON AND HIS GOONS.
WAY TO GO, BOY! GOOD SAVE! WHEN IN TROUBLE...DIVERT ATTENTION TO THE FAT GUY!
SMAK!
DAD! THAT'S SO CRUEL! YOU KNOW, YOU'RE NO SKINNY-MINI YOURSELF.
OOOHHH, LISA! WHEN YOU'RE YOUNG, THE FAT KID IS ALWAYS FUNNY. WHEN YOU BECOME AN ADULT, BEING OVERWEIGHT IS TRAGIC...
...SO PLEASE DON'T MAKE FUN OF MY AMPLE FIGURE, OR YOU'LL MAKE DADDY CRY, LISA.
YOU'RE MISSING THE POINT, DAD! WHAT ARE YOU GOING TO DO ABOUT...
BRAAAP!
WHILE YOU TWO WERE TALKING ABOUT BEING TUBBY, I INHALED ALL THE PORK CHOPS, STUFFING, AND POTATOES. TAKE THAT, HOMER.
D'OH!

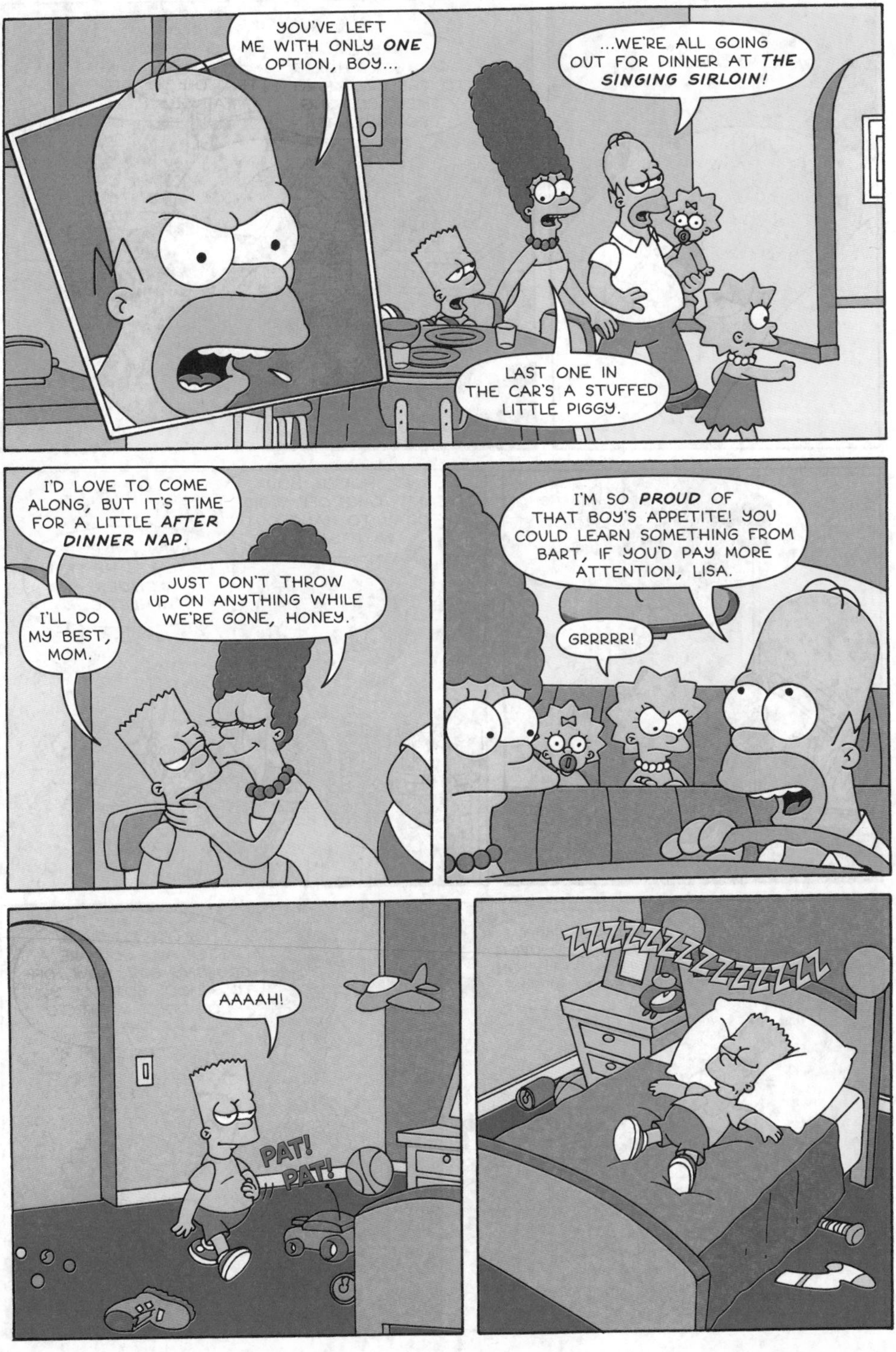
YOU'VE LEFT ME WITH ONLY ONE OPTION, BOY...
...WE'RE ALL GOING OUT FOR DINNER AT THE SINGING SIRLOIN!
LAST ONE IN THE CAR'S A STUFFED LITTLE PIGGY.
I'D LOVE TO COME ALONG, BUT IT'S TIME FOR A LITTLE AFTER DINNER NAP.
JUST DON'T THROW UP ON ANYTHING WHILE WE'RE GONE, HONEY.
I'LL DO MY BEST, MOM.
I'M SO PROUD OF THAT BOY'S APPETITE! YOU COULD LEARN SOMETHING FROM BART, IF YOU'D PAY MORE ATTENTION, LISA.
GRRRRR!
AAAAH!
PAT! PAT!
ZZZZZZZZZZZZZZZZZ

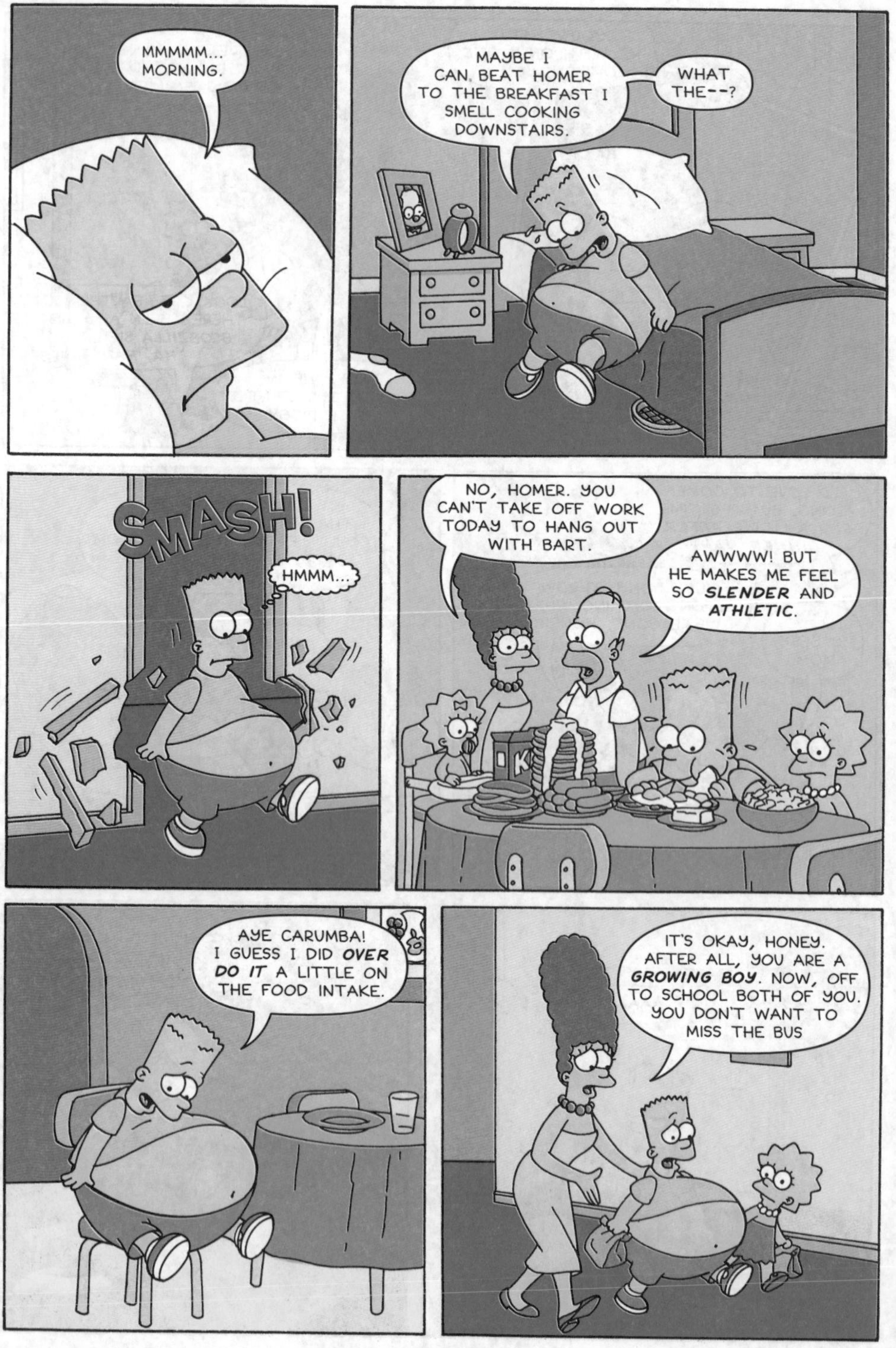
MMMMM...
MORNING.
MAYBE I CAN BEAT HOMER TO THE BREAKFAST I SMELL COOKING DOWNSTAIRS.
WHAT THE--?
SMASH!
HMMM...
NO, HOMER. YOU CAN'T TAKE OFF WORK TODAY TO HANG OUT WITH BART.
AWWWW! BUT HE MAKES ME FEEL SO **SLENDER** AND **ATHLETIC**.
AYE CARUMBA! I GUESS I DID **OVER DO IT** A LITTLE ON THE FOOD INTAKE.
IT'S OKAY, HONEY. AFTER ALL, YOU ARE A **GROWING BOY**. NOW, OFF TO SCHOOL BOTH OF YOU. YOU DON'T WANT TO MISS THE BUS

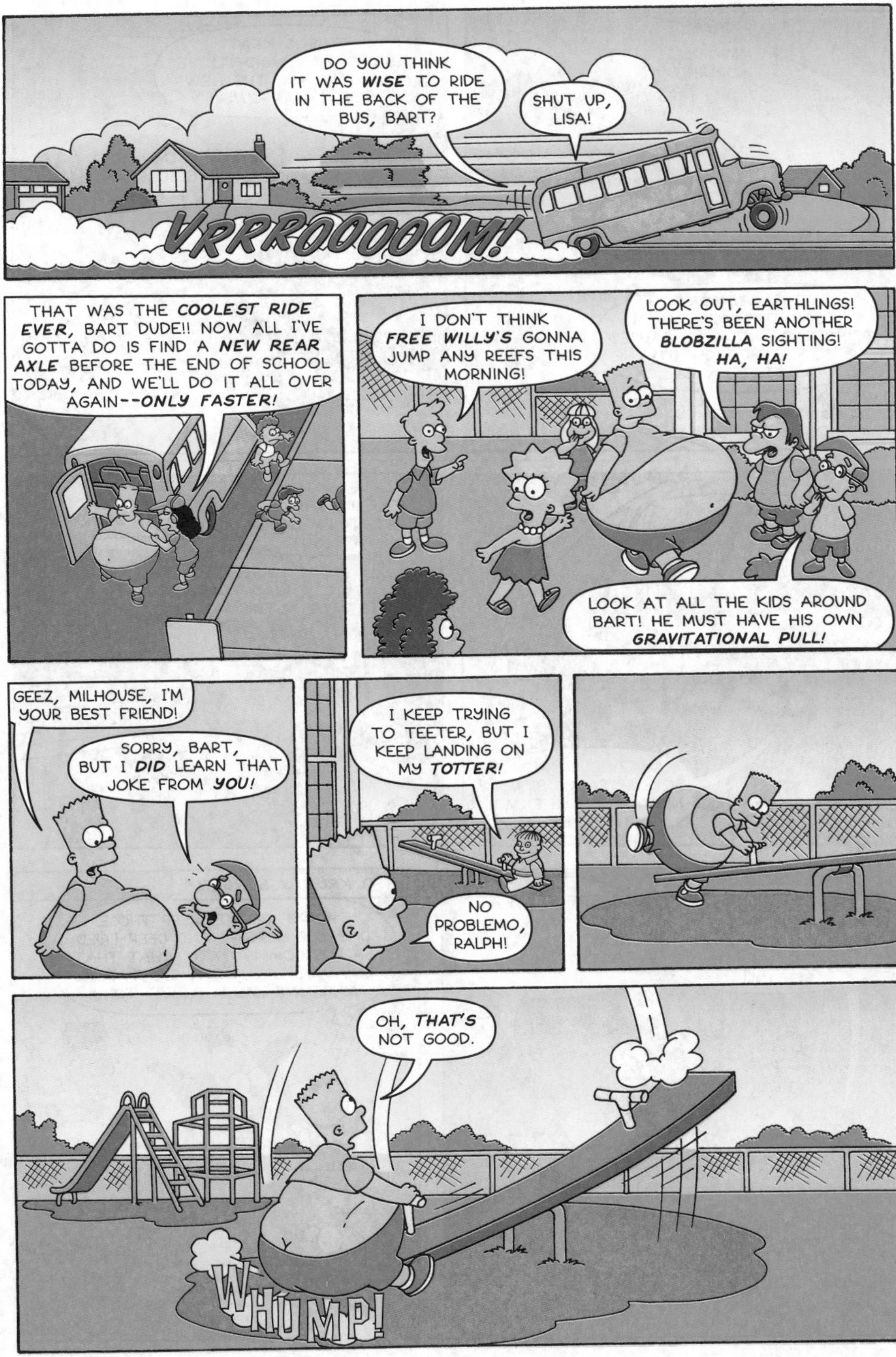
DO YOU THINK IT WAS WISE TO RIDE IN THE BACK OF THE BUS, BART?
SHUT UP, LISA!
VRRROOOOOOM!
THAT WAS THE COOLEST RIDE EVER, BART DUDE!! NOW ALL I'VE GOTTA DO IS FIND A NEW REAR AXLE BEFORE THE END OF SCHOOL TODAY, AND WE'LL DO IT ALL OVER AGAIN--ONLY FASTER!
I DON'T THINK FREE WILLY'S GONNA JUMP ANY REEFS THIS MORNING!
LOOK OUT, EARTHLINGS! THERE'S BEEN ANOTHER BLOBZILLA SIGHTING! HA, HA!
LOOK AT ALL THE KIDS AROUND BART! HE MUST HAVE HIS OWN GRAVITATIONAL PULL!
GEEZ, MILHOUSE, I'M YOUR BEST FRIEND!
SORRY, BART, BUT I DID LEARN THAT JOKE FROM YOU!
I KEEP TRYING TO TEETER, BUT I KEEP LANDING ON MY TOTTER!
NO PROBLEMO, RALPH!
OH, THAT'S NOT GOOD.
WHUMP!

THE *TREMORS* BEGAN THIS MORNING IN SPRINGFIELD AND HAVE CAUSED PROBLEMS THROUGHOUT THE TRI-STATE AREA...

THIS IS *KENT BROCKMAN*, AND I'LL BE BRINGING YOU THE NEWS *AS IT HAPPENS*...

LOOK! I'M LIKE A CHICKEN WITH NO WINGS!

WHUMP!

AMAZING FLYING BOY UPSTAGES STAR NEWS ANCHOR! FILM AT ELEVEN!

I'VE GOTTA GET SOMETHING TO EAT, OR I'M GONNA PASS OUT.

WHAT ABOUT YOUR LUNCH?

I ATE IT ON THE WAY TO THE BUS THIS MORNING.

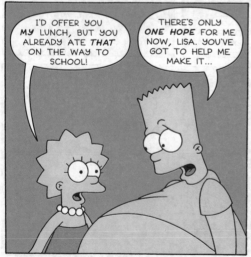

I'D OFFER YOU *MY* LUNCH, BUT YOU ALREADY ATE *THAT* ON THE WAY TO SCHOOL!

THERE'S ONLY *ONE HOPE* FOR ME NOW, LISA. YOU'VE GOT TO HELP ME MAKE IT...

"...TO *KRUSTY BURGER*."

HURRY, PEOPLE! KEEP THOSE DAY-OLD BURGERS AND DEEP-FRIED SALADS COMING! WITH WHAT THAT BOY WILL EAT, I CAN CLEAR UP MY *GAMBLING TAB* WITH FAT TONY!

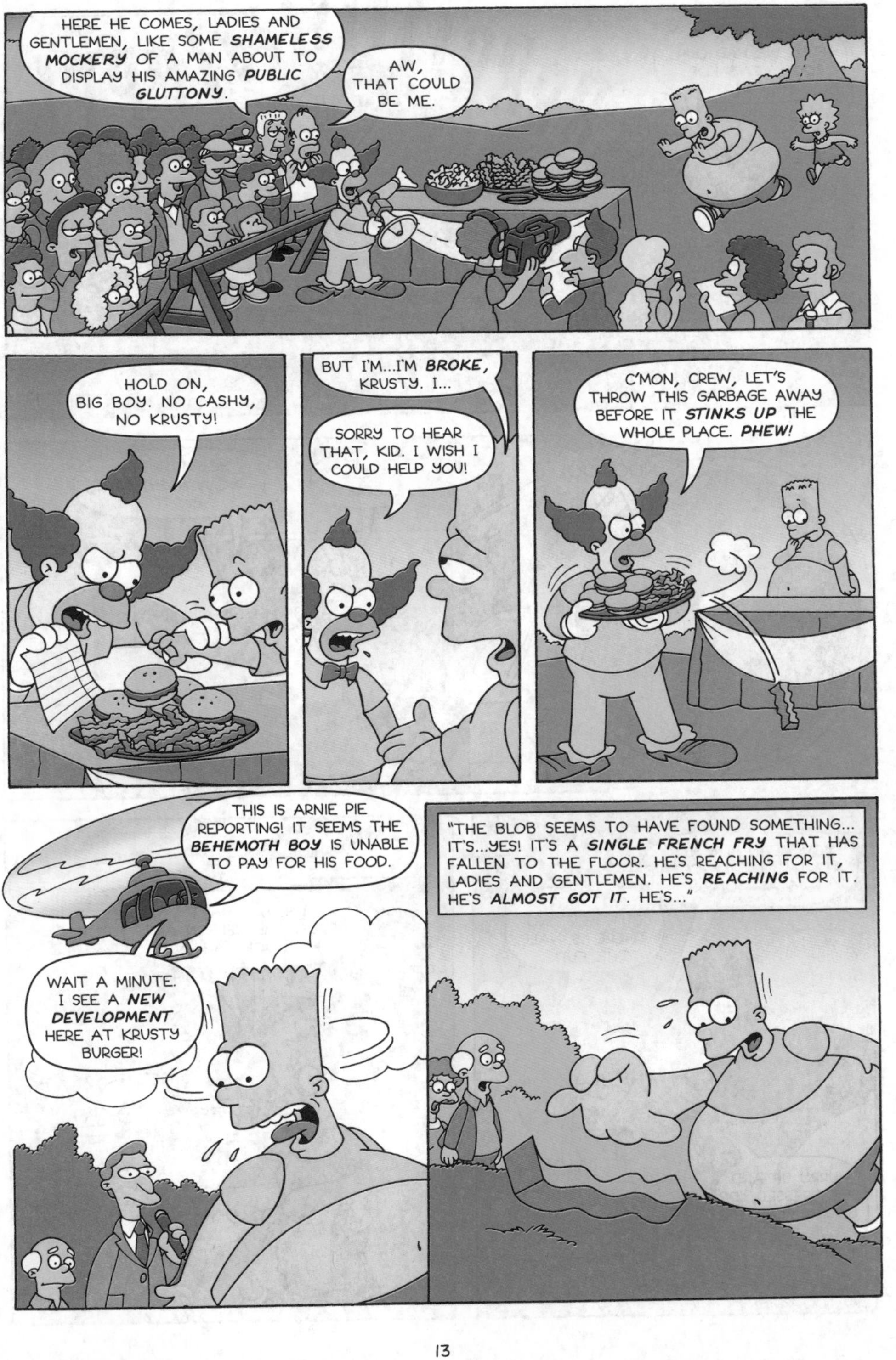
HERE HE COMES, LADIES AND GENTLEMEN, LIKE SOME **SHAMELESS MOCKERY** OF A MAN ABOUT TO DISPLAY HIS AMAZING **PUBLIC GLUTTONY**.
AW, THAT COULD BE ME.
HOLD ON, BIG BOY. NO CASHY, NO KRUSTY!
BUT I'M...I'M **BROKE**, KRUSTY. I...
SORRY TO HEAR THAT, KID. I WISH I COULD HELP YOU!
C'MON, CREW, LET'S THROW THIS GARBAGE AWAY BEFORE IT **STINKS UP** THE WHOLE PLACE. **PHEW!**
THIS IS ARNIE PIE REPORTING! IT SEEMS THE **BEHEMOTH BOY** IS UNABLE TO PAY FOR HIS FOOD.
WAIT A MINUTE. I SEE A **NEW DEVELOPMENT** HERE AT KRUSTY BURGER!
"THE BLOB SEEMS TO HAVE FOUND SOMETHING... IT'S...YES! IT'S A **SINGLE FRENCH FRY** THAT HAS FALLEN TO THE FLOOR. HE'S REACHING FOR IT, LADIES AND GENTLEMEN. HE'S **REACHING** FOR IT. HE'S **ALMOST GOT IT**. HE'S..."

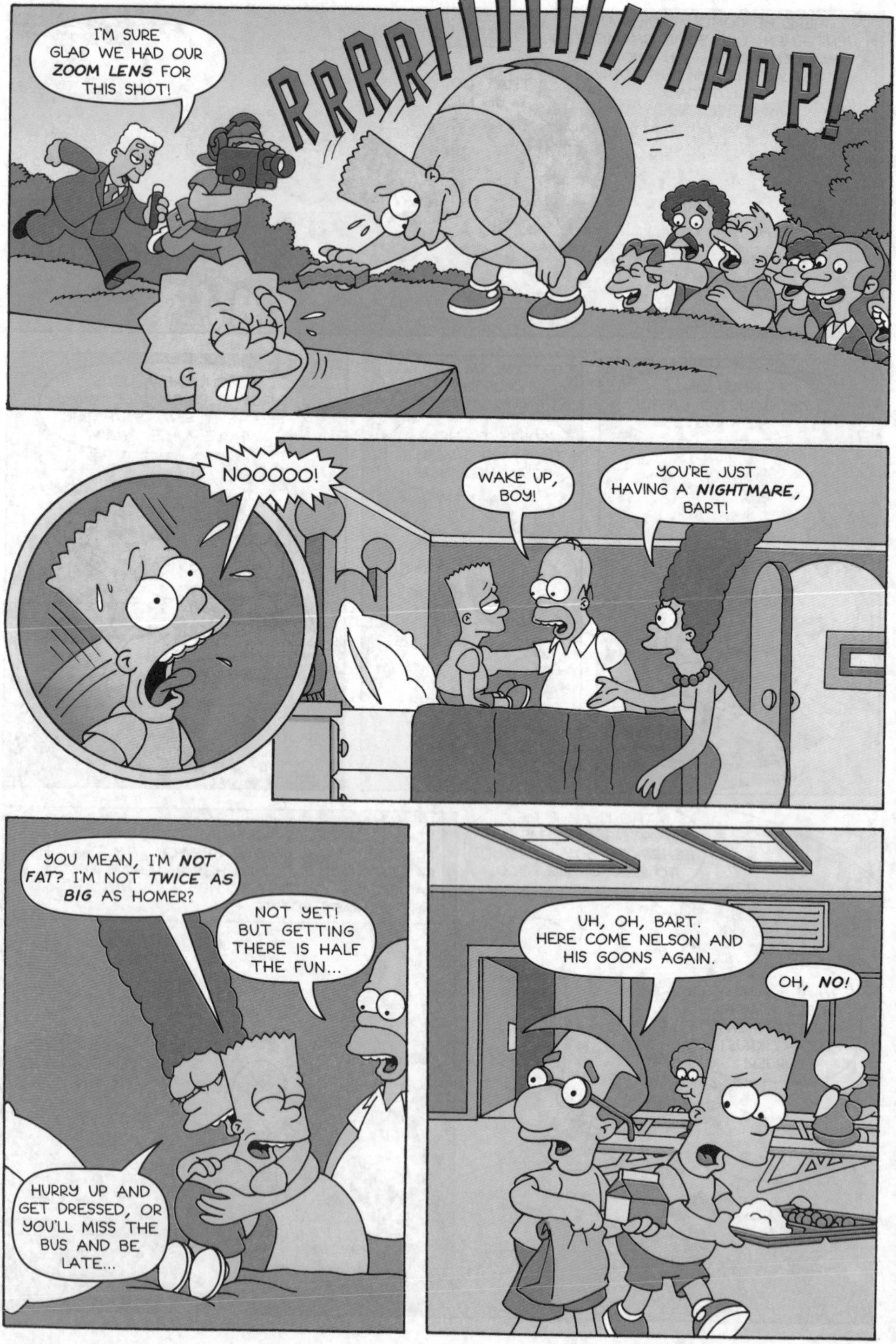

I'M SURE GLAD WE HAD OUR **ZOOM LENS** FOR THIS SHOT!
RRRRIIIIIIIIIIPPPP!
NOOOOO!
WAKE UP, BOY!
YOU'RE JUST HAVING A ***NIGHTMARE,*** BART!
YOU MEAN, I'M ***NOT*** ***FAT?*** I'M NOT ***TWICE AS BIG*** AS HOMER?
NOT YET! BUT GETTING THERE IS HALF THE FUN...
HURRY UP AND GET DRESSED, OR YOU'LL MISS THE BUS AND BE LATE...
UH, OH, BART. HERE COME NELSON AND HIS GOONS AGAIN.
OH, ***NO!***

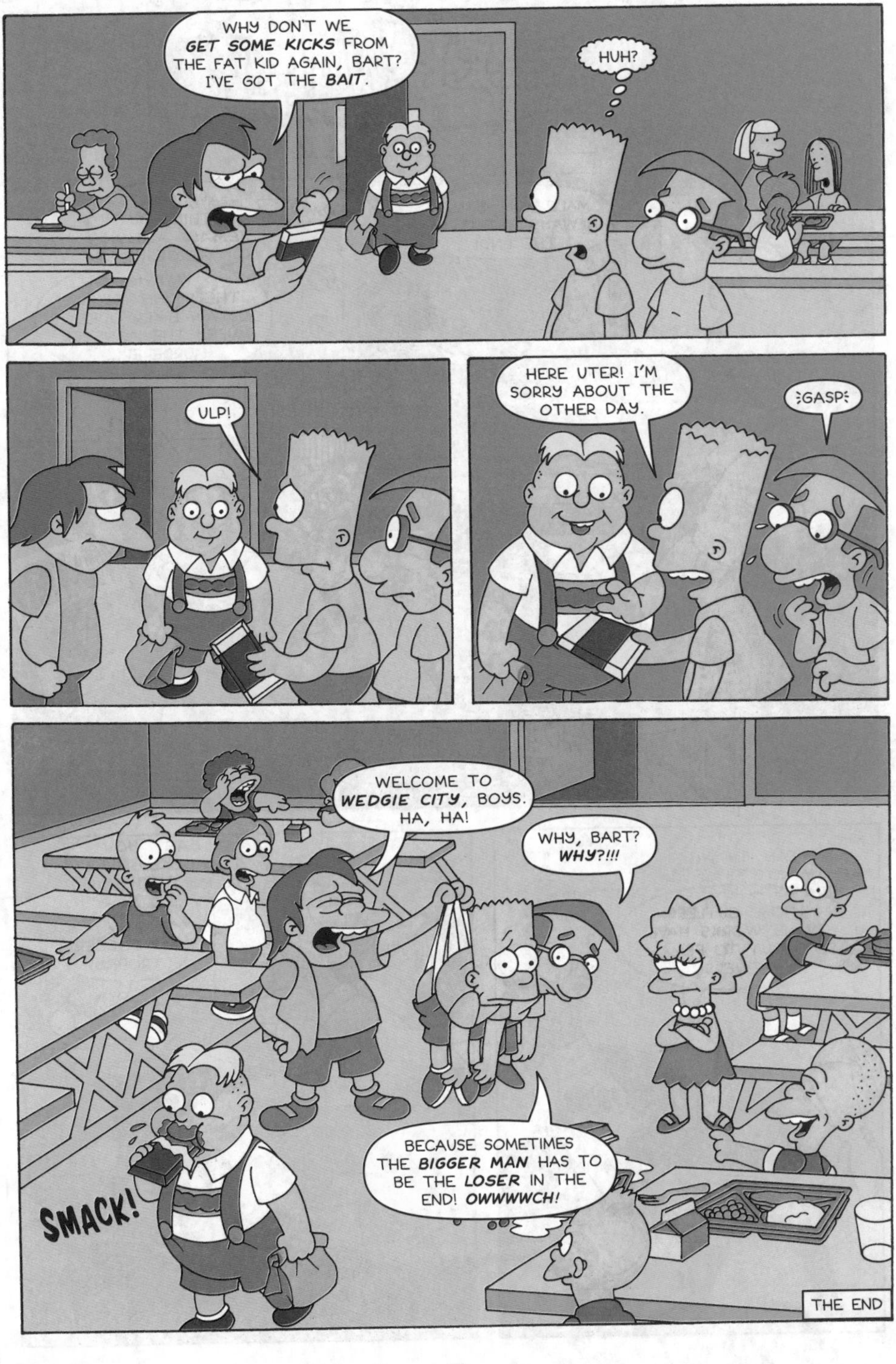
WHY DON'T WE GET SOME KICKS FROM THE FAT KID AGAIN, BART? I'VE GOT THE BAIT.
HUH?
ULP!
HERE UTER! I'M SORRY ABOUT THE OTHER DAY.
GASP
WELCOME TO WEDGIE CITY, BOYS. HA, HA!
WHY, BART? WHY?!!!
BECAUSE SOMETIMES THE BIGGER MAN HAS TO BE THE LOSER IN THE END! OWWWWCH!
SMACK!
THE END

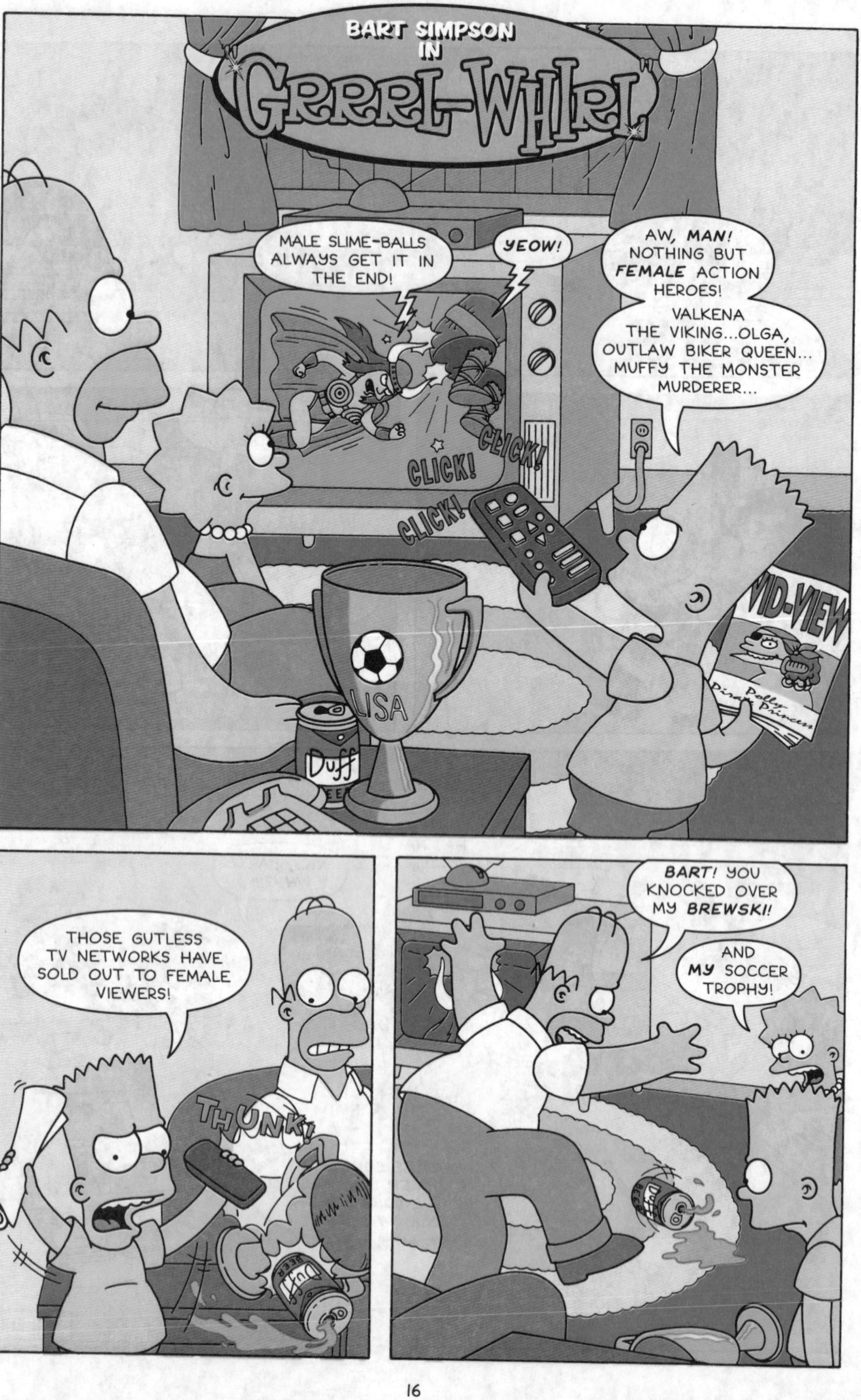
BART SIMPSON IN
GRRRL-WHIRL
MALE SLIME-BALLS ALWAYS GET IT IN THE END!
YEOW!
AW, MAN! NOTHING BUT FEMALE ACTION HEROES!
VALKENA THE VIKING...OLGA, OUTLAW BIKER QUEEN... MUFFY THE MONSTER MURDERER...
CLICK!
CLICK!
CLICK!
LISA
Duff
VID-VIEW
Dolly Pirate Princess
THOSE GUTLESS TV NETWORKS HAVE SOLD OUT TO FEMALE VIEWERS!
THUNK!
BART! YOU KNOCKED OVER MY BREWSKI!
AND MY SOCCER TROPHY!

THE BEER CAN BE REPLACED, BUT THIS TROPHY CAN'T!

HOMER, I WANT YOU TO BUILD A CASE TO DISPLAY AND PROTECT ALL OF LISA'S SOCCER TROPHIES.

D'OH! NOW SEE WHAT YOU'VE DONE?!

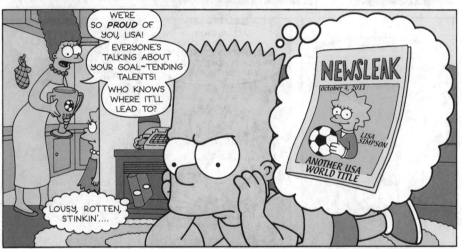

WE'RE SO PROUD OF YOU, LISA! EVERYONE'S TALKING ABOUT YOUR GOAL-TENDING TALENTS! WHO KNOWS WHERE IT'LL LEAD TO?

LOUSY, ROTTEN, STINKIN'....

NEWSLEAK

October 4, 2011

LISA SIMPSON

ANOTHER USA WORLD TITLE

IS THERE NO END TO THIS "GIRL POWER"?!

BURPO COMICS

YES WE'RE OPEN

THANK GOODNESS THERE'S STILL BURPO, MY GIRL-HATING, HOAGIE-EATING HERO!

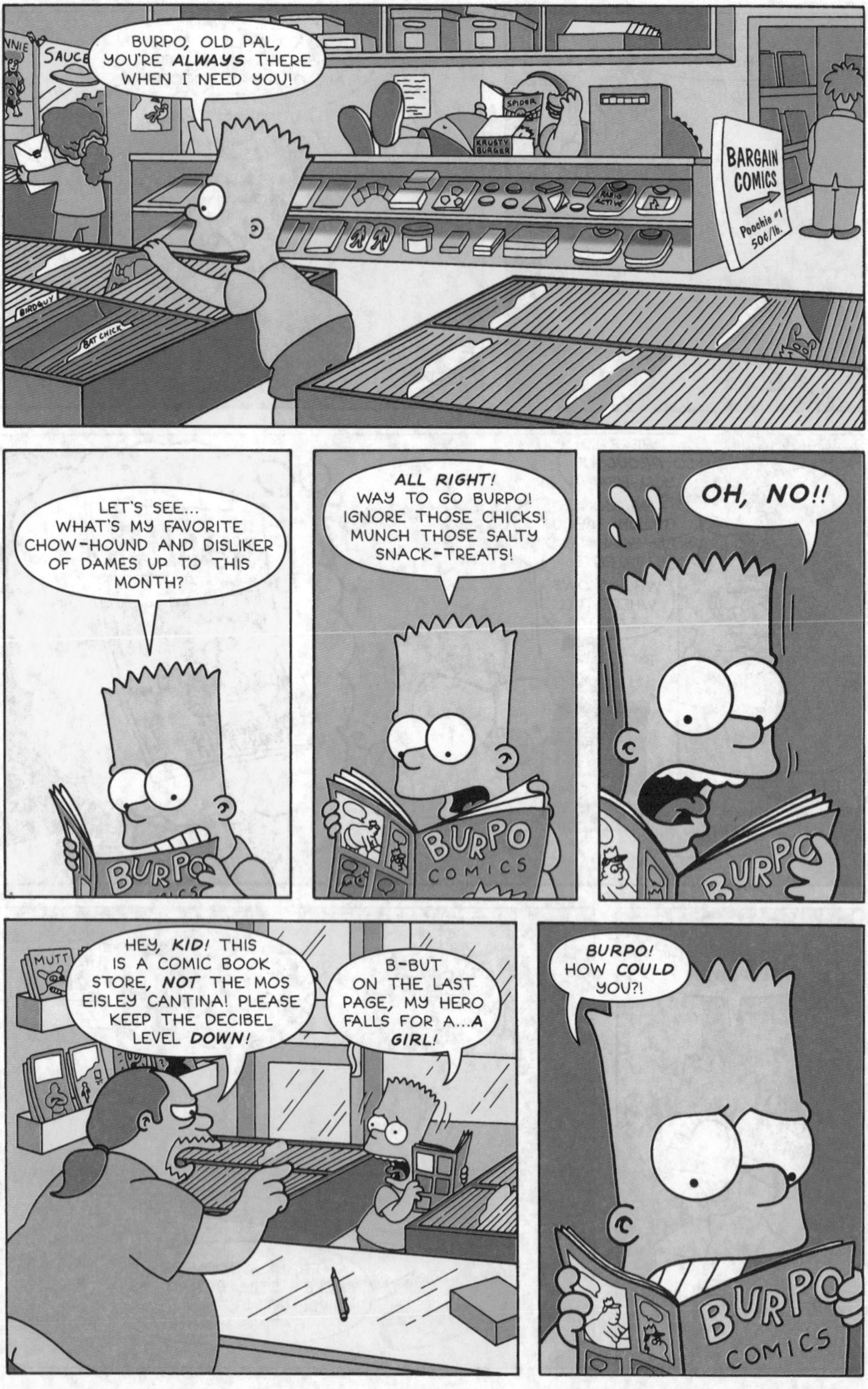
BURPO, OLD PAL, YOU'RE ALWAYS THERE WHEN I NEED YOU!
SAUCE
SPIDER
KRUSTY BURGER
RADIO ACTIVE
BARGAIN COMICS
Poochie #1 50¢/lb.
BIRDGUY
BAT CHICK
LET'S SEE... WHAT'S MY FAVORITE CHOW-HOUND AND DISLIKER OF DAMES UP TO THIS MONTH?
BURPO
ALL RIGHT! WAY TO GO BURPO! IGNORE THOSE CHICKS! MUNCH THOSE SALTY SNACK-TREATS!
BURPO COMICS
OH, NO!!
BURPO
MUTT
HEY, KID! THIS IS A COMIC BOOK STORE, NOT THE MOS EISLEY CANTINA! PLEASE KEEP THE DECIBEL LEVEL DOWN!
B-BUT ON THE LAST PAGE, MY HERO FALLS FOR A...A GIRL!
BURPO! HOW COULD YOU?!
BURPO COMICS

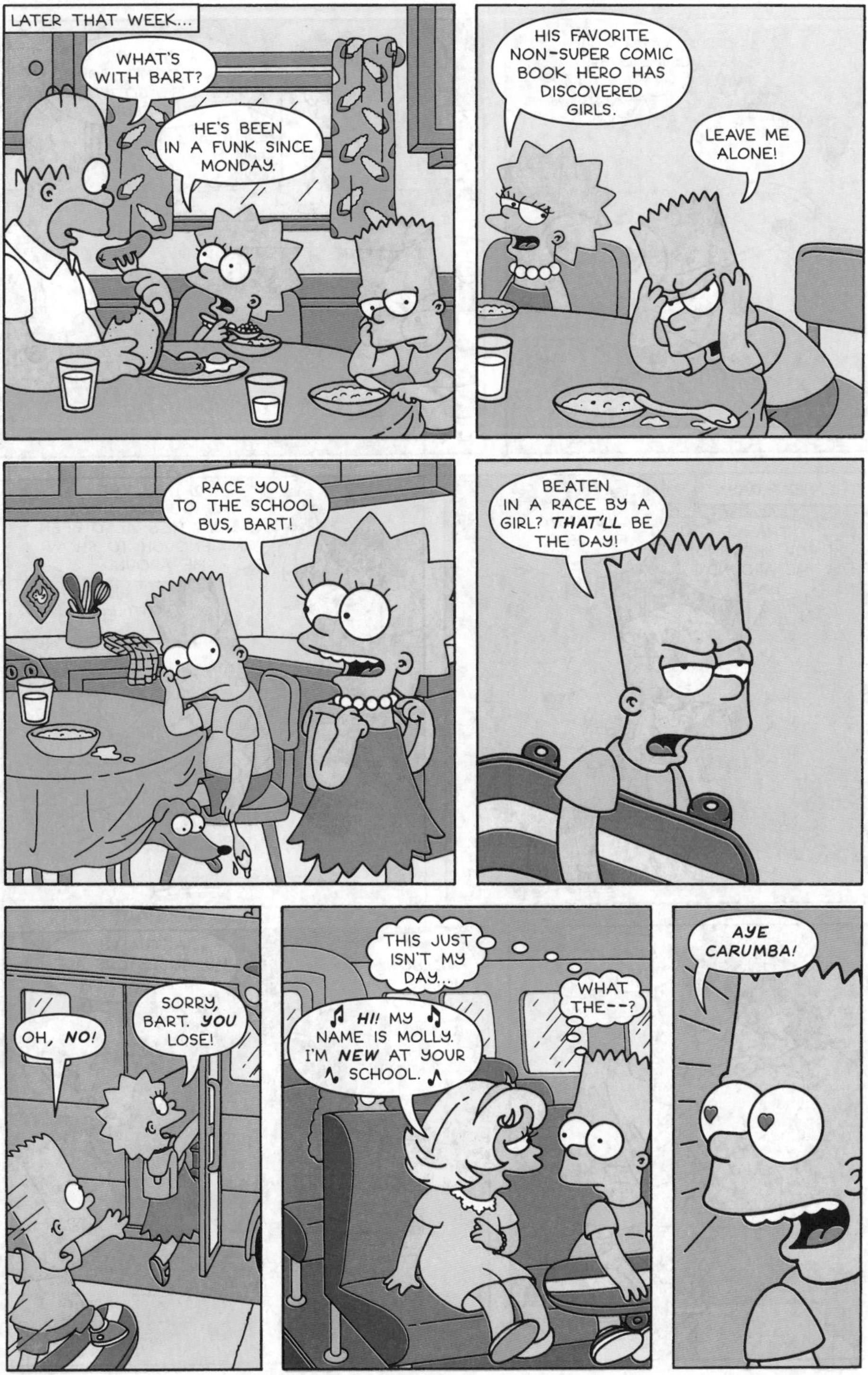
LATER THAT WEEK...
WHAT'S WITH BART?
HE'S BEEN IN A FUNK SINCE MONDAY.
HIS FAVORITE NON-SUPER COMIC BOOK HERO HAS DISCOVERED GIRLS.
LEAVE ME ALONE!
RACE YOU TO THE SCHOOL BUS, BART!
BEATEN IN A RACE BY A GIRL? *THAT'LL* BE THE DAY!
OH, *NO!*
SORRY, BART. *YOU* LOSE!
THIS JUST ISN'T MY DAY...
♪ *HI!* MY ♪ NAME IS MOLLY. I'M *NEW* AT YOUR ♪ SCHOOL. ♪
WHAT THE--?
AYE CARUMBA!

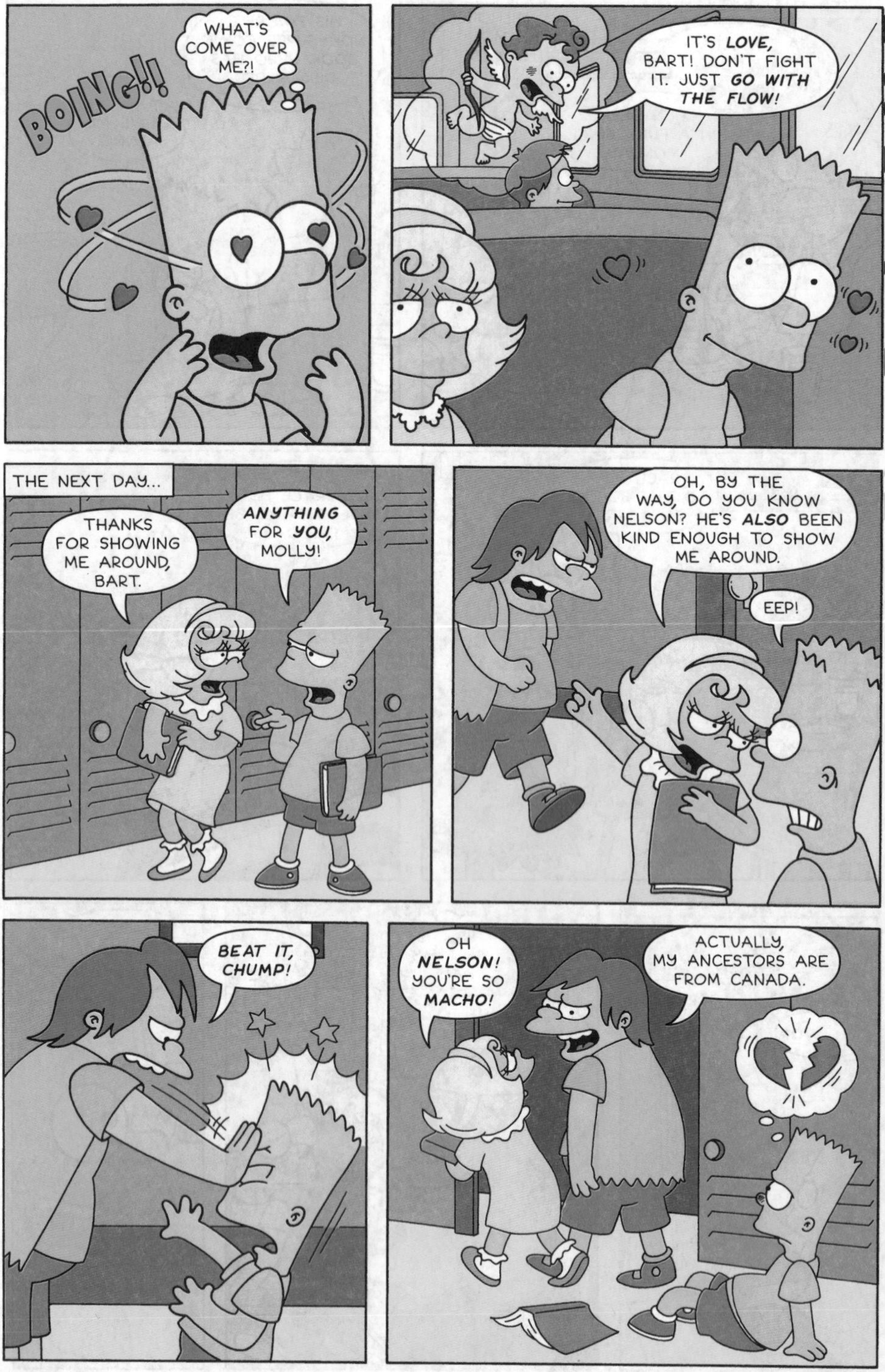
BOING!!
WHAT'S COME OVER ME?!
IT'S LOVE, BART! DON'T FIGHT IT. JUST GO WITH THE FLOW!
THE NEXT DAY...
THANKS FOR SHOWING ME AROUND, BART.
ANYTHING FOR YOU, MOLLY!
OH, BY THE WAY, DO YOU KNOW NELSON? HE'S ALSO BEEN KIND ENOUGH TO SHOW ME AROUND.
EEP!
BEAT IT, CHUMP!
OH NELSON! YOU'RE SO MACHO!
ACTUALLY, MY ANCESTORS ARE FROM CANADA.

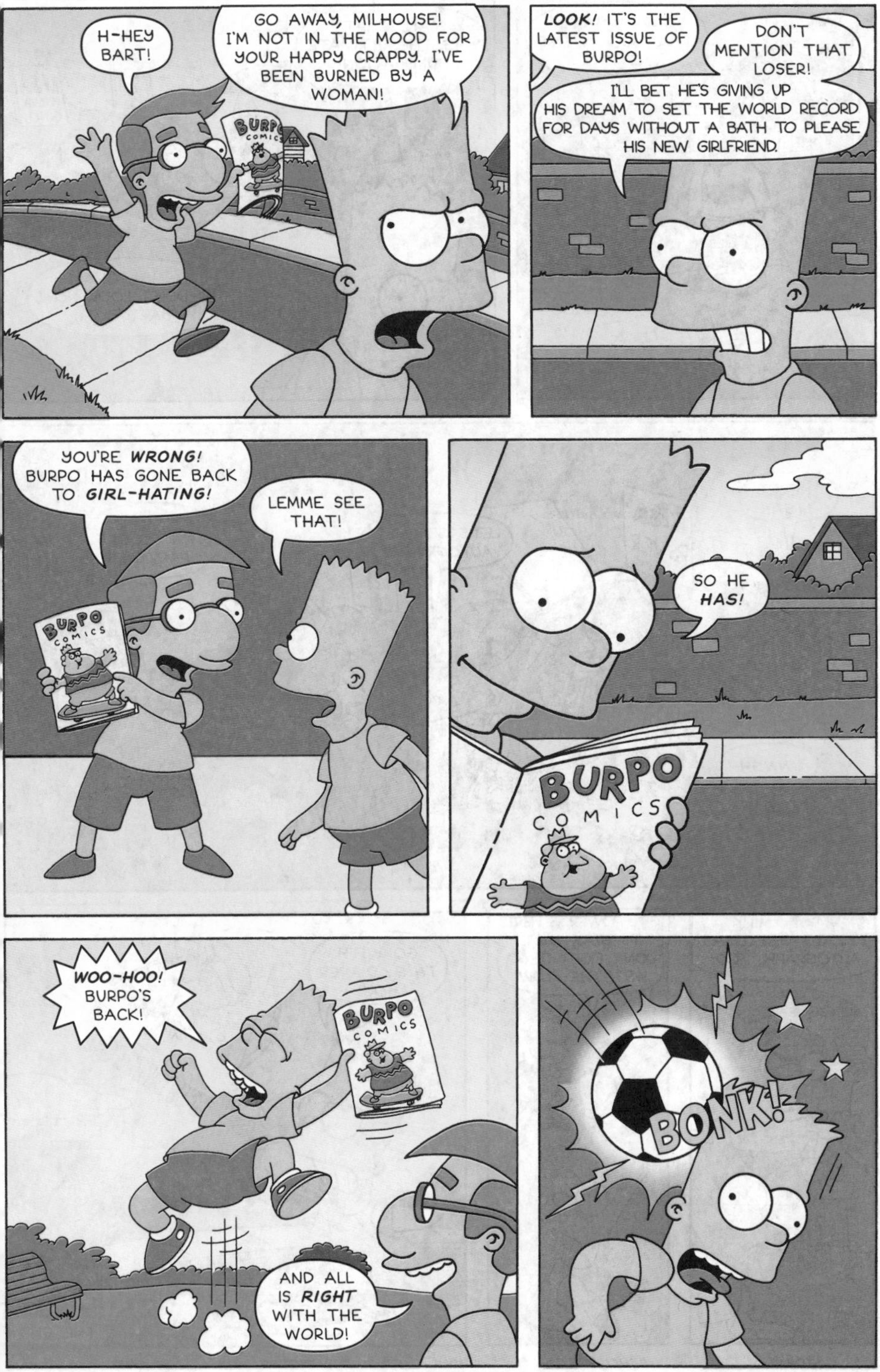
H-HEY BART!
GO AWAY, MILHOUSE! I'M NOT IN THE MOOD FOR YOUR HAPPY CRAPPY. I'VE BEEN BURNED BY A WOMAN!
BURPO COMICS
LOOK! IT'S THE LATEST ISSUE OF BURPO!
DON'T MENTION THAT LOSER!
I'LL BET HE'S GIVING UP HIS DREAM TO SET THE WORLD RECORD FOR DAYS WITHOUT A BATH TO PLEASE HIS NEW GIRLFRIEND.
YOU'RE WRONG! BURPO HAS GONE BACK TO GIRL-HATING!
LEMME SEE THAT!
BURPO COMICS
SO HE HAS!
BURPO COMICS
WOO-HOO! BURPO'S BACK!
BURPO COMICS
AND ALL IS RIGHT WITH THE WORLD!
BONK!

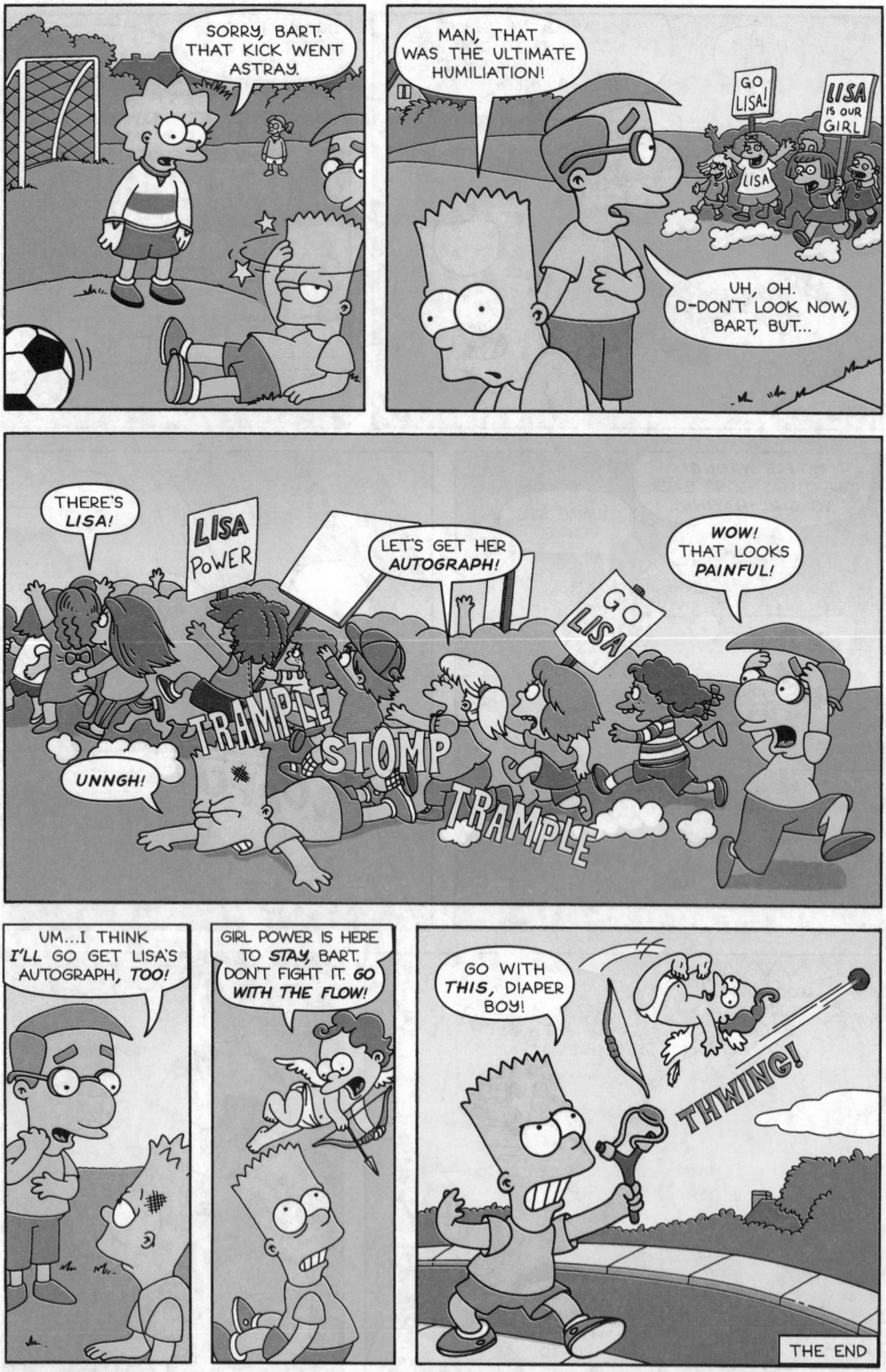
SORRY, BART. THAT KICK WENT ASTRAY.
MAN, THAT WAS THE ULTIMATE HUMILIATION!
GO LISA!
LISA IS OUR GIRL
LISA
UH, OH. D-DON'T LOOK NOW, BART, BUT...
THERE'S LISA!
LISA POWER
LET'S GET HER AUTOGRAPH!
GO LISA
WOW! THAT LOOKS PAINFUL!
TRAMPLE
STOMP
TRAMPLE
UNNGH!
UM...I THINK I'LL GO GET LISA'S AUTOGRAPH, TOO!
GIRL POWER IS HERE TO STAY, BART. DON'T FIGHT IT. GO WITH THE FLOW!
GO WITH THIS, DIAPER BOY!
THWING!
THE END

STORY GEORGE GLADIR *PENCILS* CAROLINE KELLY *INKS* MIKE ROTE *LETTERS* KAREN BATES *COLORS* BATES/VILLANUEVA

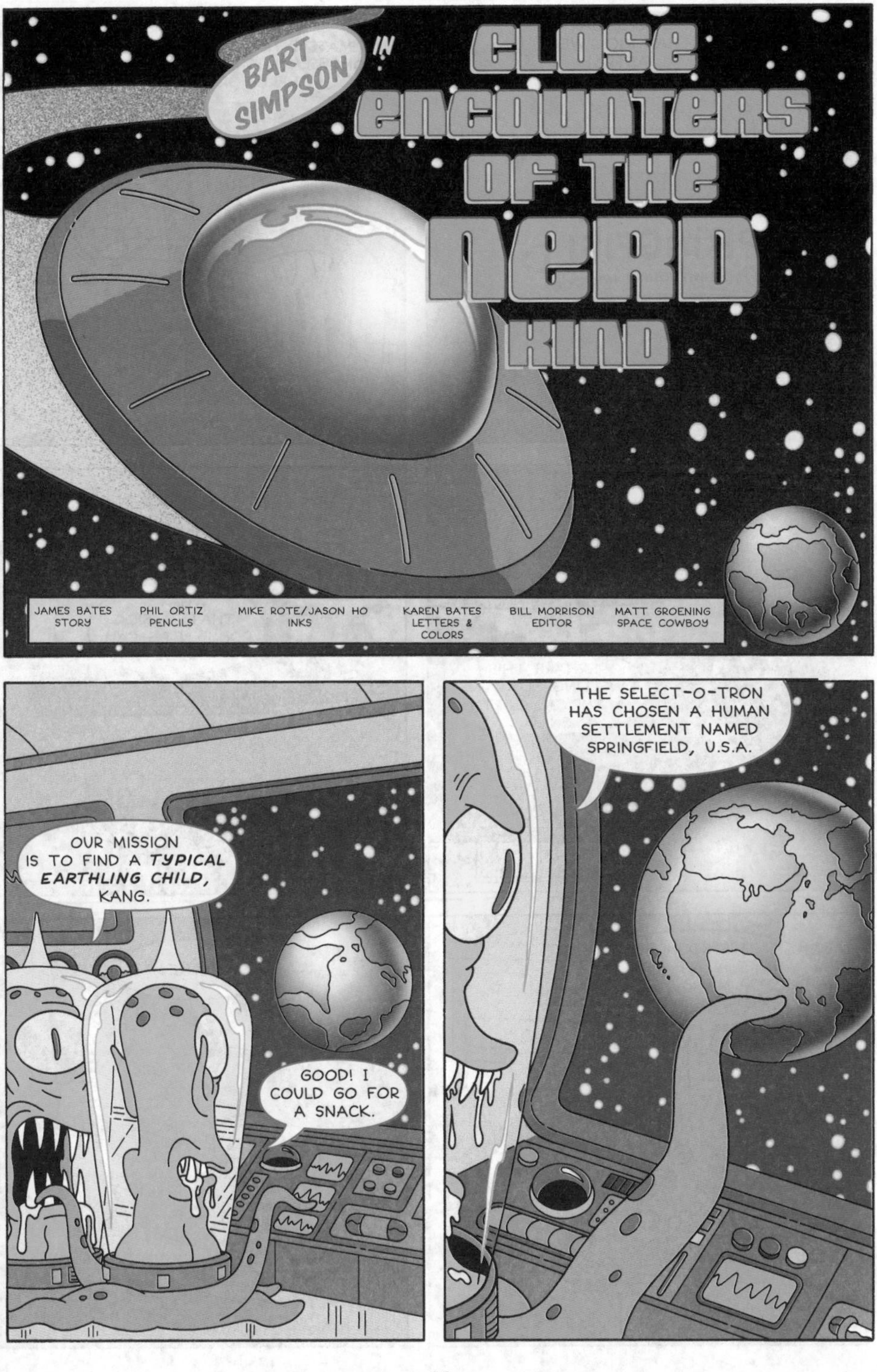
BART SIMPSON IN
CLOSE ENCOUNTERS OF THE NERD KIND
JAMES BATES STORY
PHIL ORTIZ PENCILS
MIKE ROTE/JASON HO INKS
KAREN BATES LETTERS & COLORS
BILL MORRISON EDITOR
MATT GROENING SPACE COWBOY
OUR MISSION IS TO FIND A TYPICAL EARTHLING CHILD, KANG.
GOOD! I COULD GO FOR A SNACK.
THE SELECT-O-TRON HAS CHOSEN A HUMAN SETTLEMENT NAMED SPRINGFIELD, U.S.A.

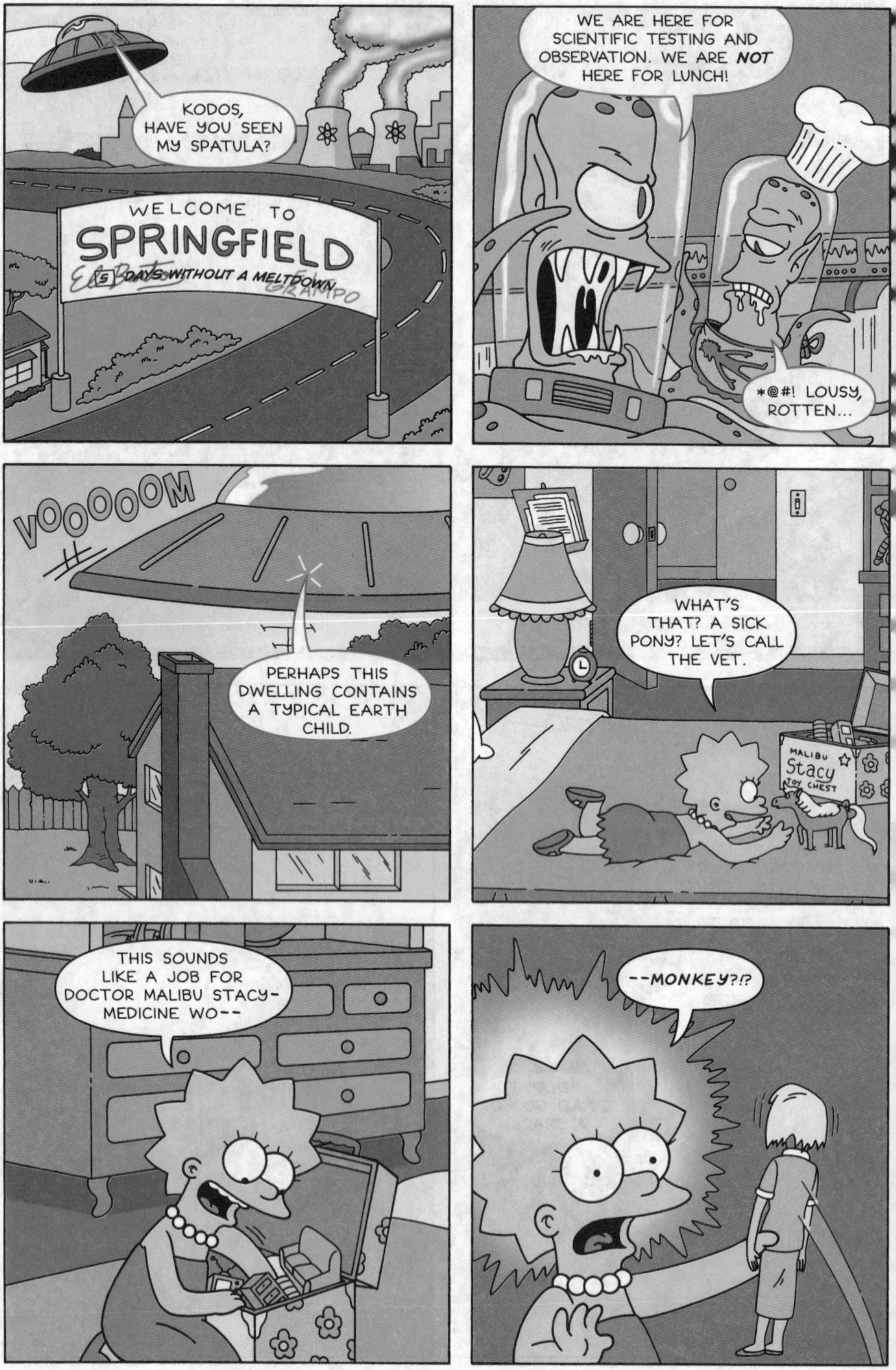
KODOS, HAVE YOU SEEN MY SPATULA?
WELCOME TO
SPRINGFIELD
5 DAYS WITHOUT A MELTDOWN
WE ARE HERE FOR SCIENTIFIC TESTING AND OBSERVATION. WE ARE ***NOT*** HERE FOR LUNCH!
*@#! LOUSY, ROTTEN...
VOOOOOM
PERHAPS THIS DWELLING CONTAINS A TYPICAL EARTH CHILD.
WHAT'S THAT? A SICK PONY? LET'S CALL THE VET.
MALIBU Stacy TOY CHEST
THIS SOUNDS LIKE A JOB FOR DOCTOR MALIBU STACY-MEDICINE WO--
--***MONKEY***?!?

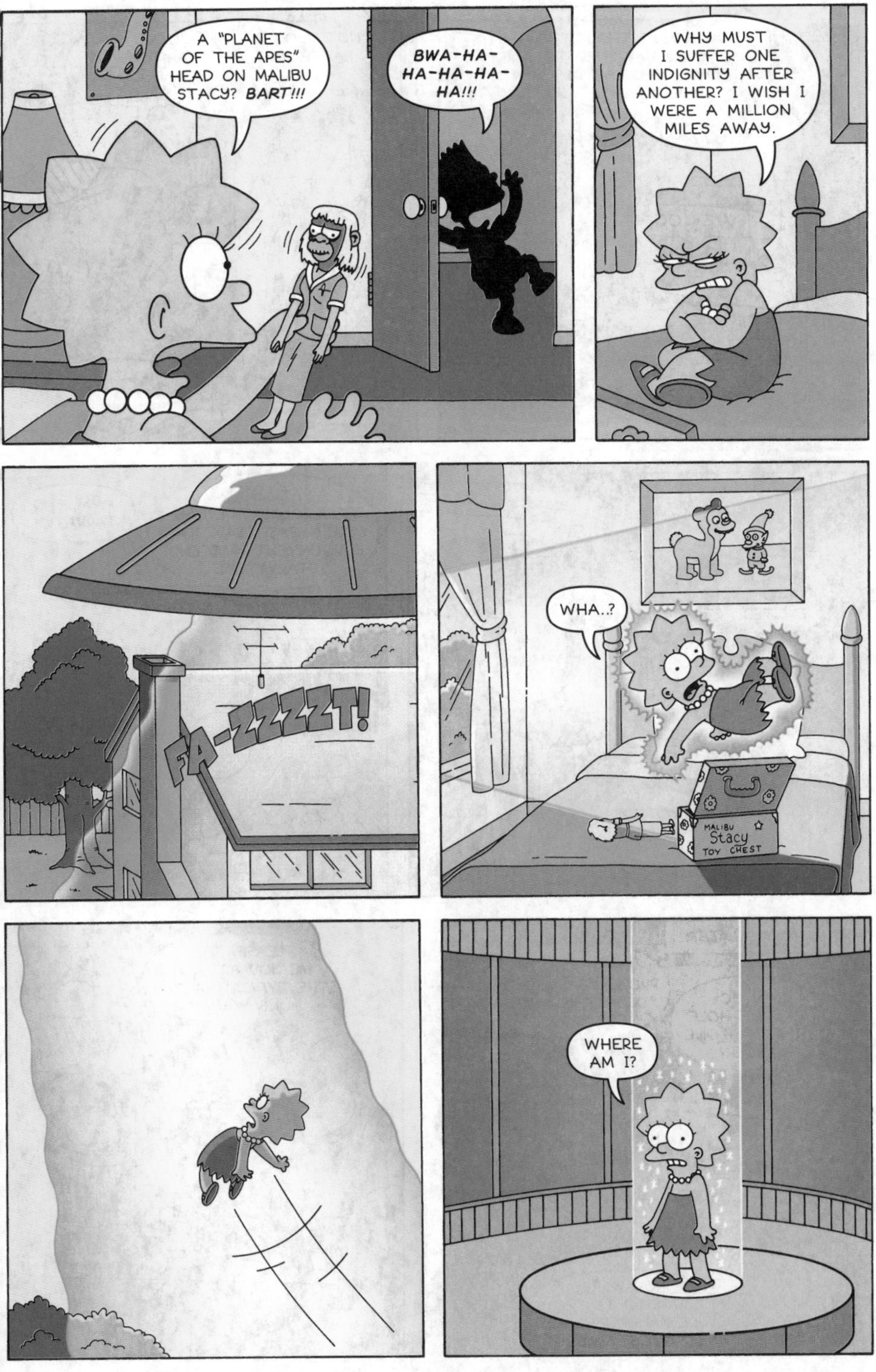
A "PLANET OF THE APES" HEAD ON MALIBU STACY? BART!!!
BWA-HA-HA-HA-HA-HA!!!
WHY MUST I SUFFER ONE INDIGNITY AFTER ANOTHER? I WISH I WERE A MILLION MILES AWAY.
FA-ZZZZT!
WHA..?
MALIBU Stacy TOY CHEST
WHERE AM I?

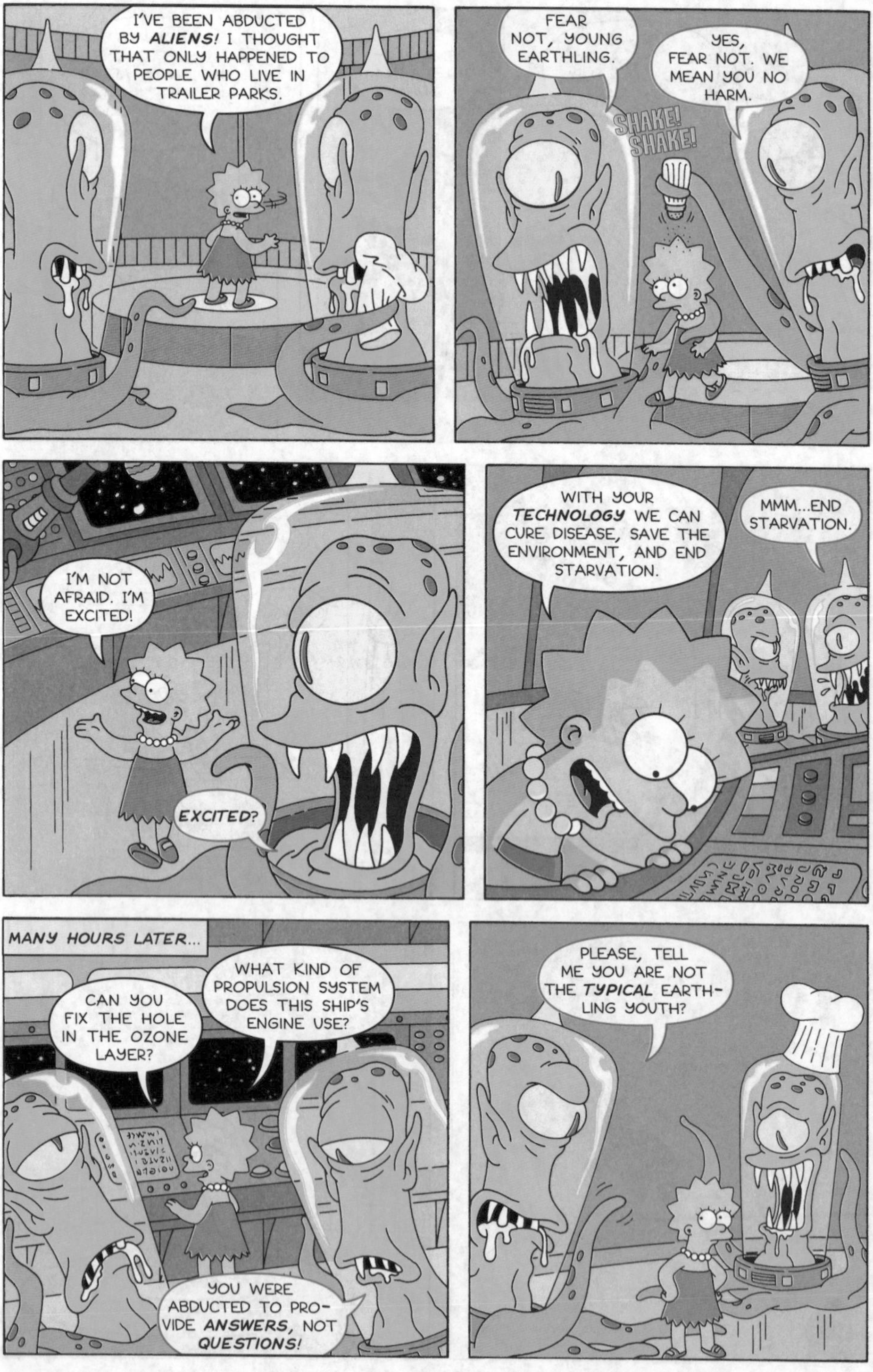
I'VE BEEN ABDUCTED BY ALIENS! I THOUGHT THAT ONLY HAPPENED TO PEOPLE WHO LIVE IN TRAILER PARKS.
FEAR NOT, YOUNG EARTHLING.
YES, FEAR NOT. WE MEAN YOU NO HARM.
SHAKE! SHAKE!
I'M NOT AFRAID. I'M EXCITED!
EXCITED?
WITH YOUR TECHNOLOGY WE CAN CURE DISEASE, SAVE THE ENVIRONMENT, AND END STARVATION.
MMM...END STARVATION.
MANY HOURS LATER...
CAN YOU FIX THE HOLE IN THE OZONE LAYER?
WHAT KIND OF PROPULSION SYSTEM DOES THIS SHIP'S ENGINE USE?
YOU WERE ABDUCTED TO PROVIDE ANSWERS, NOT QUESTIONS!
PLEASE, TELL ME YOU ARE NOT THE TYPICAL EARTHLING YOUTH?

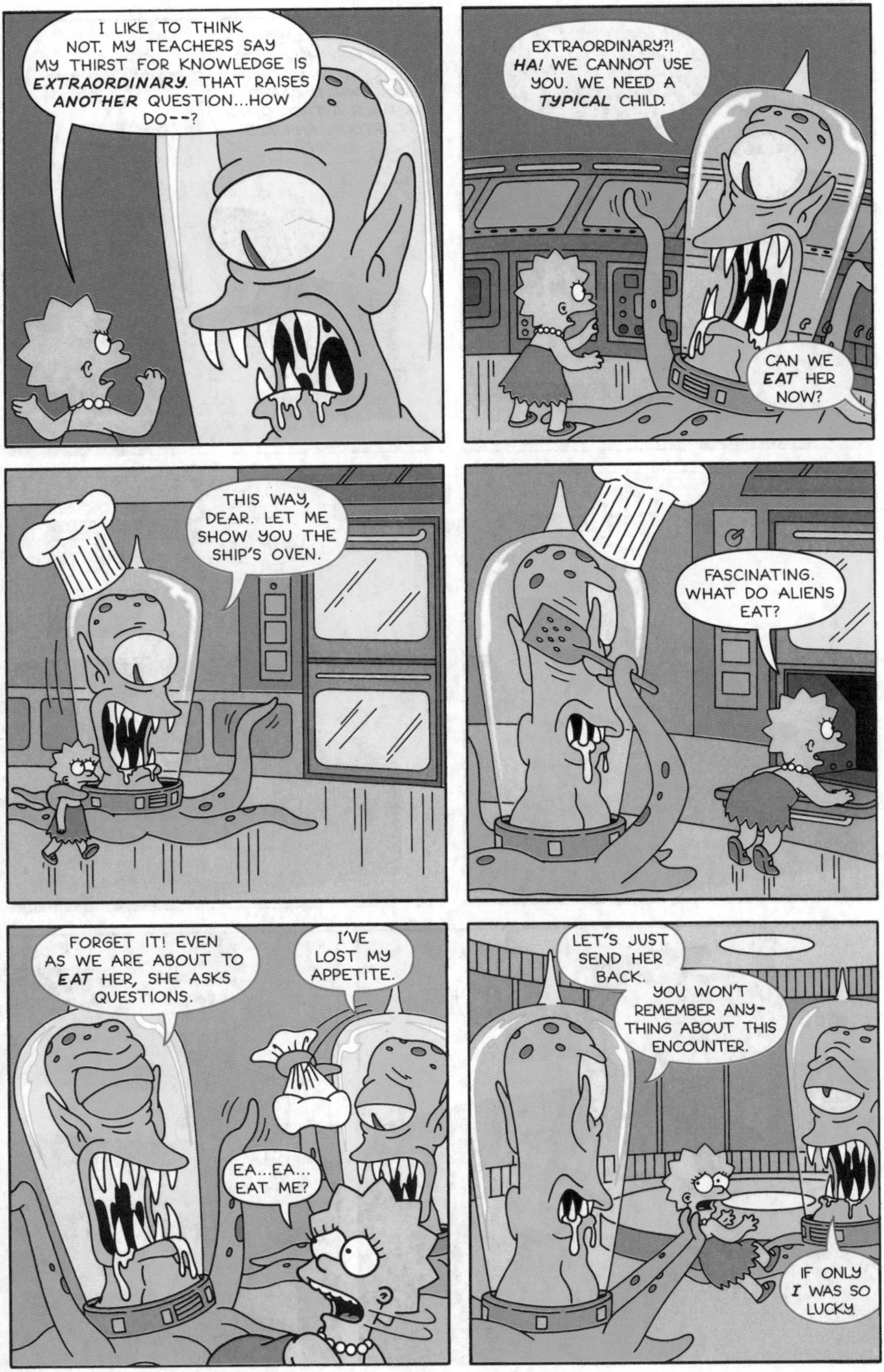

I LIKE TO THINK NOT. MY TEACHERS SAY MY THIRST FOR KNOWLEDGE IS **EXTRAORDINARY**. THAT RAISES **ANOTHER** QUESTION...HOW DO--?
EXTRAORDINARY?! **HA!** WE CANNOT USE YOU. WE NEED A **TYPICAL** CHILD.
CAN WE **EAT** HER NOW?
THIS WAY, DEAR. LET ME SHOW YOU THE SHIP'S OVEN.
FASCINATING. WHAT DO ALIENS EAT?
FORGET IT! EVEN AS WE ARE ABOUT TO **EAT** HER, SHE ASKS QUESTIONS.
I'VE LOST MY APPETITE.
EA...EA... EAT ME?
LET'S JUST SEND HER BACK.
YOU WON'T REMEMBER ANY-THING ABOUT THIS ENCOUNTER.
IF ONLY **I** WAS SO LUCKY.

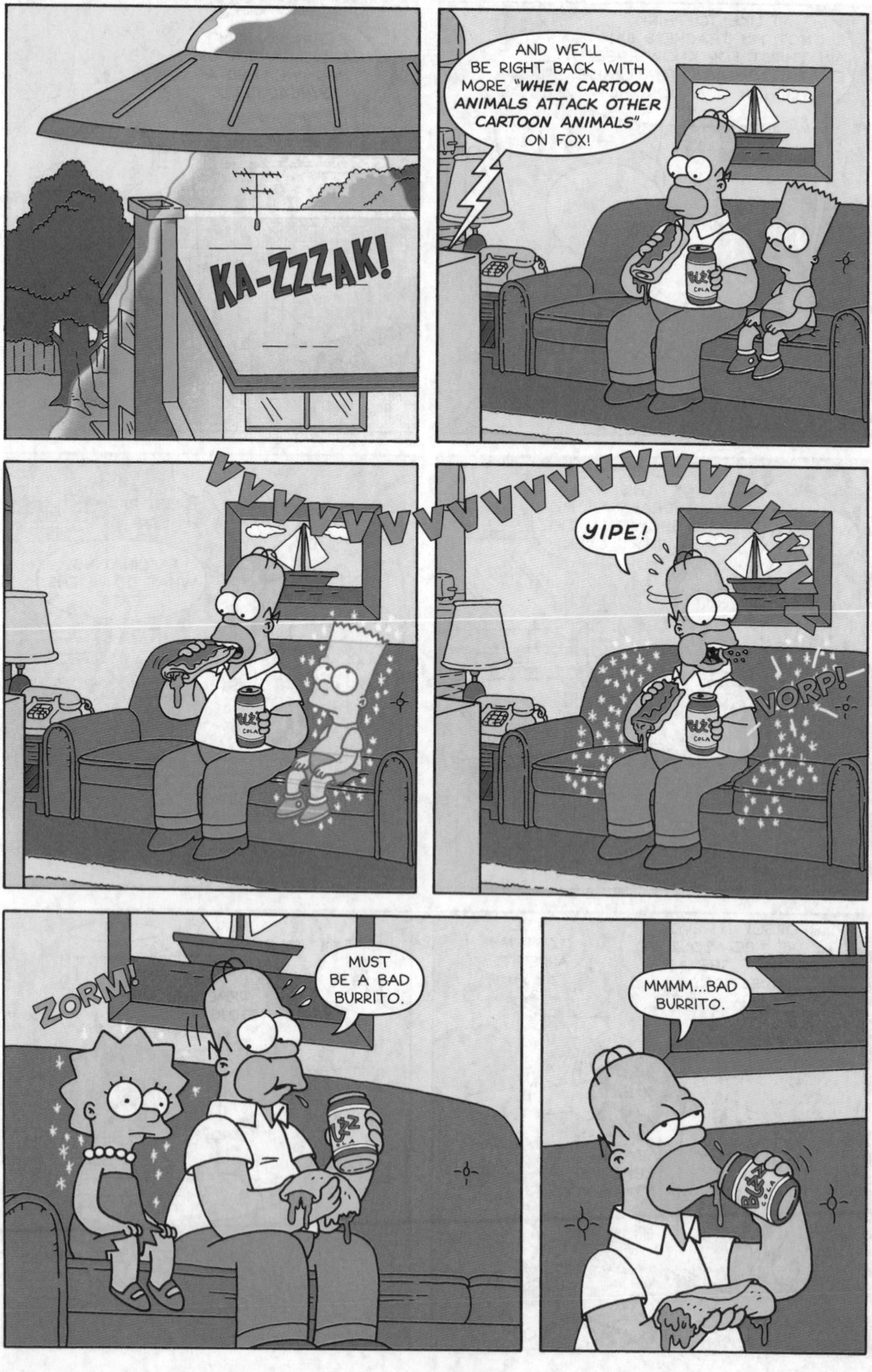
KA-ZZZAK!
AND WE'LL BE RIGHT BACK WITH MORE "WHEN CARTOON ANIMALS ATTACK OTHER CARTOON ANIMALS" ON FOX!
VVVVVVVVVVVVVVVVVVVVVV
YIPE!
VORP!
ZORM!
MUST BE A BAD BURRITO.
MMMM...BAD BURRITO.

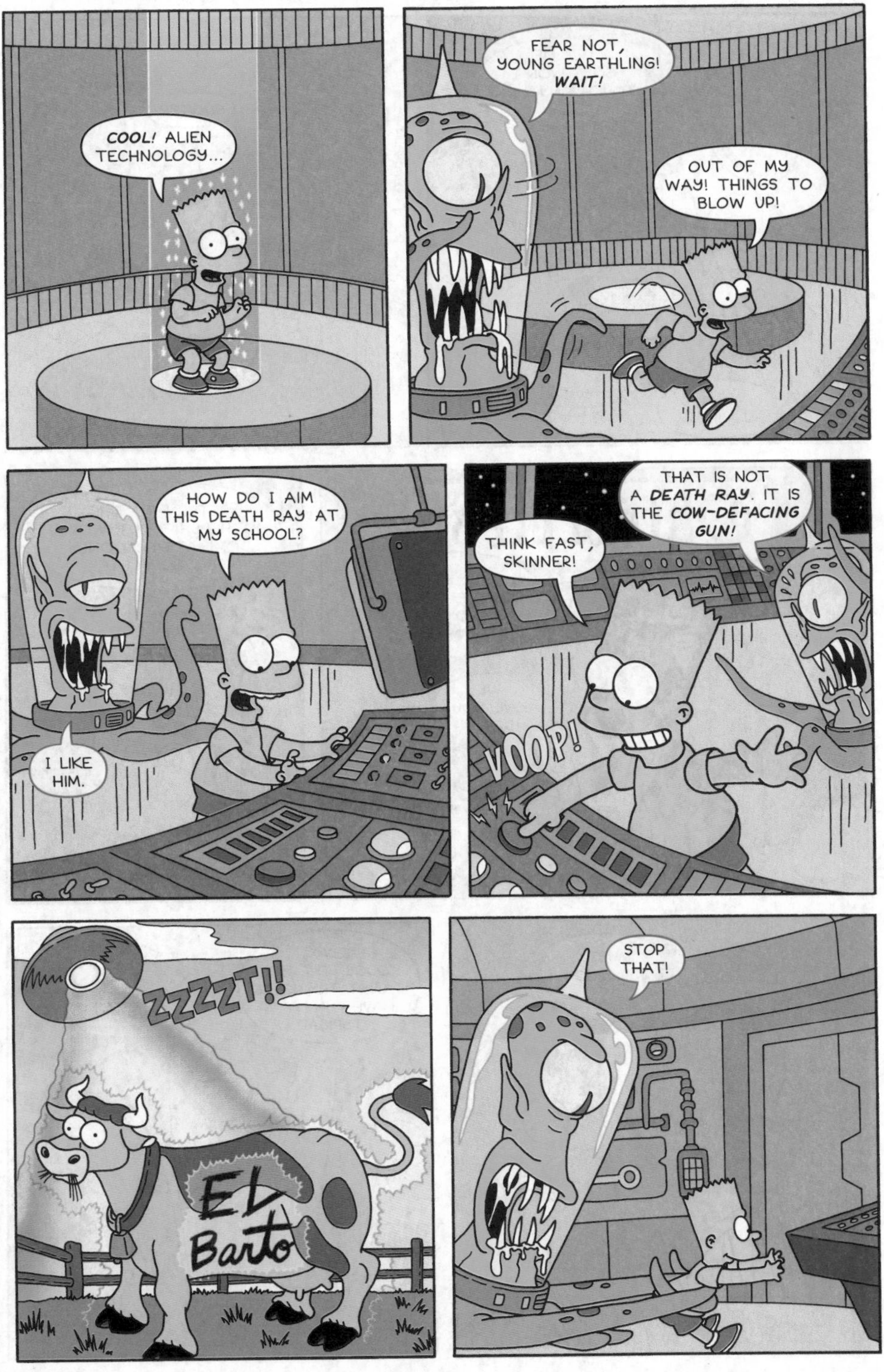
COOL! ALIEN TECHNOLOGY...
FEAR NOT, YOUNG EARTHLING! WAIT!
OUT OF MY WAY! THINGS TO BLOW UP!
HOW DO I AIM THIS DEATH RAY AT MY SCHOOL?
I LIKE HIM.
THINK FAST, SKINNER!
THAT IS NOT A DEATH RAY. IT IS THE COW-DEFACING GUN!
VOOP!
ZZZZT!!
EL Barto
STOP THAT!

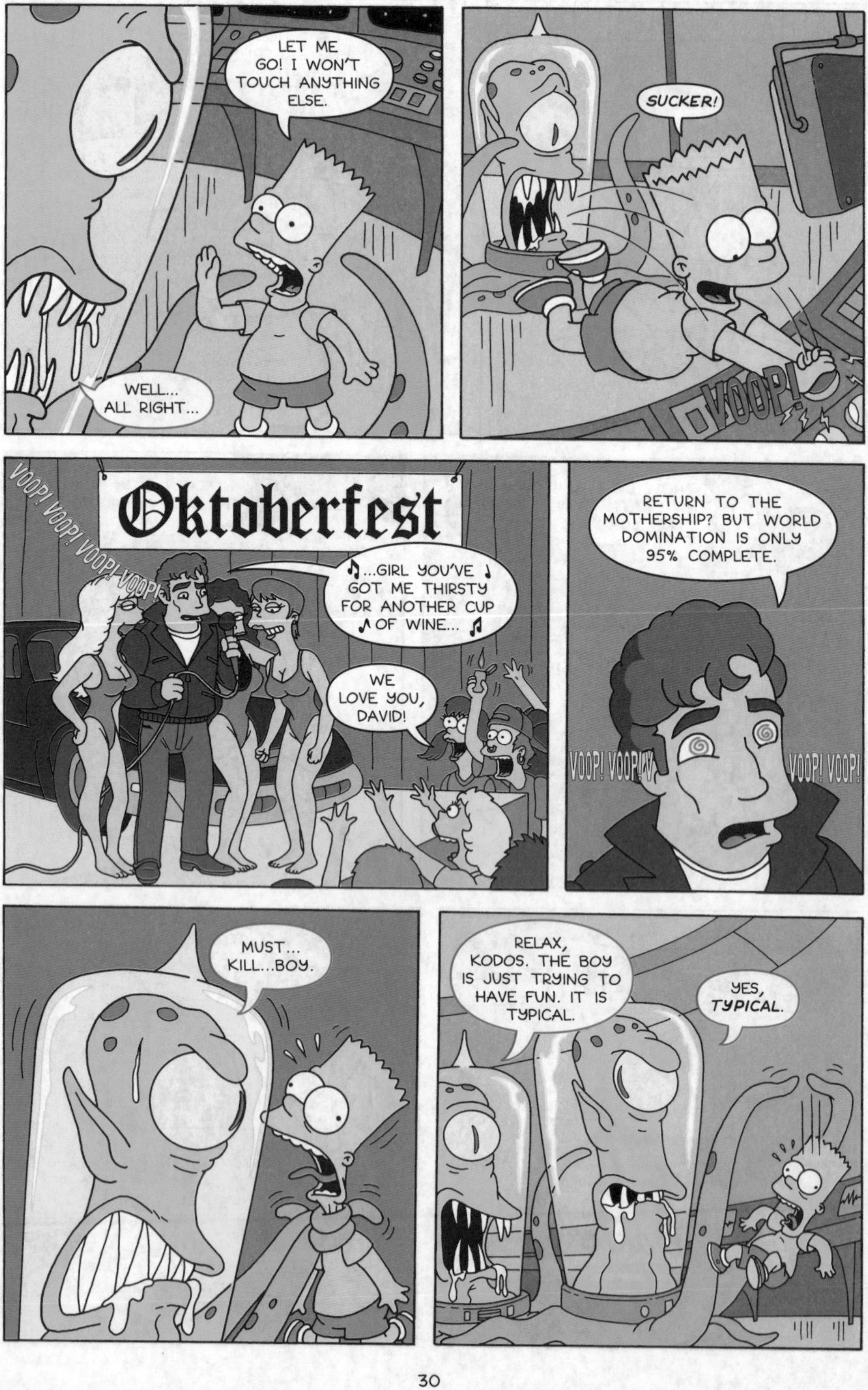
LET ME GO! I WON'T TOUCH ANYTHING ELSE.
WELL... ALL RIGHT...
SUCKER!
VOOP!
Oktoberfest
VOOP! VOOP! VOOP! VOOP!
♫ ...GIRL YOU'VE ♩ GOT ME THIRSTY FOR ANOTHER CUP ♪ OF WINE... ♫
WE LOVE YOU, DAVID!
RETURN TO THE MOTHERSHIP? BUT WORLD DOMINATION IS ONLY 95% COMPLETE.
VOOP! VOOP!
VOOP! VOOP!
MUST... KILL...BOY.
RELAX, KODOS. THE BOY IS JUST TRYING TO HAVE FUN. IT IS TYPICAL.
YES, *TYPICAL*.

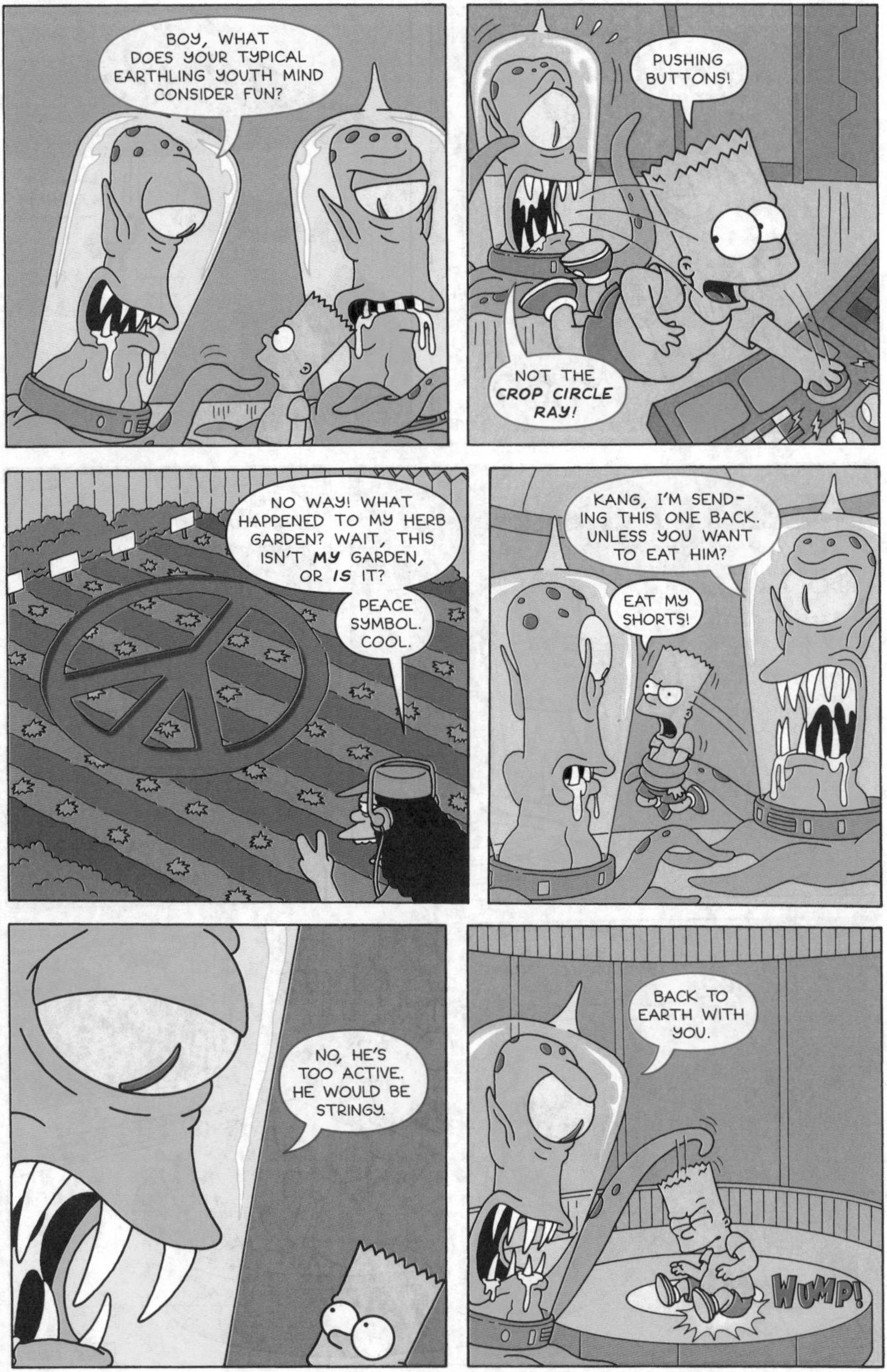
BOY, WHAT DOES YOUR TYPICAL EARTHLING YOUTH MIND CONSIDER FUN?
PUSHING BUTTONS!
NOT THE CROP CIRCLE RAY!
NO WAY! WHAT HAPPENED TO MY HERB GARDEN? WAIT, THIS ISN'T MY GARDEN, OR IS IT?
PEACE SYMBOL. COOL.
KANG, I'M SENDING THIS ONE BACK. UNLESS YOU WANT TO EAT HIM?
EAT MY SHORTS!
NO, HE'S TOO ACTIVE. HE WOULD BE STRINGY.
BACK TO EARTH WITH YOU.
WUMP!

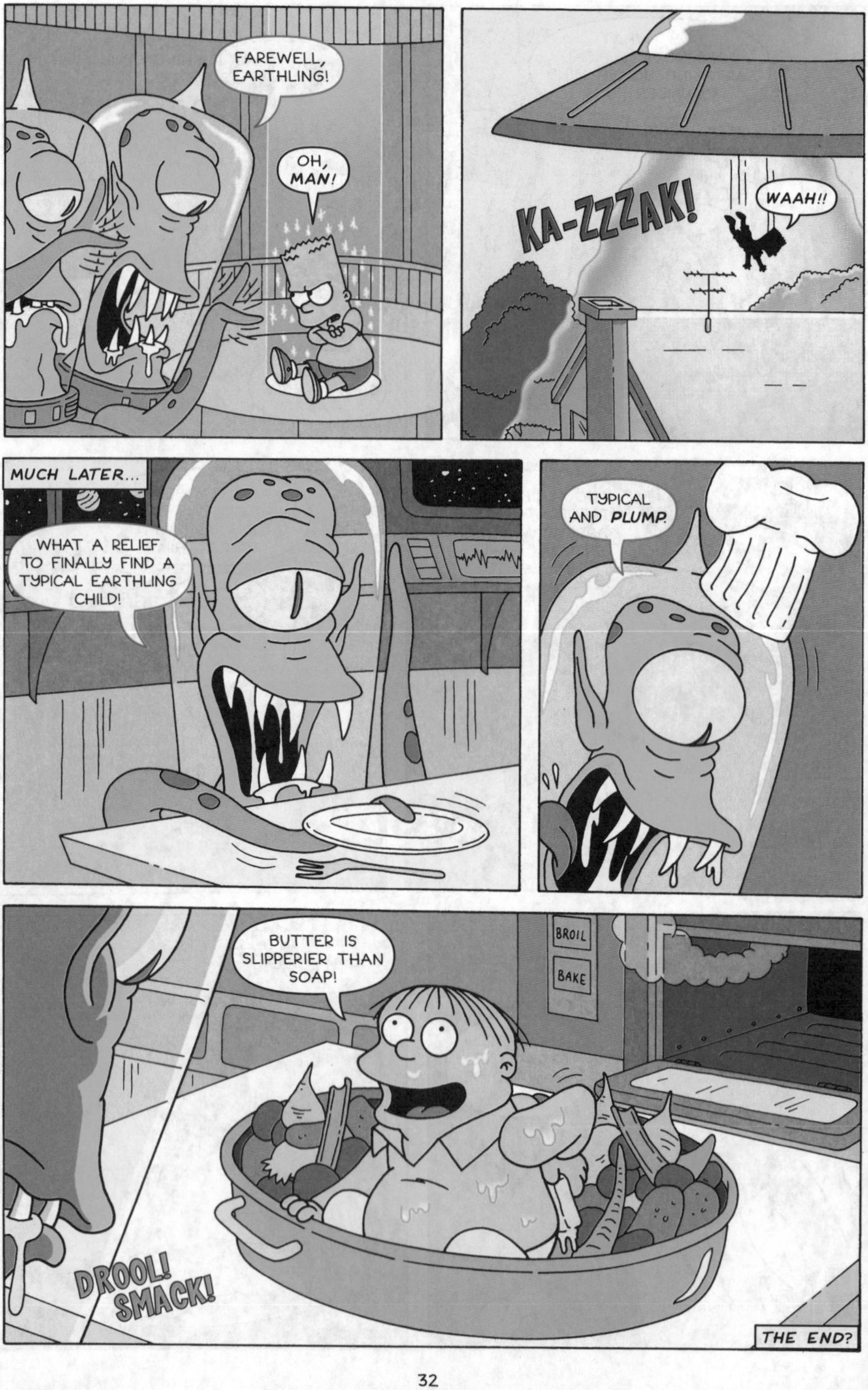
FAREWELL, EARTHLING!
OH, MAN!
KA-ZZZAK!
WAAH!!
MUCH LATER...
WHAT A RELIEF TO FINALLY FIND A TYPICAL EARTHLING CHILD!
TYPICAL AND PLUMP.
BUTTER IS SLIPPERIER THAN SOAP!
BROIL
BAKE
DROOL! SMACK!
THE END?

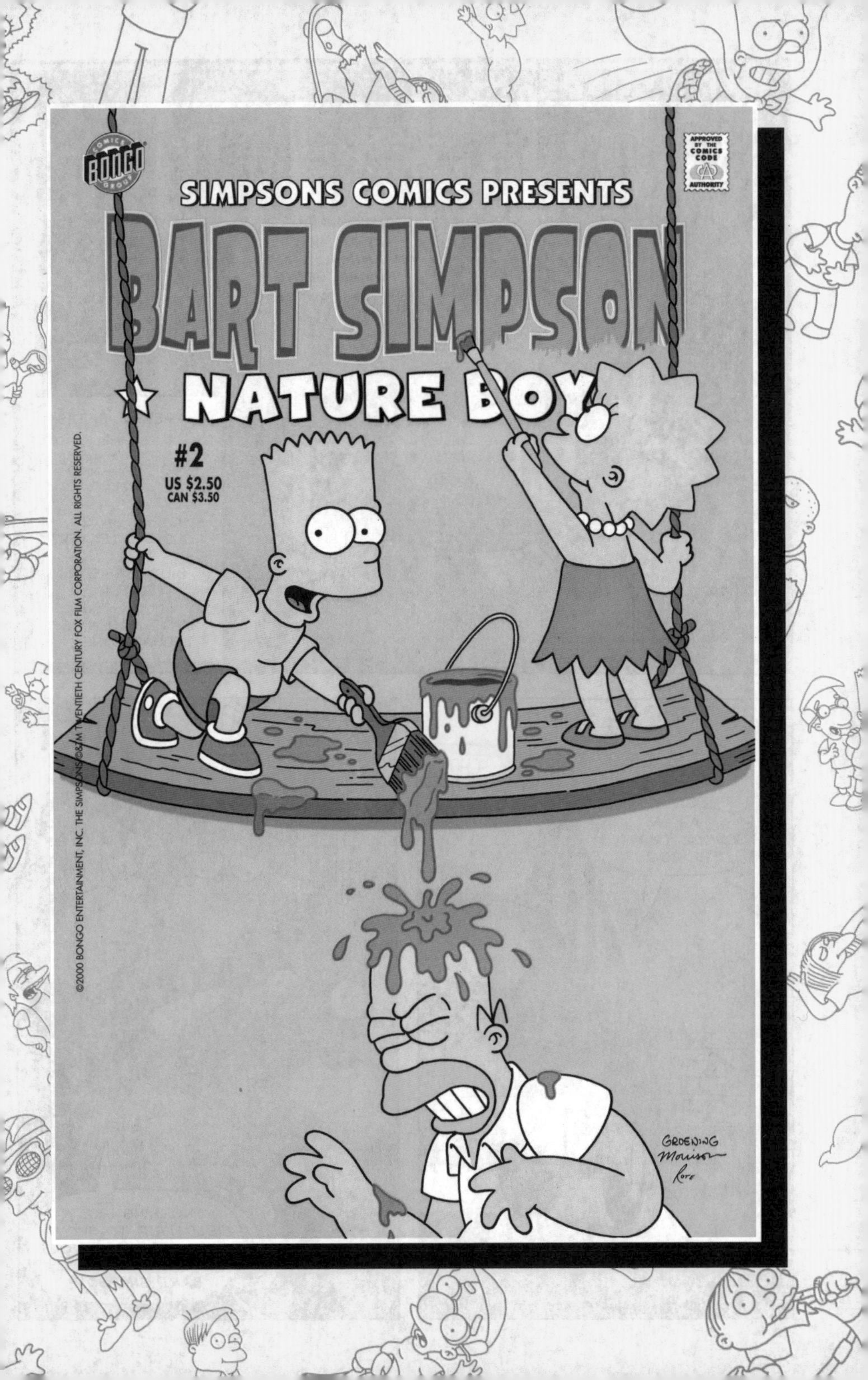
BONGO COMICS GROUP
APPROVED BY THE COMICS CODE AUTHORITY
SIMPSONS COMICS PRESENTS
BART SIMPSON
NATURE BOY
#2
US $2.50
CAN $3.50
©2000 BONGO ENTERTAINMENT, INC. THE SIMPSONS ©&TM TWENTIETH CENTURY FOX FILM CORPORATION. ALL RIGHTS RESERVED.
GROENING
Morrison
Rote

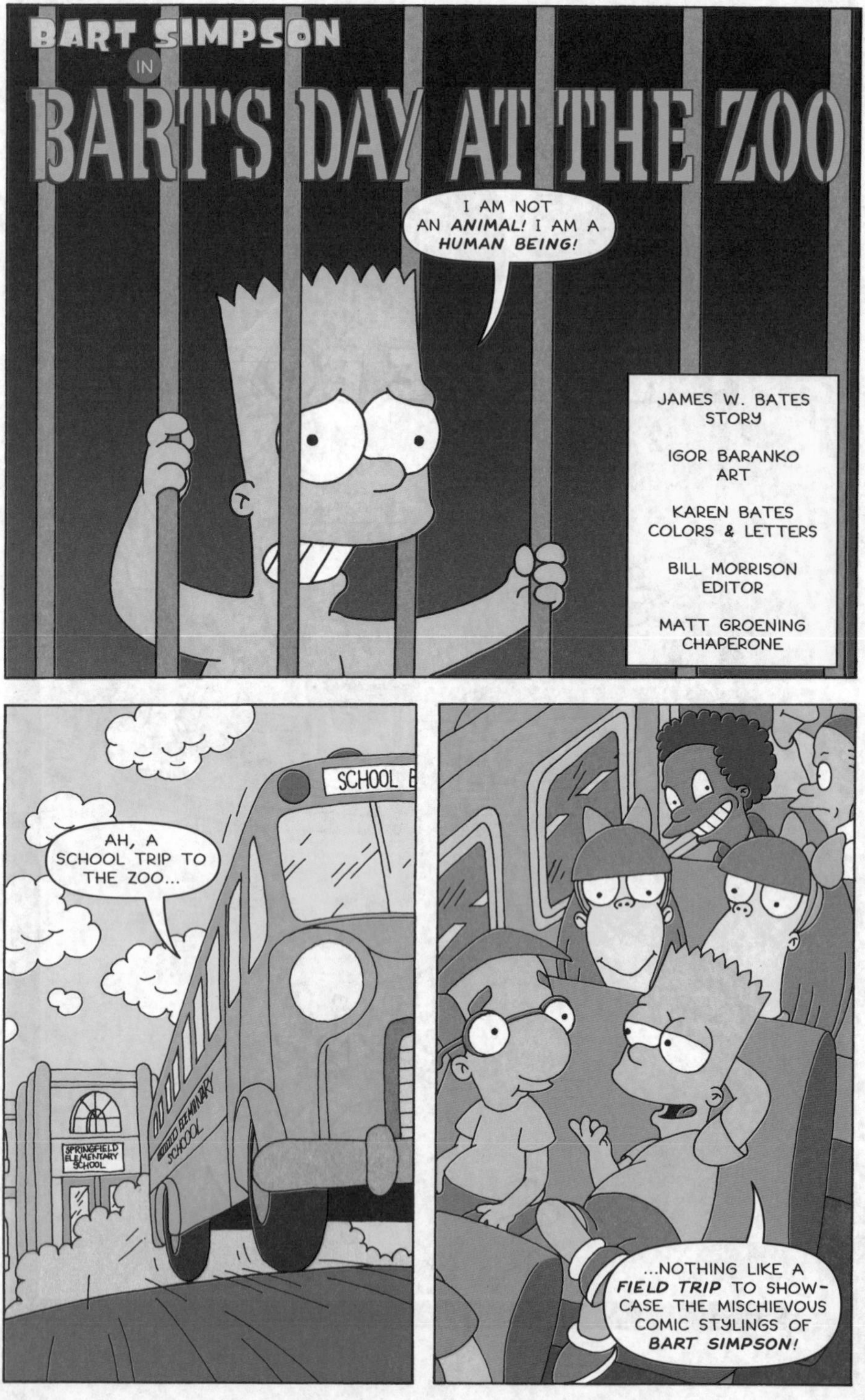
BART SIMPSON
IN
BART'S DAY AT THE ZOO
I AM NOT AN *ANIMAL!* I AM A *HUMAN BEING!*
JAMES W. BATES STORY
IGOR BARANKO ART
KAREN BATES COLORS & LETTERS
BILL MORRISON EDITOR
MATT GROENING CHAPERONE
SCHOOL B
AH, A SCHOOL TRIP TO THE ZOO...
SPRINGFIELD ELEMENTARY SCHOOL
...NOTHING LIKE A *FIELD TRIP* TO SHOW-CASE THE MISCHIEVOUS COMIC STYLINGS OF *BART SIMPSON!*

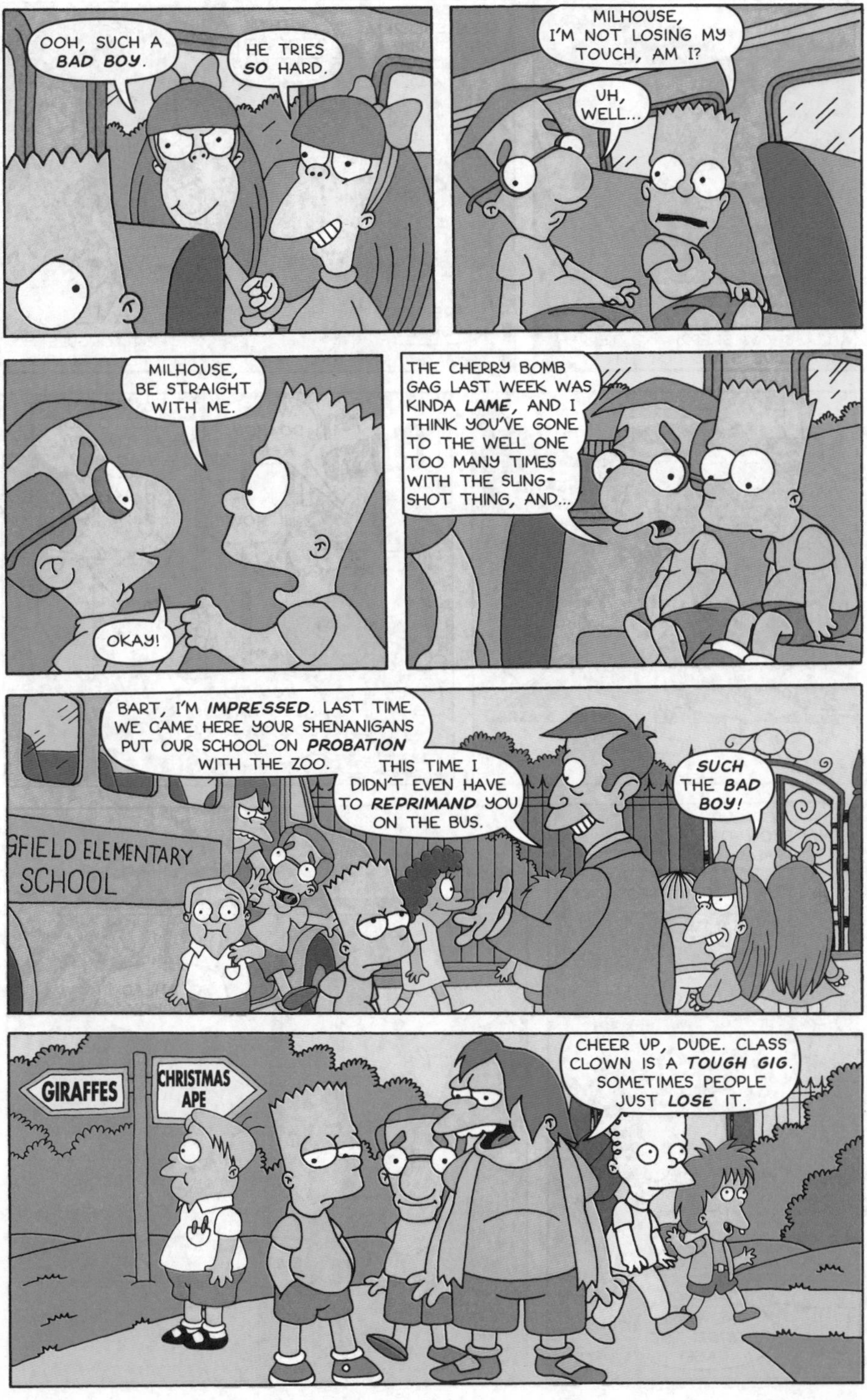
OOH, SUCH A BAD BOY.
HE TRIES SO HARD.
MILHOUSE, I'M NOT LOSING MY TOUCH, AM I?
UH, WELL...
MILHOUSE, BE STRAIGHT WITH ME.
OKAY!
THE CHERRY BOMB GAG LAST WEEK WAS KINDA LAME, AND I THINK YOU'VE GONE TO THE WELL ONE TOO MANY TIMES WITH THE SLING-SHOT THING, AND...
BART, I'M IMPRESSED. LAST TIME WE CAME HERE YOUR SHENANIGANS PUT OUR SCHOOL ON PROBATION WITH THE ZOO.
THIS TIME I DIDN'T EVEN HAVE TO REPRIMAND YOU ON THE BUS.
SUCH THE BAD BOY!
GFIELD ELEMENTARY SCHOOL
GIRAFFES
CHRISTMAS APE
CHEER UP, DUDE. CLASS CLOWN IS A TOUGH GIG. SOMETIMES PEOPLE JUST LOSE IT.

I DON'T CARE WHAT IT TAKES, *I'LL* SHOW YOU. I'LL SHOW SHERRI AND TERRI. I'VE *STILL* GOT IT!

HAVE YOU SEEN SHERRI AND TERRI?

I THINK THEY WENT *THAT* WAY.

UH, RALPH, ARE YOU OKAY?

THEIR TONGUES FEEL LIKE SANDPAPER.

SHERRI! TERRI!

WHAT DO *YOU* WANT?

I'M GONNA PROVE TO YOU THAT I'M *STILL* A *BAD BOY.*

HOW?

YOU TELL *ME.* WHAT DO YOU WANT ME TO DO?

WRITE YOUR NAME ON THE WALL.

THAT'S *ALL?* NO PROBLEMO.

THE WALL *INSIDE* THE CAGE!

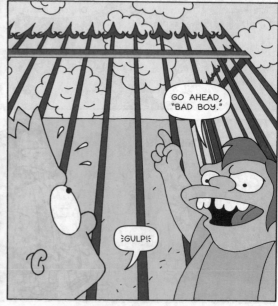

GO AHEAD, "BAD BOY."

≒GULP!≒

36

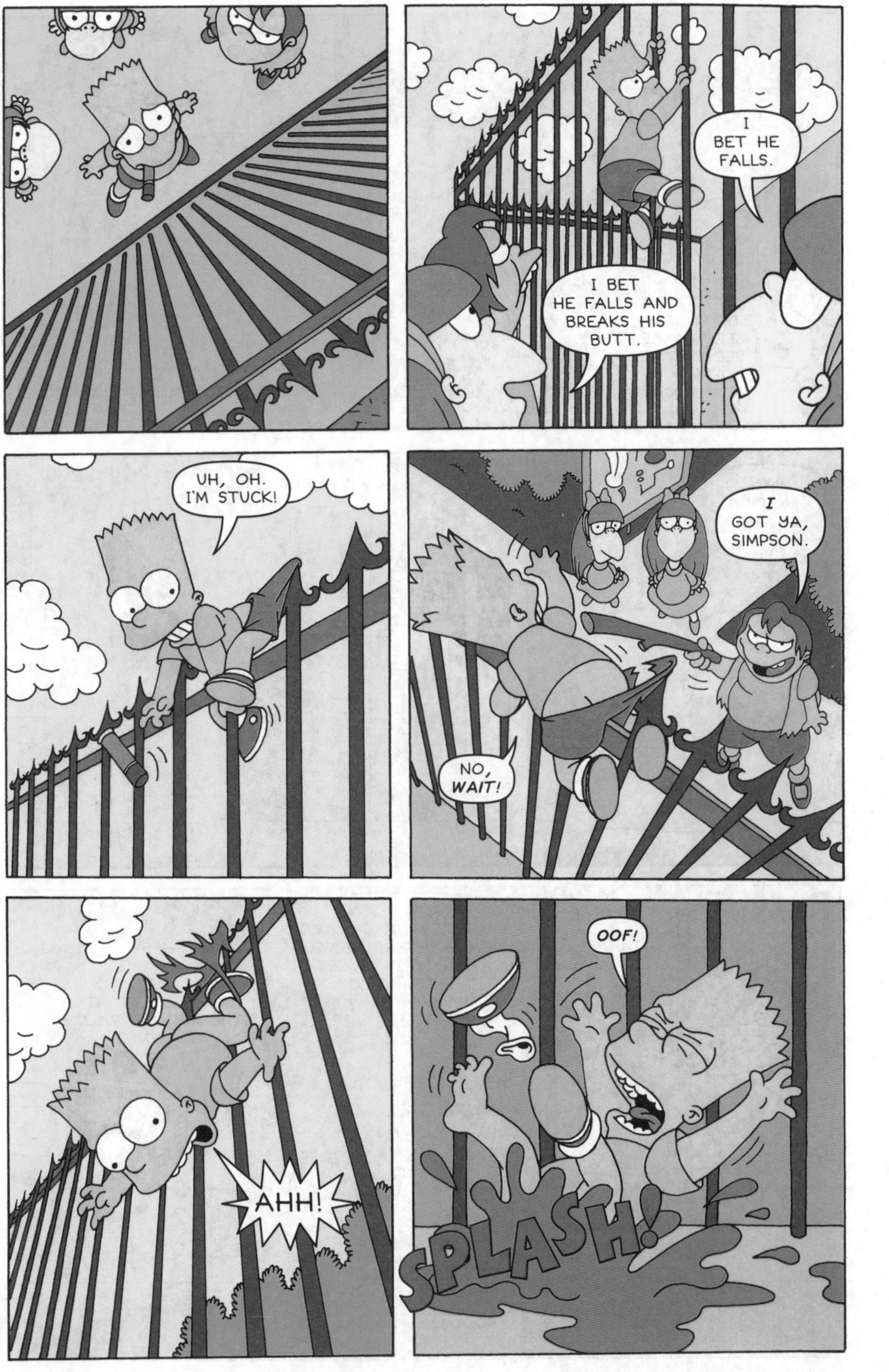
I BET HE FALLS.
I BET HE FALLS AND BREAKS HIS BUTT.
UH, OH. I'M STUCK!
I GOT YA, SIMPSON.
NO, WAIT!
AHH!
OOF!
SPLASH!

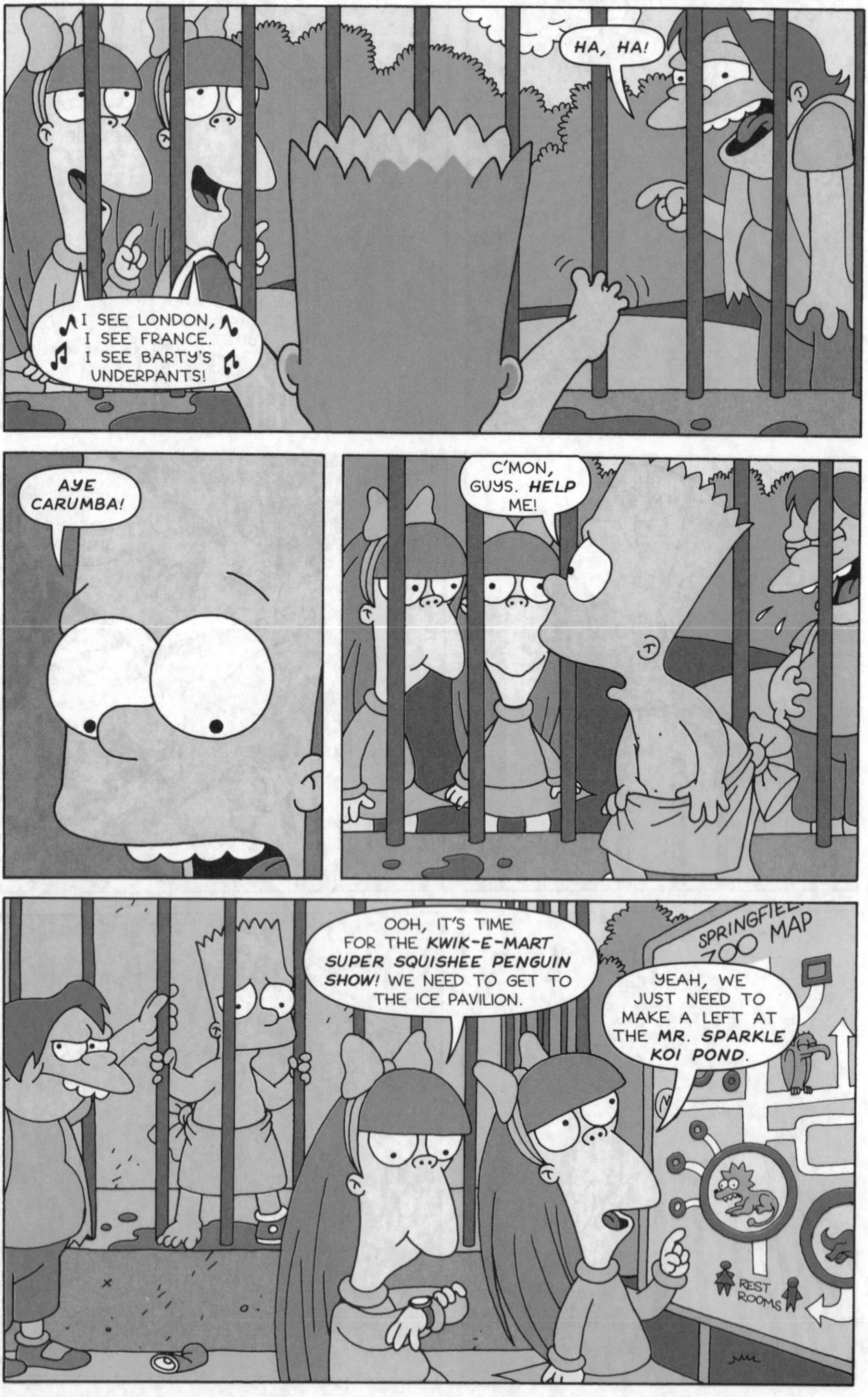
HA, HA!
I SEE LONDON, I SEE FRANCE. I SEE BARTY'S UNDERPANTS!
AYE CARUMBA!
C'MON, GUYS. HELP ME!
OOH, IT'S TIME FOR THE KWIK-E-MART SUPER SQUISHEE PENGUIN SHOW! WE NEED TO GET TO THE ICE PAVILION.
YEAH, WE JUST NEED TO MAKE A LEFT AT THE MR. SPARKLE KOI POND.
SPRINGFIELD ZOO MAP
REST ROOMS

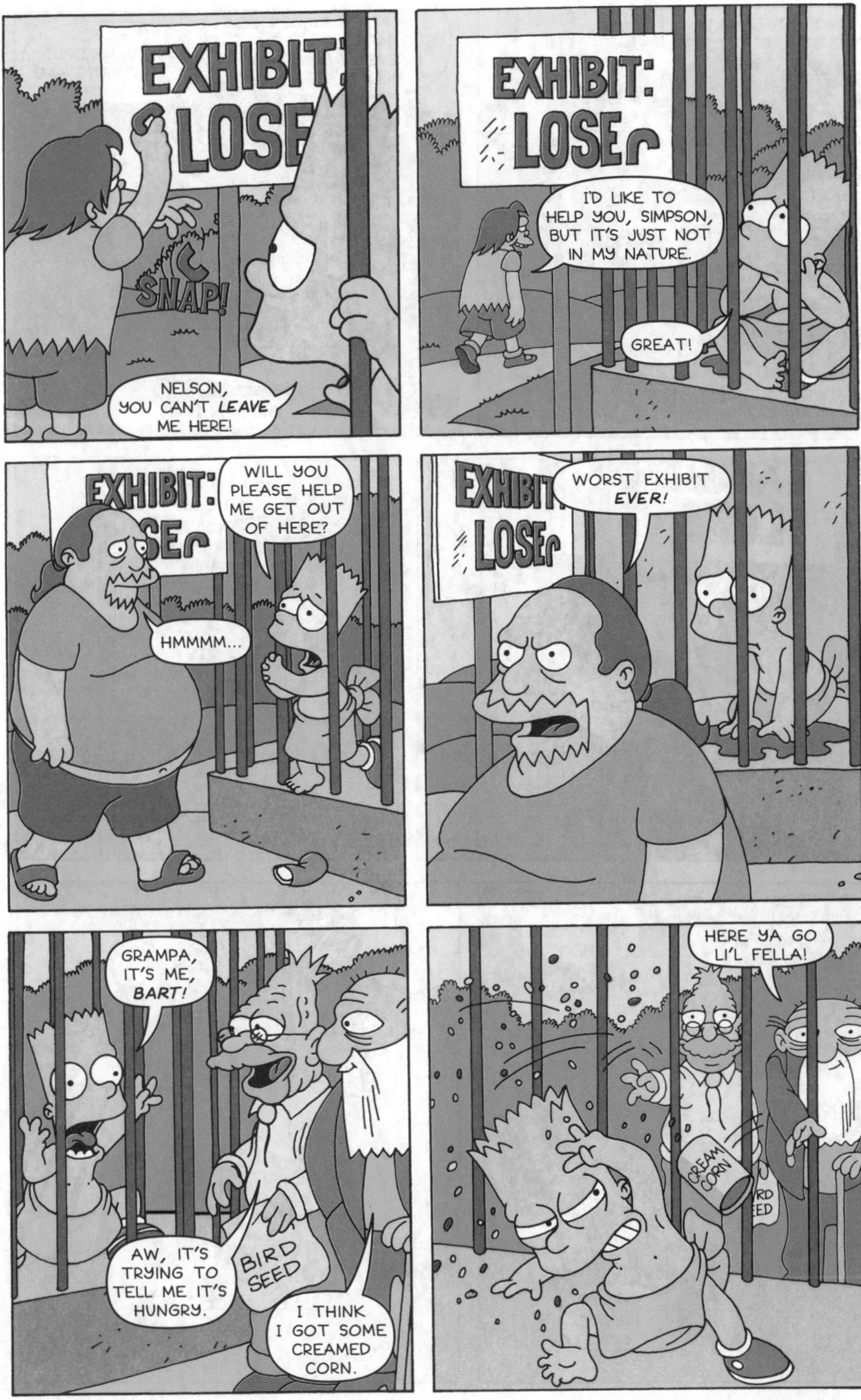
EXHIBIT: LOSE
SNAP!
NELSON, YOU CAN'T *LEAVE* ME HERE!
EXHIBIT: LOSER
I'D LIKE TO HELP YOU, SIMPSON, BUT IT'S JUST NOT IN MY NATURE.
GREAT!
WILL YOU PLEASE HELP ME GET OUT OF HERE?
HMMMM...
WORST EXHIBIT *EVER!*
GRAMPA, IT'S ME, *BART!*
AW, IT'S TRYING TO TELL ME IT'S HUNGRY.
BIRD SEED
I THINK I GOT SOME CREAMED CORN.
HERE YA GO LI'L FELLA!
CREAM CORN

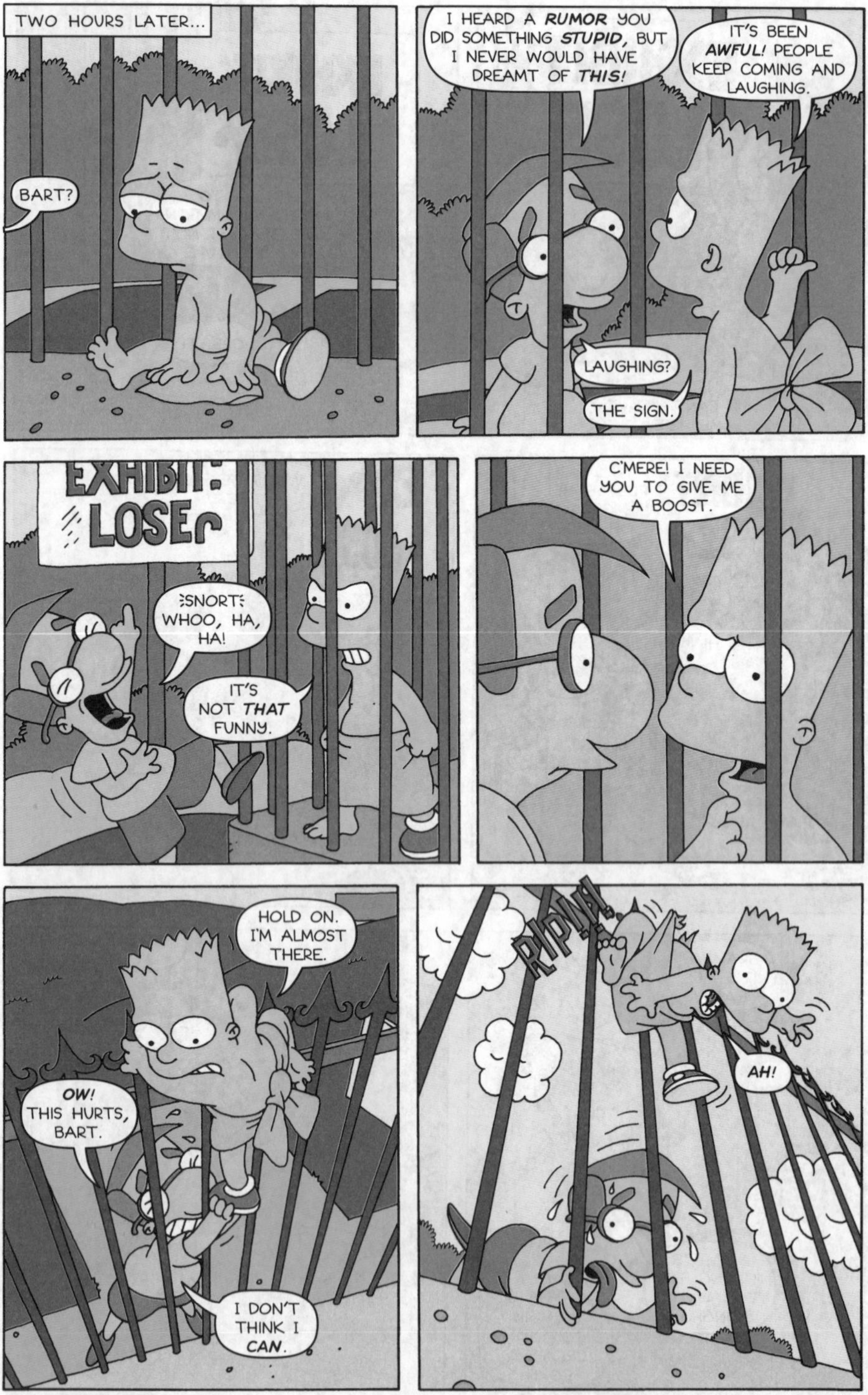
TWO HOURS LATER...
BART?
I HEARD A RUMOR YOU DID SOMETHING STUPID, BUT I NEVER WOULD HAVE DREAMT OF THIS!
IT'S BEEN AWFUL! PEOPLE KEEP COMING AND LAUGHING.
LAUGHING?
THE SIGN.
EXHIBIT: LOSER
SNORT WHOO, HA, HA!
IT'S NOT THAT FUNNY.
C'MERE! I NEED YOU TO GIVE ME A BOOST.
HOLD ON. I'M ALMOST THERE.
OW! THIS HURTS, BART.
I DON'T THINK I CAN.
RIPP!
AH!

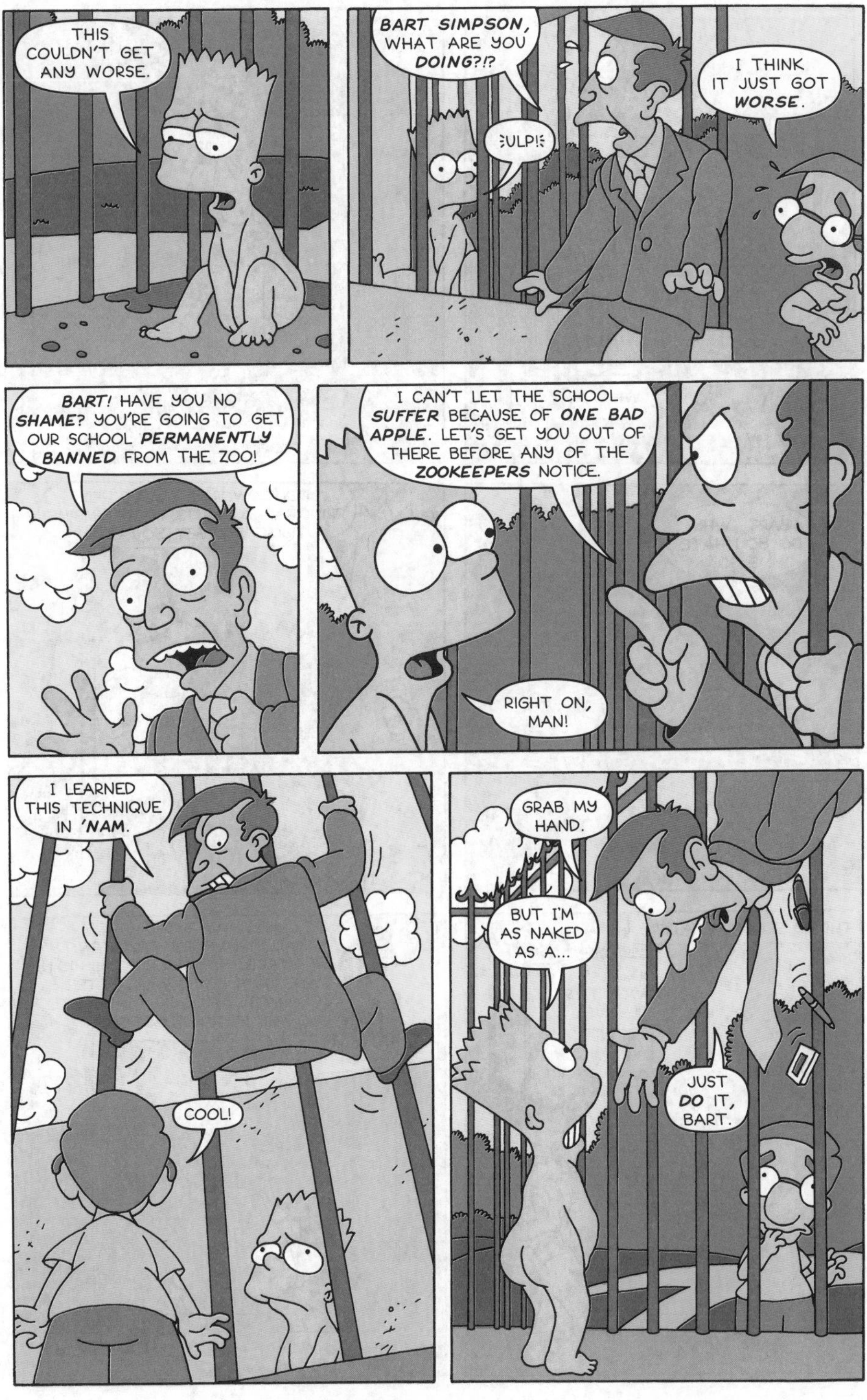
THIS COULDN'T GET ANY WORSE.
BART SIMPSON, WHAT ARE YOU DOING?!?
ULP!
I THINK IT JUST GOT WORSE.
BART! HAVE YOU NO SHAME? YOU'RE GOING TO GET OUR SCHOOL PERMANENTLY BANNED FROM THE ZOO!
I CAN'T LET THE SCHOOL SUFFER BECAUSE OF ONE BAD APPLE. LET'S GET YOU OUT OF THERE BEFORE ANY OF THE ZOOKEEPERS NOTICE.
RIGHT ON, MAN!
I LEARNED THIS TECHNIQUE IN 'NAM.
COOL!
GRAB MY HAND.
BUT I'M AS NAKED AS A...
JUST DO IT, BART.

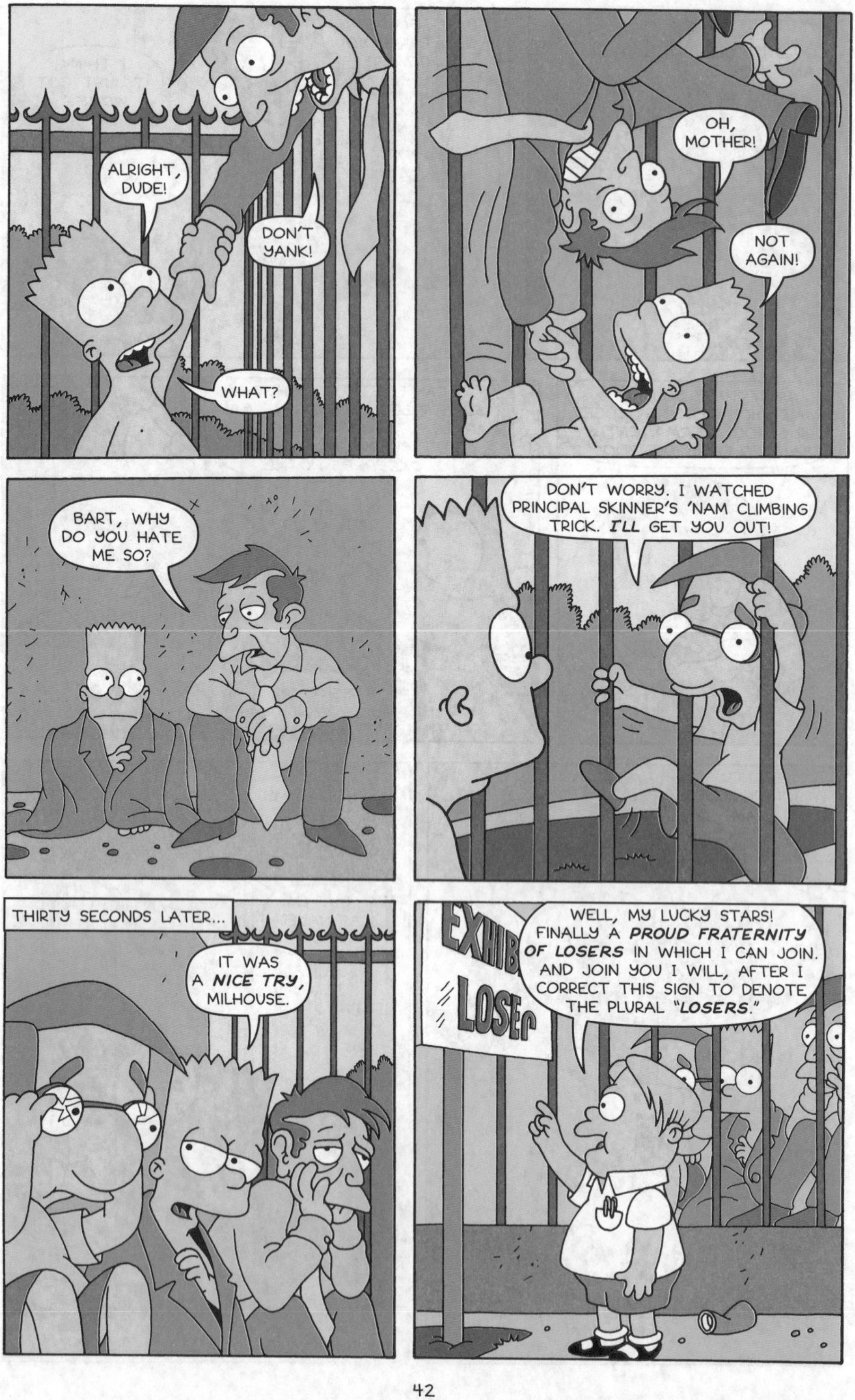

ALRIGHT, DUDE!
DON'T YANK!
WHAT?
OH, MOTHER!
NOT AGAIN!
BART, WHY DO YOU HATE ME SO?
DON'T WORRY. I WATCHED PRINCIPAL SKINNER'S 'NAM CLIMBING TRICK. *I'LL* GET YOU OUT!
THIRTY SECONDS LATER...
IT WAS A ***NICE TRY***, MILHOUSE.
EXHIB
LOSEr
WELL, MY LUCKY STARS! FINALLY A ***PROUD FRATERNITY OF LOSERS*** IN WHICH I CAN JOIN. AND JOIN YOU I WILL, AFTER I CORRECT THIS SIGN TO DENOTE THE PLURAL "***LOSERS***."

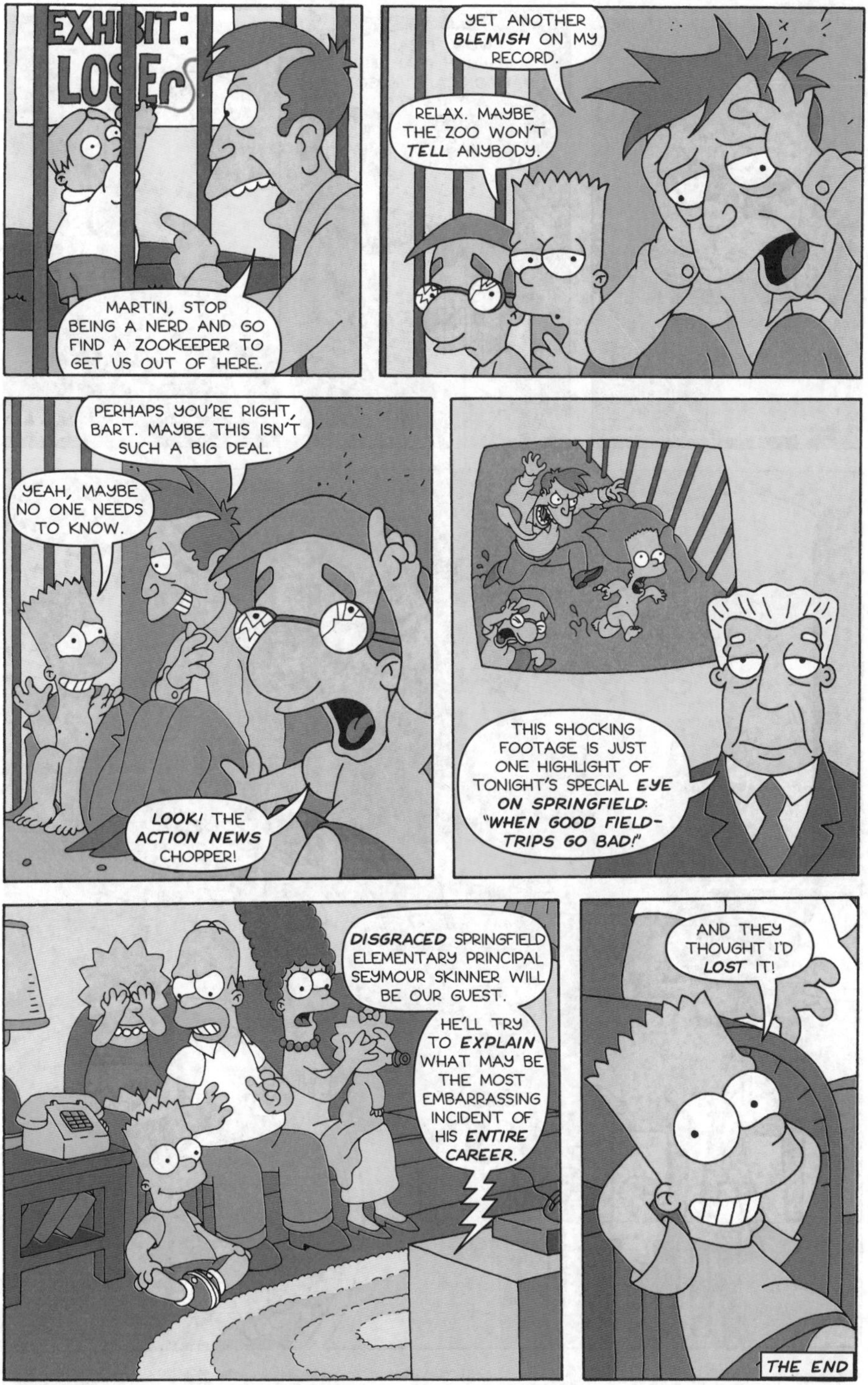
EXHIBIT: LOSER
MARTIN, STOP BEING A NERD AND GO FIND A ZOOKEEPER TO GET US OUT OF HERE.
YET ANOTHER BLEMISH ON MY RECORD.
RELAX. MAYBE THE ZOO WON'T TELL ANYBODY.
PERHAPS YOU'RE RIGHT, BART. MAYBE THIS ISN'T SUCH A BIG DEAL.
YEAH, MAYBE NO ONE NEEDS TO KNOW.
LOOK! THE ACTION NEWS CHOPPER!
THIS SHOCKING FOOTAGE IS JUST ONE HIGHLIGHT OF TONIGHT'S SPECIAL EYE ON SPRINGFIELD: "WHEN GOOD FIELD-TRIPS GO BAD!"
DISGRACED SPRINGFIELD ELEMENTARY PRINCIPAL SEYMOUR SKINNER WILL BE OUR GUEST.
HE'LL TRY TO EXPLAIN WHAT MAY BE THE MOST EMBARRASSING INCIDENT OF HIS ENTIRE CAREER.
AND THEY THOUGHT I'D LOST IT!
THE END

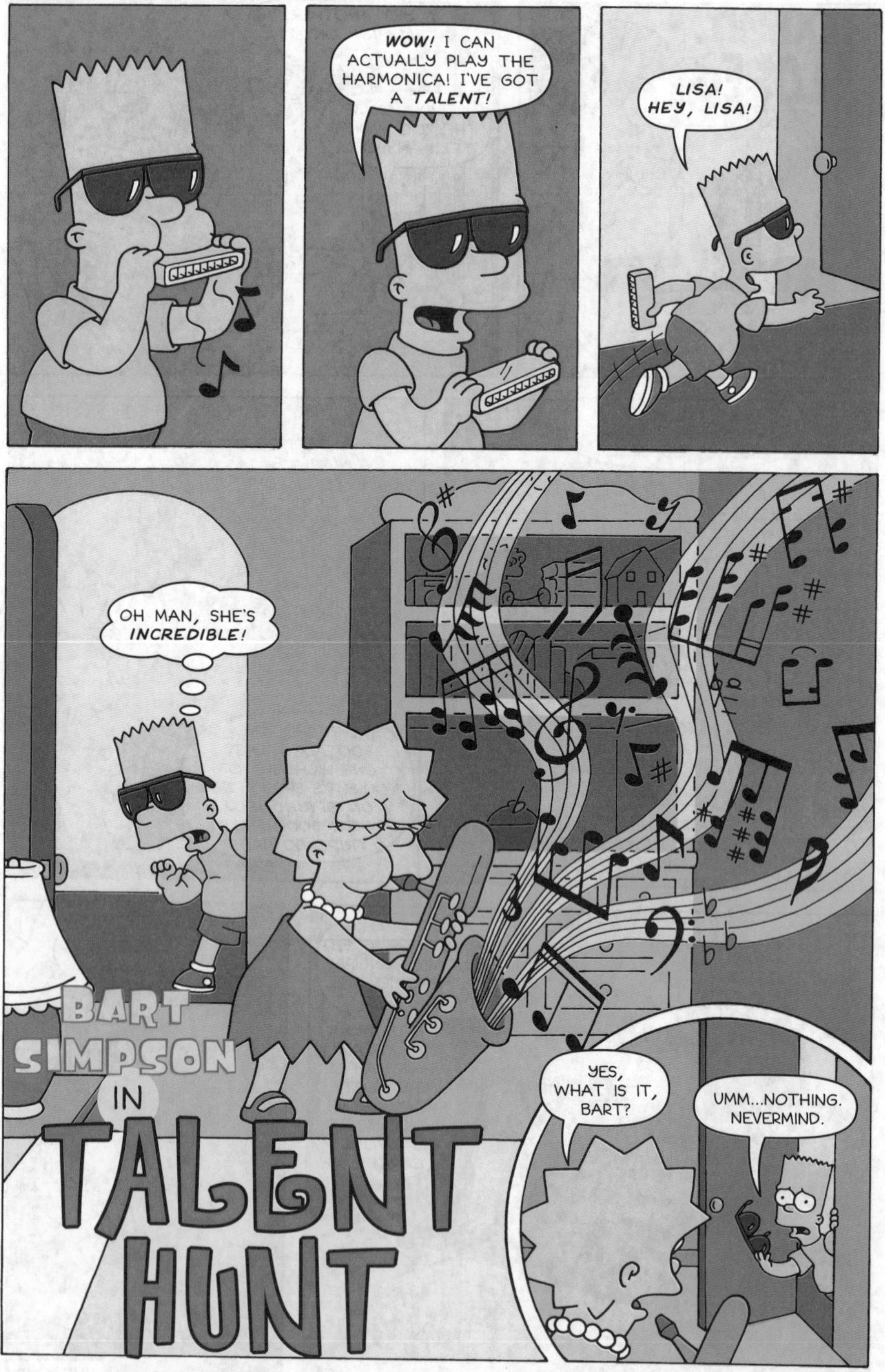
WOW! I CAN ACTUALLY PLAY THE HARMONICA! I'VE GOT A TALENT!
LISA! HEY, LISA!
OH MAN, SHE'S INCREDIBLE!
BART SIMPSON IN TALENT HUNT
YES, WHAT IS IT, BART?
UMM...NOTHING. NEVERMIND.

GEORGE GLADIR SCRIPT · FRANCIS DINGLASAN PENCILS · MIKE DE CARLO INKS · ART VILLANUEVA COLORS · KAREN BATES LETTERS · BILL MORRISON EDITOR · MATT GROENING TALENT SCOUT

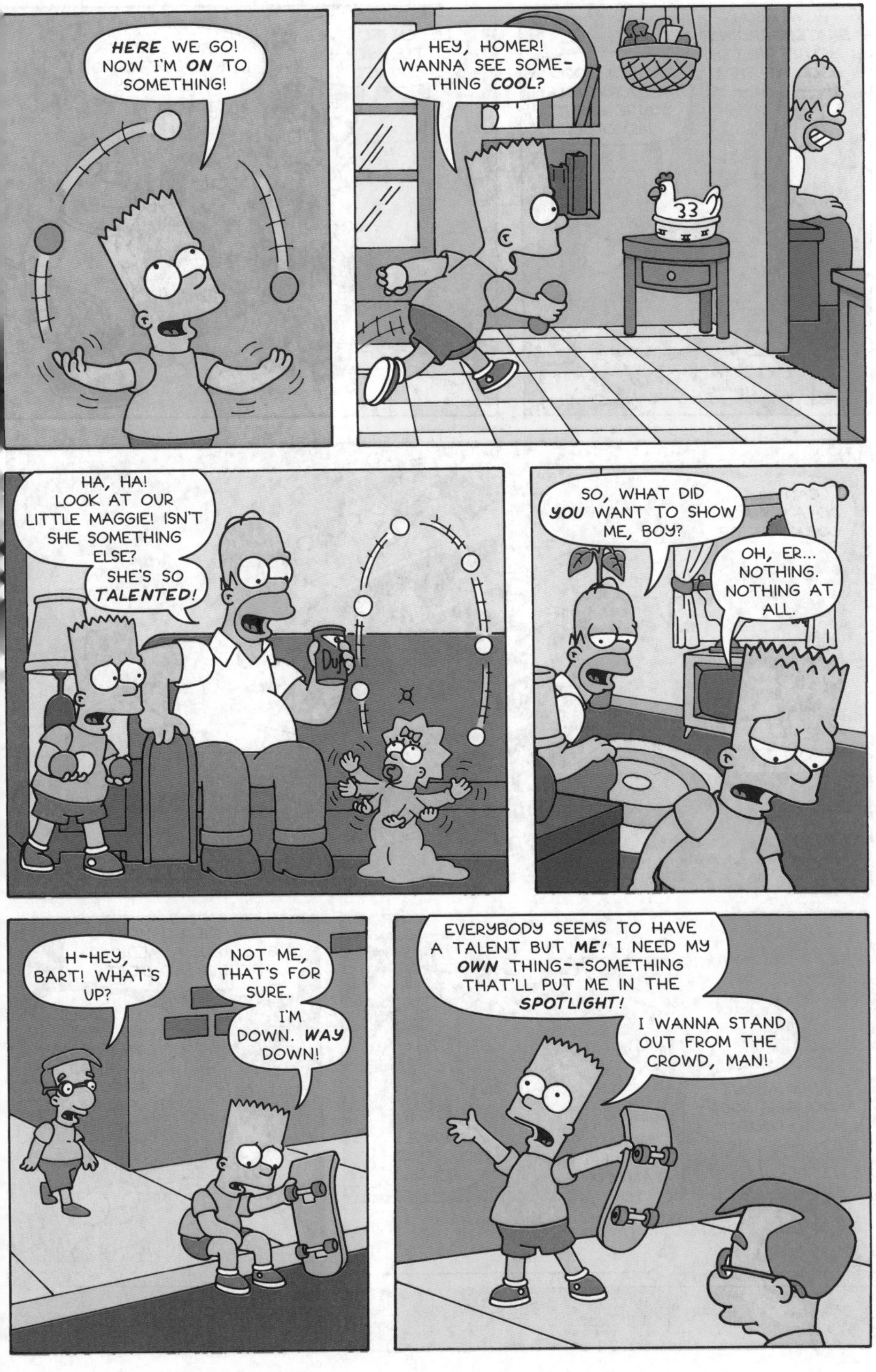
HERE WE GO! NOW I'M ON TO SOMETHING!
HEY, HOMER! WANNA SEE SOME-THING COOL?
33
HA, HA! LOOK AT OUR LITTLE MAGGIE! ISN'T SHE SOMETHING ELSE?
SHE'S SO TALENTED!
SO, WHAT DID YOU WANT TO SHOW ME, BOY?
OH, ER... NOTHING. NOTHING AT ALL.
H-HEY, BART! WHAT'S UP?
NOT ME, THAT'S FOR SURE.
I'M DOWN. WAY DOWN!
EVERYBODY SEEMS TO HAVE A TALENT BUT ME! I NEED MY OWN THING--SOMETHING THAT'LL PUT ME IN THE SPOTLIGHT!
I WANNA STAND OUT FROM THE CROWD, MAN!

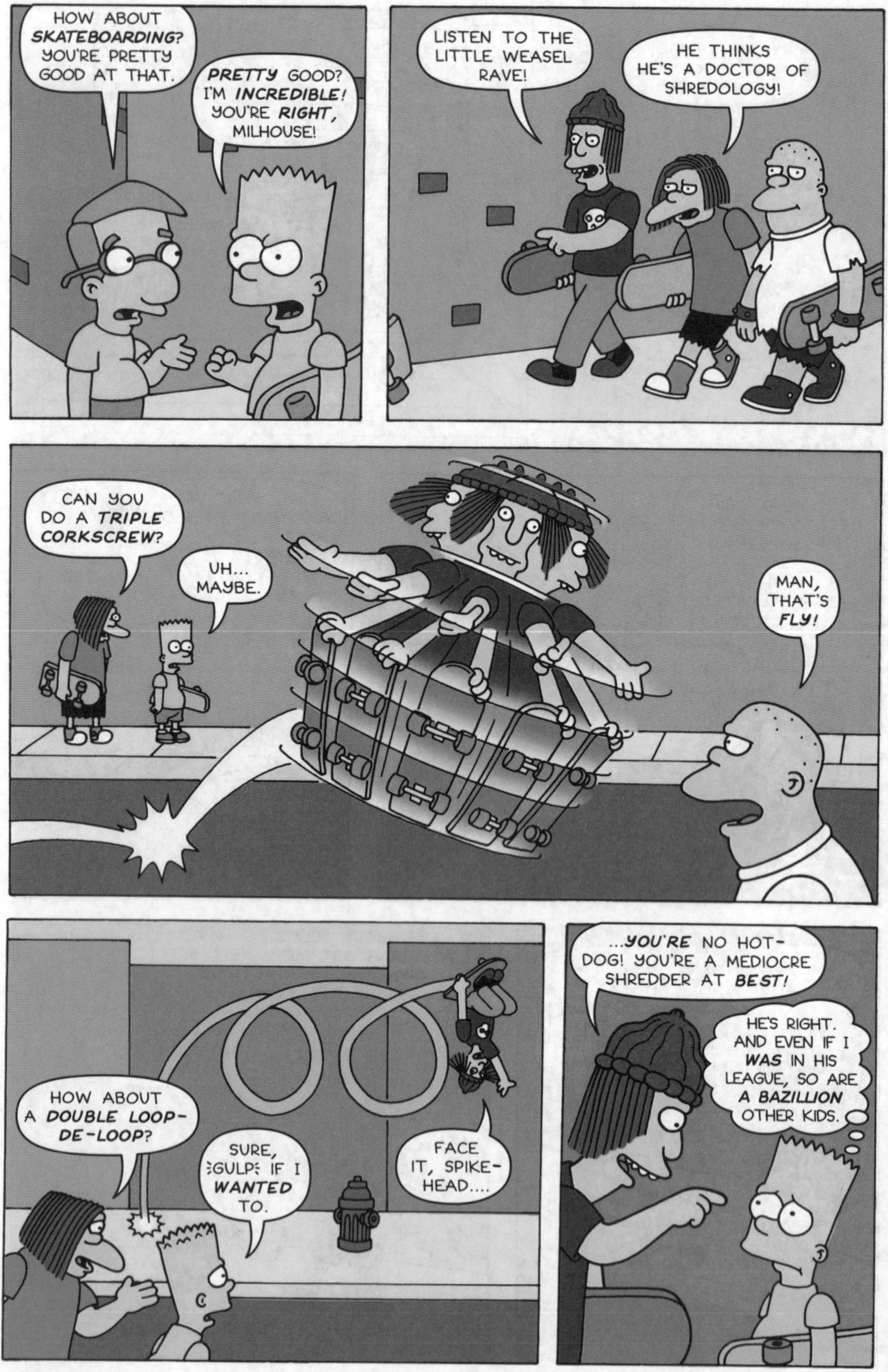
HOW ABOUT SKATEBOARDING? YOU'RE PRETTY GOOD AT THAT.
PRETTY GOOD? I'M INCREDIBLE! YOU'RE RIGHT, MILHOUSE!
LISTEN TO THE LITTLE WEASEL RAVE!
HE THINKS HE'S A DOCTOR OF SHREDOLOGY!
CAN YOU DO A TRIPLE CORKSCREW?
UH... MAYBE.
MAN, THAT'S FLY!
HOW ABOUT A DOUBLE LOOP-DE-LOOP?
SURE, ;GULP; IF I WANTED TO.
FACE IT, SPIKE-HEAD....
...YOU'RE NO HOT-DOG! YOU'RE A MEDIOCRE SHREDDER AT BEST!
HE'S RIGHT. AND EVEN IF I WAS IN HIS LEAGUE, SO ARE A BAZILLION OTHER KIDS.

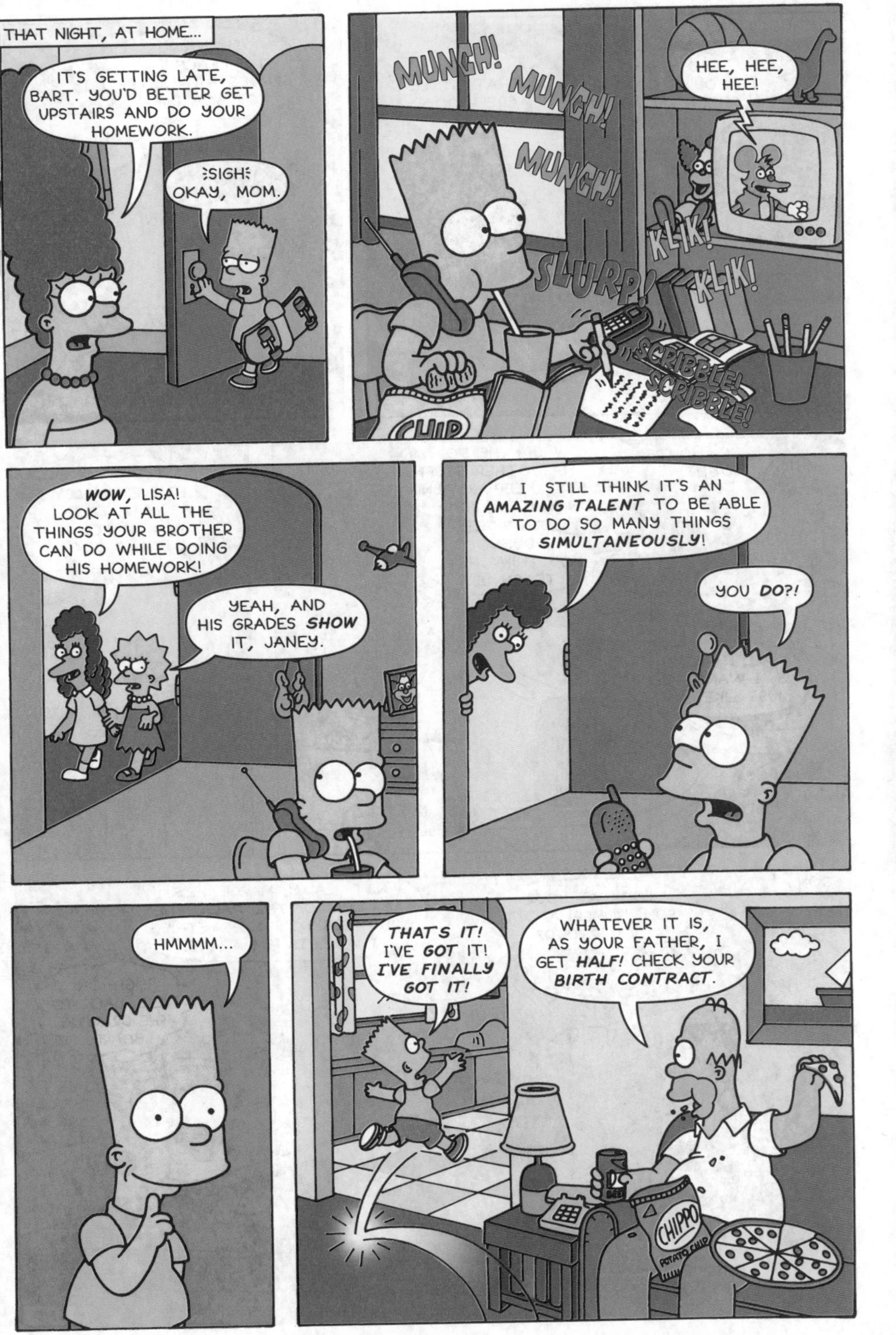
THAT NIGHT, AT HOME...
IT'S GETTING LATE, BART. YOU'D BETTER GET UPSTAIRS AND DO YOUR HOMEWORK.
:SIGH: OKAY, MOM.
MUNCH! MUNCH! MUNCH!
HEE, HEE, HEE!
SLURP!
KLIK! KLIK!
SCRIBBLE! SCRIBBLE!
CHIP
WOW, LISA! LOOK AT ALL THE THINGS YOUR BROTHER CAN DO WHILE DOING HIS HOMEWORK!
YEAH, AND HIS GRADES SHOW IT, JANEY.
I STILL THINK IT'S AN AMAZING TALENT TO BE ABLE TO DO SO MANY THINGS SIMULTANEOUSLY!
YOU DO?!
HMMMM...
THAT'S IT! I'VE GOT IT! I'VE FINALLY GOT IT!
WHATEVER IT IS, AS YOUR FATHER, I GET HALF! CHECK YOUR BIRTH CONTRACT.
CHIPPO POTATO CHIP

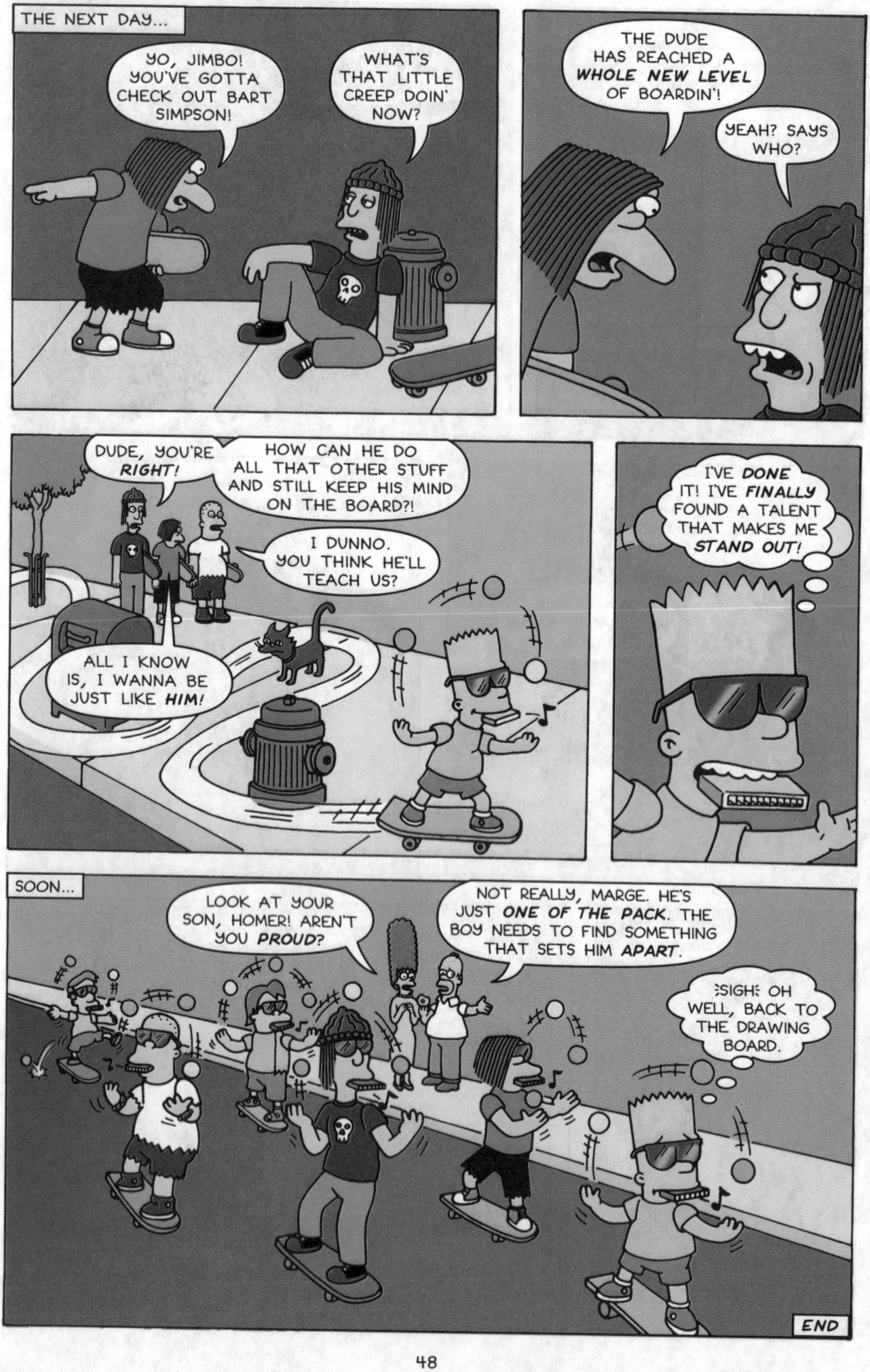
THE NEXT DAY...
YO, JIMBO! YOU'VE GOTTA CHECK OUT BART SIMPSON!
WHAT'S THAT LITTLE CREEP DOIN' NOW?
THE DUDE HAS REACHED A WHOLE NEW LEVEL OF BOARDIN'!
YEAH? SAYS WHO?
DUDE, YOU'RE RIGHT!
HOW CAN HE DO ALL THAT OTHER STUFF AND STILL KEEP HIS MIND ON THE BOARD?!
I DUNNO. YOU THINK HE'LL TEACH US?
ALL I KNOW IS, I WANNA BE JUST LIKE HIM!
I'VE DONE IT! I'VE FINALLY FOUND A TALENT THAT MAKES ME STAND OUT!
SOON...
LOOK AT YOUR SON, HOMER! AREN'T YOU PROUD?
NOT REALLY, MARGE. HE'S JUST ONE OF THE PACK. THE BOY NEEDS TO FIND SOMETHING THAT SETS HIM APART.
SIGH OH WELL, BACK TO THE DRAWING BOARD.
END

NG-HEY!, NON-ADULT TYPE PERSONS WITH THE *READING* AND THE *FUNNING!* IMAGINE WHAT WOULD HAPPEN IF SUDDENLY YOU WERE *LOTS* OF YOU WITH EXTRA FEET AND ARMS AND !VOYVING! AND !YOINKS!? THAT'S WHAT HAPPENS IN THIS ISSUE'S *PROFESSOR FRINK'S TENUOUSLY TRUTHFUL TALES*.

SPRINGFIELD INSTITUTE OF SCIENCE PERSONS

TRY OUR QUANTUM PHYSICS SEMINARS!

(SCIENTIST HAS LESS THAN $20 IN REGISTER)

BART SIMPSON IN MAXIMUM BART!

Professon Frink "He makes you think!"

CLONING CHAMBER NO FOOD OR DRINK

HEY, *PROFESSOR!* I BROUGHT BACK THAT 4TH DIMENSIONAL *FAKE VOMIT* YOU LOANED ME!

HMM...HE'S NOT HERE! WELL, I DOUBT HE'LL MIND IF I JUST *PUMP UP THE JAMS* A LITTLE...

NUCLEAR-POWERED SOUND PROJECTOR. CAUTION!

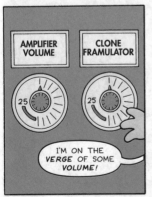

AMPLIFIER VOLUME

CLONE FRAMULATOR

25   25

I'M ON THE *VERGE* OF SOME *VOLUME!*

HEY! NOTHING'S *HAPPENING!*

AMPLIFIER VOLUME

CLON FRAM

25

OOPS! TURNED THE *WRONG DIAL!* HERE WE GO!

GAIL SIMONE SCRIPT

DAN DECARLO LAYOUTS

MIKE ROTE PENCILS & INKS

ART VILLANUEVA COLORS

KAREN BATES LETTERS

BILL MORRISON EDITOR

MATT GROENING ONE IN A MILLION

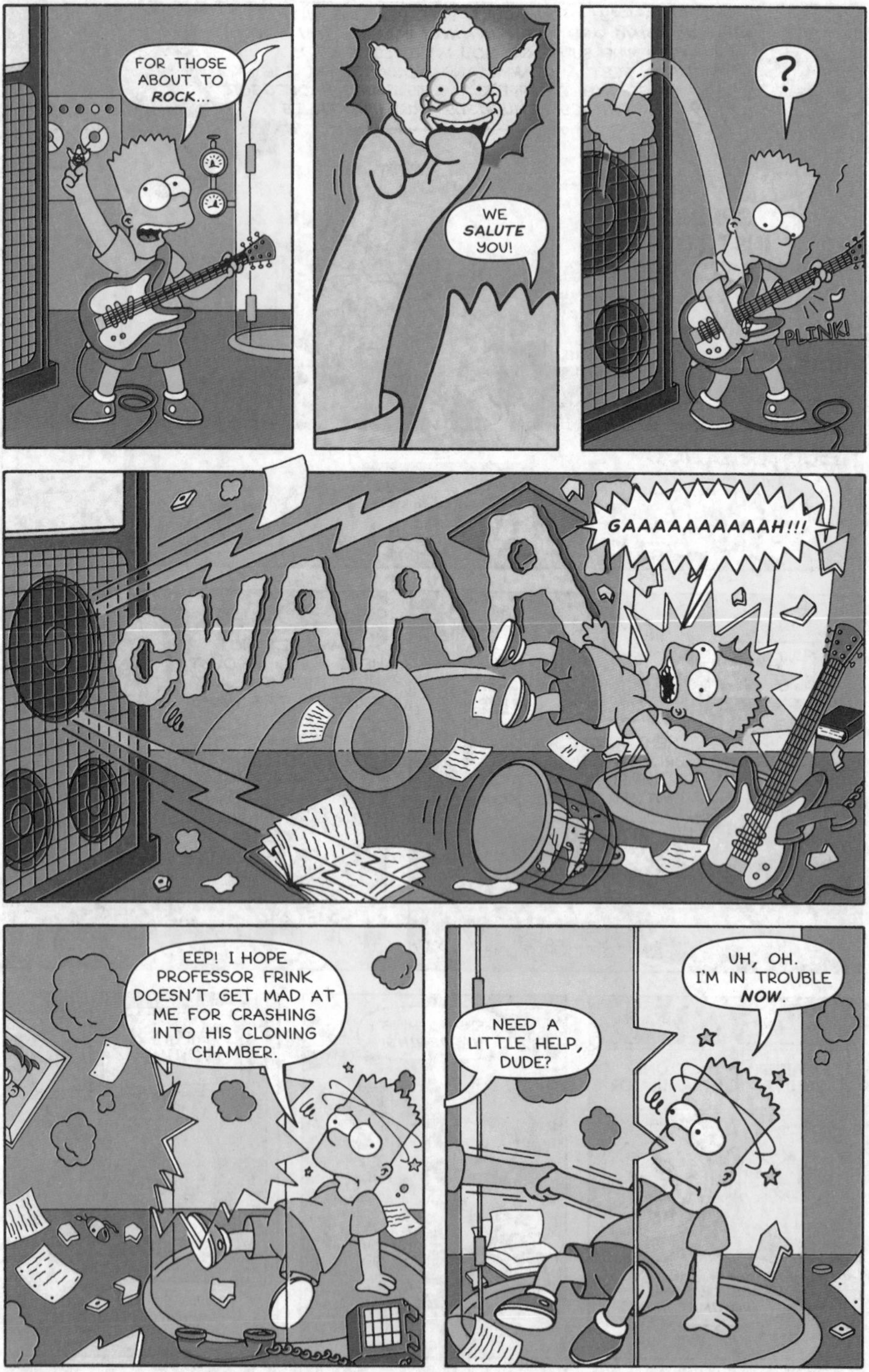
FOR THOSE ABOUT TO ROCK...
WE SALUTE YOU!
?
PLINK!
CWAAA
GAAAAAAAAAAH!!!
EEP! I HOPE PROFESSOR FRINK DOESN'T GET MAD AT ME FOR CRASHING INTO HIS CLONING CHAMBER.
UH, OH. I'M IN TROUBLE NOW.
NEED A LITTLE HELP, DUDE?

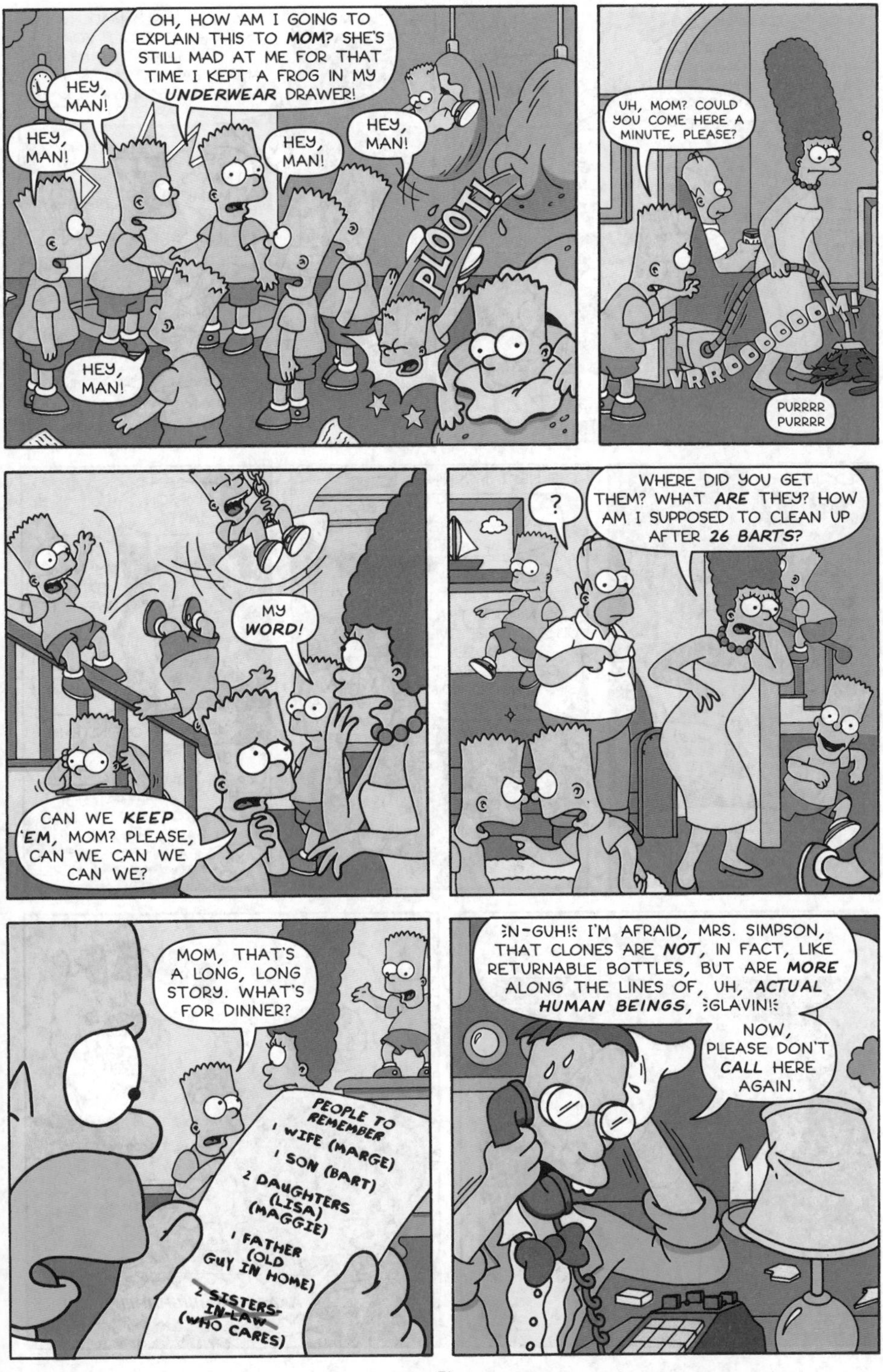
OH, HOW AM I GOING TO EXPLAIN THIS TO MOM? SHE'S STILL MAD AT ME FOR THAT TIME I KEPT A FROG IN MY UNDERWEAR DRAWER!
HEY, MAN!
HEY, MAN!
HEY, MAN!
HEY, MAN!
HEY, MAN!
PLOOT!
UH, MOM? COULD YOU COME HERE A MINUTE, PLEASE?
VRROOOOOOOM!
PURRRR PURRRR
MY WORD!
CAN WE KEEP 'EM, MOM? PLEASE, CAN WE CAN WE CAN WE?
?
WHERE DID YOU GET THEM? WHAT ARE THEY? HOW AM I SUPPOSED TO CLEAN UP AFTER 26 BARTS?
MOM, THAT'S A LONG, LONG STORY. WHAT'S FOR DINNER?
PEOPLE TO REMEMBER
1 WIFE (MARGE)
1 SON (BART)
2 DAUGHTERS (LISA) (MAGGIE)
1 FATHER (OLD GUY IN HOME)
2 SISTERS-IN-LAW (WHO CARES)
N-GUH! I'M AFRAID, MRS. SIMPSON, THAT CLONES ARE NOT, IN FACT, LIKE RETURNABLE BOTTLES, BUT ARE MORE ALONG THE LINES OF, UH, ACTUAL HUMAN BEINGS, GLAVIN!
NOW, PLEASE DON'T CALL HERE AGAIN.

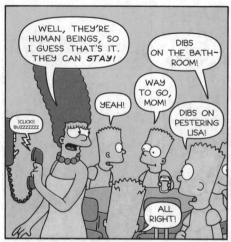

WELL, THEY'RE HUMAN BEINGS, SO I GUESS THAT'S IT. THEY CAN *STAY!*

DIBS ON THE BATH-ROOM!

YEAH!

WAY TO GO, MOM!

DIBS ON PESTERING LISA!

¡CLICK! BVZZZZZZZZ

ALL RIGHT!

SUPPERTIME...

WELL, I ONLY MADE ENOUGH MEATLOAF FOR FIVE, SO I SLICED THE MEAT AND BREAD EXTRA-THIN AND MADE SANDWICHES. BON APPETIT!

GEE. THANKS, MOM.

THANKS, MOM.

THANKS, MOM.

THANKS, MOM.

BEDTIME...

HEY! BART #23 IS HOGGING THE COVERS!

G'NIGHT, MY SPECIAL LITTLE GUYS! SLEEP TIGHT!

THE NEXT MORNING...

...HEY, BART. HEY, BART. HEY, BART. HEY, BART. HEY, BART. HEY, BART....

EXCUSE ME-- DID YOU HAPPEN TO NOTICE THAT THERE WERE OVER TWO DOZEN IDENTICAL BART SIMPSONS BOARDING YOUR BUS?

WHOA, I HAVE A *BUS*???!

...SIMPSON, BART...

THAT'S MY NAME, DON'T WEAR IT OUT!

SAY IT, DON'T SPRAY IT!

YEPPERS!

DEFINITELY!

BART IS IN THE HOUSE!

PRESENT!

YO!

BART BART BO BART, BANANA-FANA-FO-AYE, AYE!

HERE!

PAGE-

SNAP!

AAAAAAAIAIIIIGHHH!!!

52

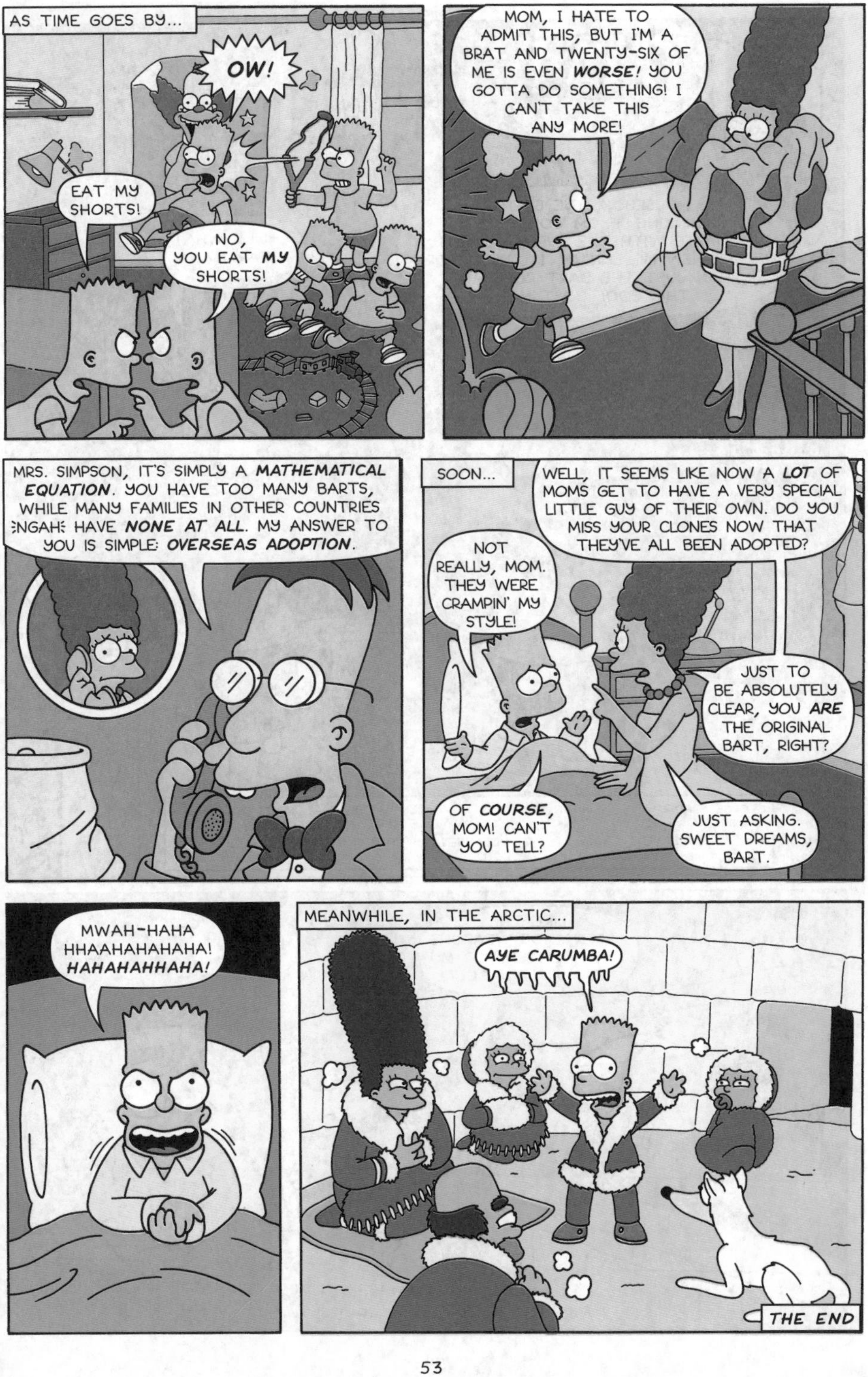
AS TIME GOES BY...
OW!
EAT MY SHORTS!
NO, YOU EAT MY SHORTS!
MOM, I HATE TO ADMIT THIS, BUT I'M A BRAT AND TWENTY-SIX OF ME IS EVEN WORSE! YOU GOTTA DO SOMETHING! I CAN'T TAKE THIS ANY MORE!
MRS. SIMPSON, IT'S SIMPLY A MATHEMATICAL EQUATION. YOU HAVE TOO MANY BARTS, WHILE MANY FAMILIES IN OTHER COUNTRIES :NGAH: HAVE NONE AT ALL. MY ANSWER TO YOU IS SIMPLE: OVERSEAS ADOPTION.
SOON...
WELL, IT SEEMS LIKE NOW A LOT OF MOMS GET TO HAVE A VERY SPECIAL LITTLE GUY OF THEIR OWN. DO YOU MISS YOUR CLONES NOW THAT THEY'VE ALL BEEN ADOPTED?
NOT REALLY, MOM. THEY WERE CRAMPIN' MY STYLE!
JUST TO BE ABSOLUTELY CLEAR, YOU ARE THE ORIGINAL BART, RIGHT?
OF COURSE, MOM! CAN'T YOU TELL?
JUST ASKING. SWEET DREAMS, BART.
MWAH-HAHA HHAAHAHAHAHA! HAHAHAHHAHA!
MEANWHILE, IN THE ARCTIC...
AYE CARUMBA!
THE END

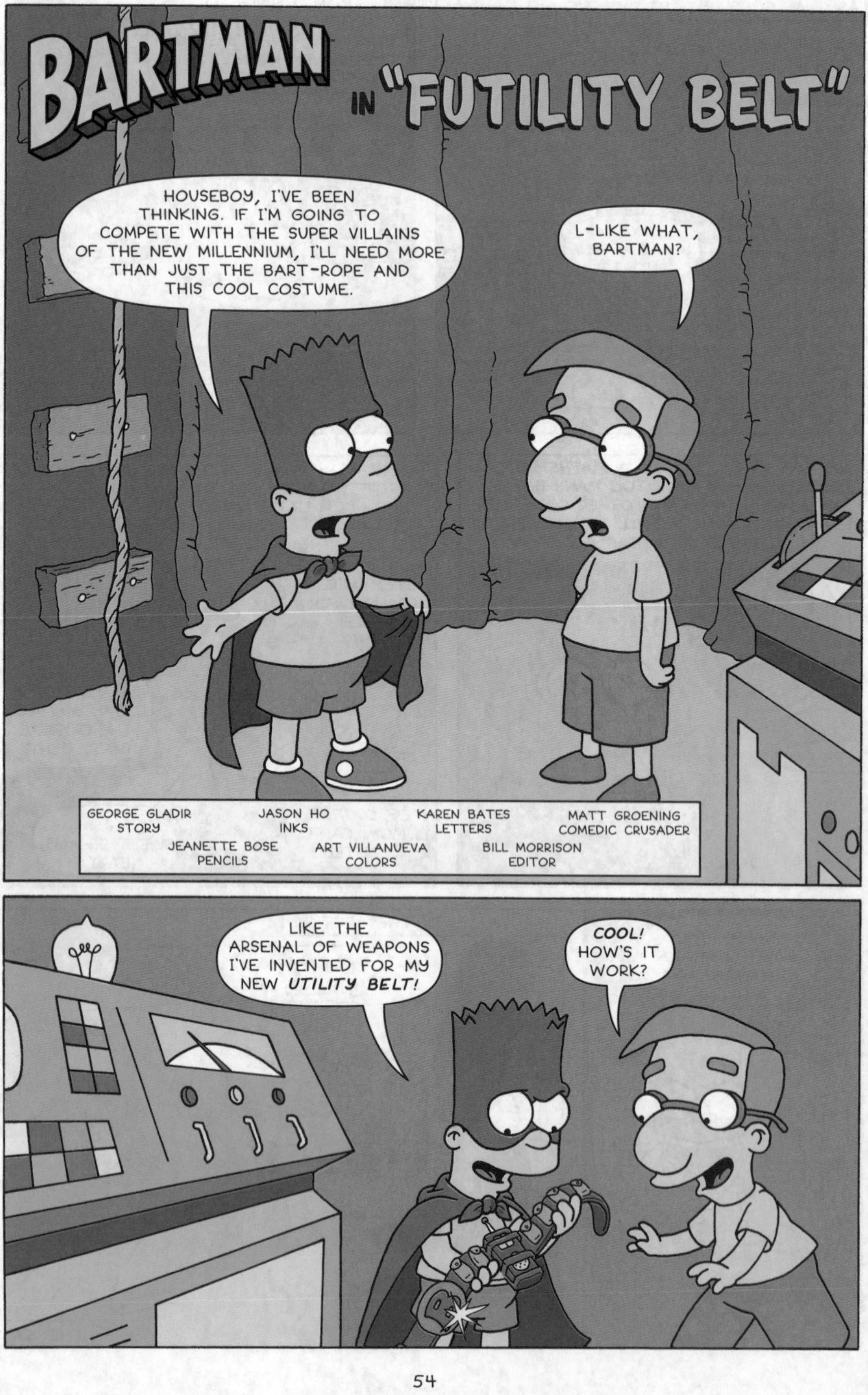
BARTMAN IN "FUTILITY BELT"
HOUSEBOY, I'VE BEEN THINKING. IF I'M GOING TO COMPETE WITH THE SUPER VILLAINS OF THE NEW MILLENNIUM, I'LL NEED MORE THAN JUST THE BART-ROPE AND THIS COOL COSTUME.
L-LIKE WHAT, BARTMAN?
GEORGE GLADIR STORY
JEANETTE BOSE PENCILS
JASON HO INKS
ART VILLANUEVA COLORS
KAREN BATES LETTERS
BILL MORRISON EDITOR
MATT GROENING COMEDIC CRUSADER
LIKE THE ARSENAL OF WEAPONS I'VE INVENTED FOR MY NEW UTILITY BELT!
COOL! HOW'S IT WORK?

EACH COMPARTMENT ON THE BELT HOLDS A DIFFERENT WEAPON.

FOR EXAMPLE, *THESE SMOKE CAPSULES* WILL HELP ME CONFUSE CRIMINALS AND GET AWAY FROM *TRUANT OFFICERS*.

THESE *STINK BOMBS* WILL HELP ME EMPTY OUT *CRIMINAL HIDEOUTS*...

...NOT TO MENTION CLASSROOMS ON *EXAM* DAY!

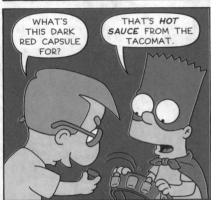

WHAT'S THIS DARK RED CAPSULE FOR?

THAT'S *HOT SAUCE* FROM THE TACOMAT.

OH, TO *BLIND* YOUR ENEMIES WITH, *RIGHT*?

NO, JUST 'CAUSE I LIKE HOT SAUCE.

NOW, I JUST NEED *ONE* MORE THING...

...A HIGH TECH SET OF WHEELS TO GET ME WHERE I'M GOING!

I'M SORRY PROFESSOR FRINK, BUT WE'VE DECIDED NOT TO BUY YOUR *JET-POWERED SKATEBOARD*.

B-BUT WHY?

THE RESULTING FLOOD OF *INJURY LAWSUITS* WOULD *BANKRUPT* MY TOY COMPANY.

⋷SIGH⋷ OH WELL, BACK TO THE DRAWING BOARD ⋷WOO-HOY⋷

KLUNK!

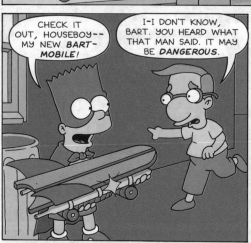

CHECK IT OUT, HOUSEBOY-- MY NEW *BART-MOBILE!*

I-I DON'T KNOW, BART. YOU HEARD WHAT THAT MAN SAID. IT MAY BE *DANGEROUS.*

NONSENSE. *KIDS* CAN'T GO *BANKRUPT.* C'MON, LET'S TEST IT!

IS IT FUELED UP ENOUGH?

WHY *WOULDN'T* IT BE?

KLIK!

WHOAH!

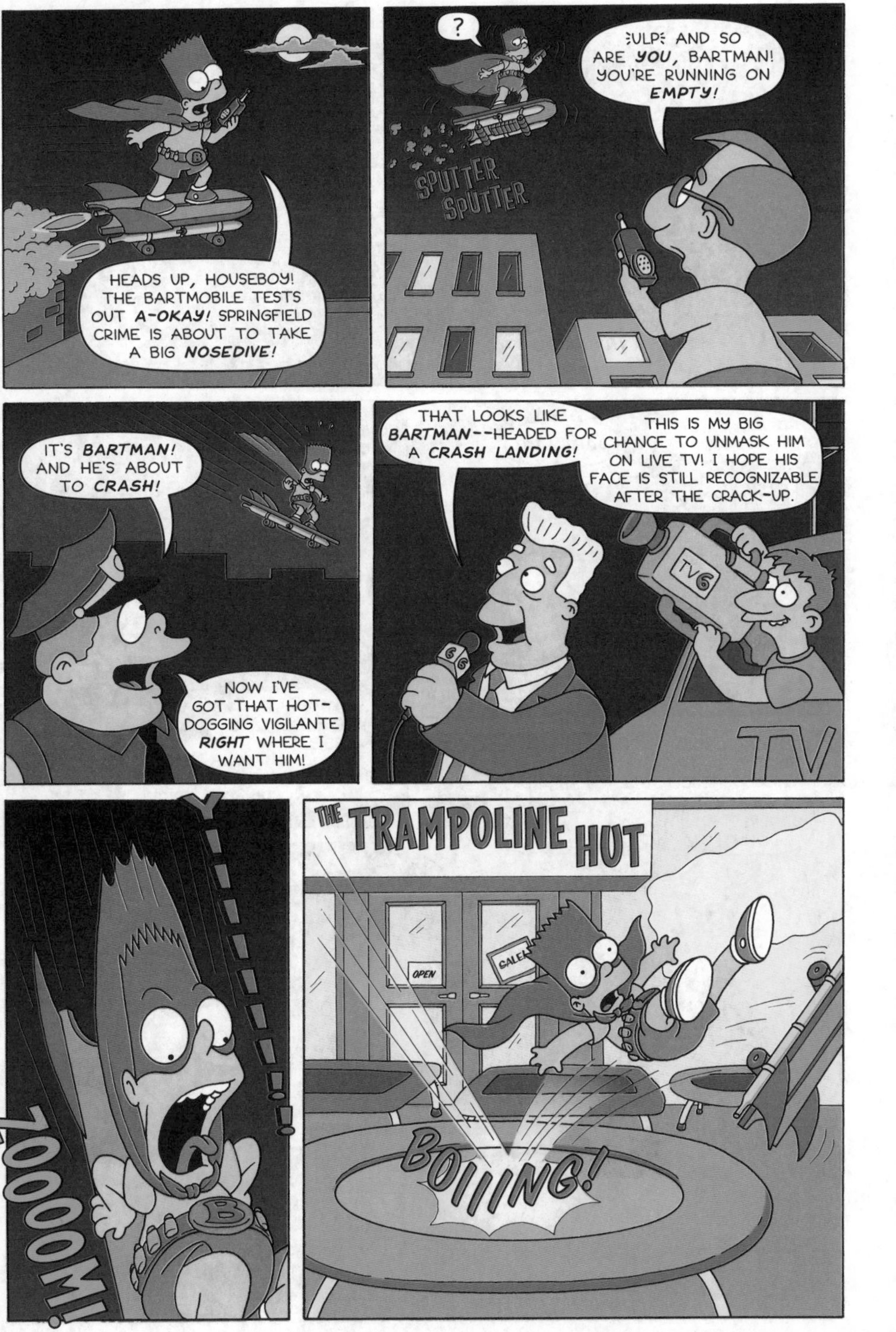
HEADS UP, HOUSEBOY! THE BARTMOBILE TESTS OUT A-OKAY! SPRINGFIELD CRIME IS ABOUT TO TAKE A BIG NOSEDIVE!
?
SPUTTER SPUTTER
ULP AND SO ARE YOU, BARTMAN! YOU'RE RUNNING ON EMPTY!
IT'S BARTMAN! AND HE'S ABOUT TO CRASH!
NOW I'VE GOT THAT HOT-DOGGING VIGILANTE RIGHT WHERE I WANT HIM!
THAT LOOKS LIKE BARTMAN--HEADED FOR A CRASH LANDING!
THIS IS MY BIG CHANCE TO UNMASK HIM ON LIVE TV! I HOPE HIS FACE IS STILL RECOGNIZABLE AFTER THE CRACK-UP.
TV6
TV
ZOOOOM!
THE TRAMPOLINE HUT
OPEN
SALE
BOIIING!

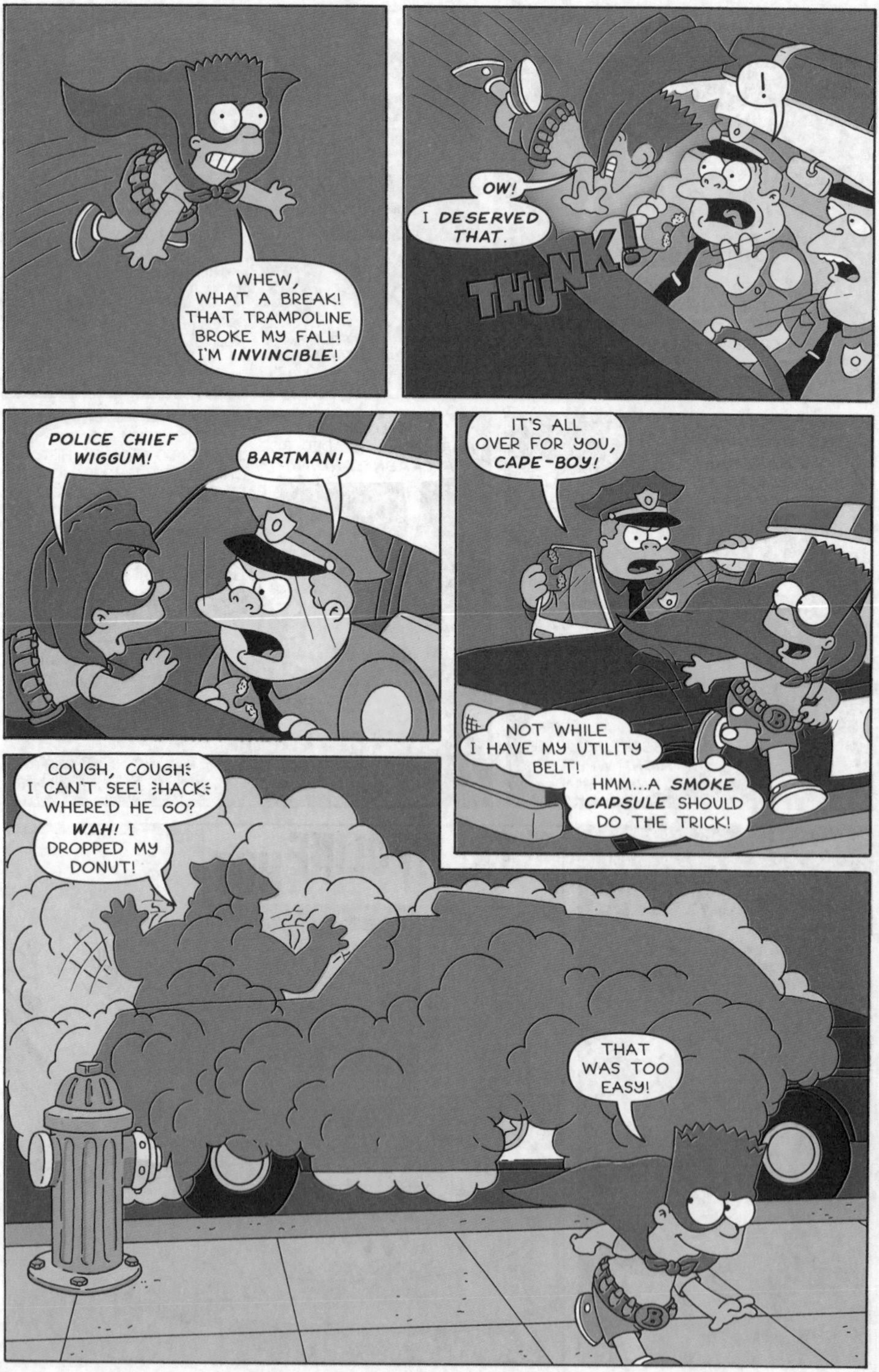
WHEW, WHAT A BREAK! THAT TRAMPOLINE BROKE MY FALL! I'M INVINCIBLE!
!
OW!
I DESERVED THAT.
THUNK!
POLICE CHIEF WIGGUM!
BARTMAN!
IT'S ALL OVER FOR YOU, CAPE-BOY!
NOT WHILE I HAVE MY UTILITY BELT!
HMM...A SMOKE CAPSULE SHOULD DO THE TRICK!
COUGH, COUGH: I CAN'T SEE! :HACK: WHERE'D HE GO? WAH! I DROPPED MY DONUT!
THAT WAS TOO EASY!

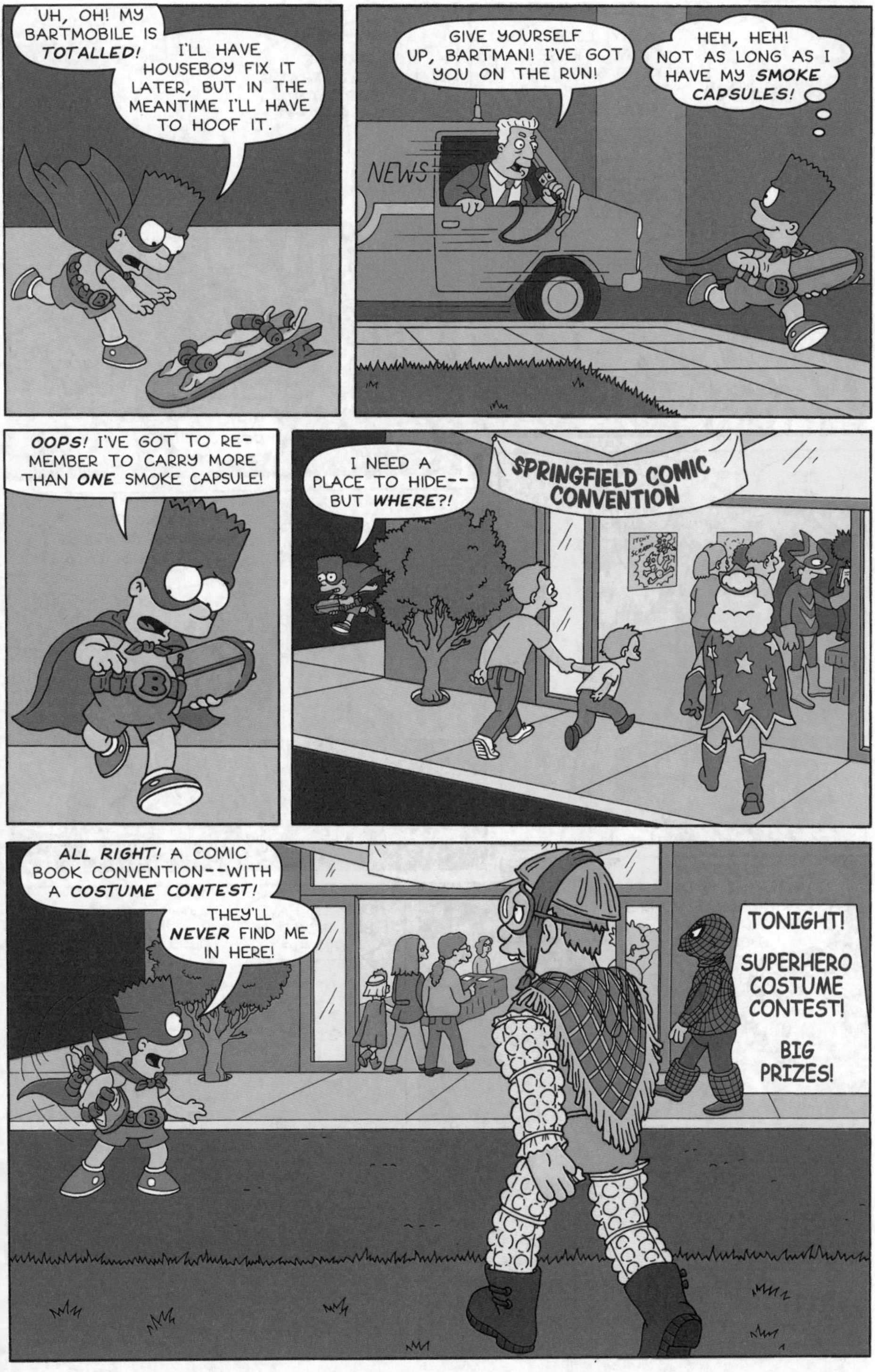
UH, OH! MY BARTMOBILE IS TOTALLED!
I'LL HAVE HOUSEBOY FIX IT LATER, BUT IN THE MEANTIME I'LL HAVE TO HOOF IT.
GIVE YOURSELF UP, BARTMAN! I'VE GOT YOU ON THE RUN!
NEWS
HEH, HEH! NOT AS LONG AS I HAVE MY SMOKE CAPSULES!
OOPS! I'VE GOT TO REMEMBER TO CARRY MORE THAN ONE SMOKE CAPSULE!
I NEED A PLACE TO HIDE--BUT WHERE?!
SPRINGFIELD COMIC CONVENTION
ALL RIGHT! A COMIC BOOK CONVENTION--WITH A COSTUME CONTEST!
THEY'LL NEVER FIND ME IN HERE!
TONIGHT!
SUPERHERO COSTUME CONTEST!
BIG PRIZES!

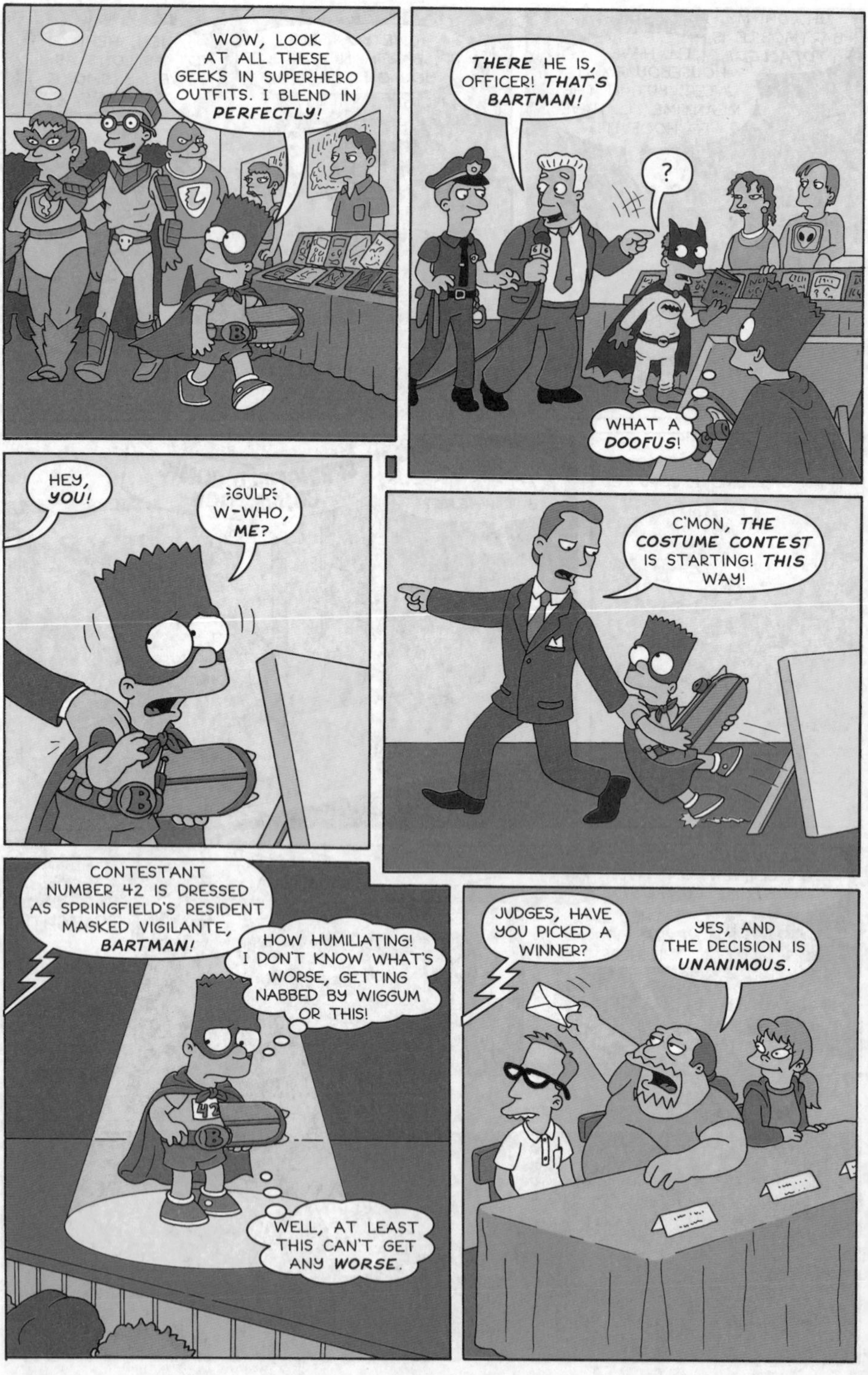
WOW, LOOK AT ALL THESE GEEKS IN SUPERHERO OUTFITS. I BLEND IN PERFECTLY!
THERE HE IS, OFFICER! THAT'S BARTMAN!
?
WHAT A DOOFUS!
HEY, YOU!
GULP W-WHO, ME?
C'MON, THE COSTUME CONTEST IS STARTING! THIS WAY!
CONTESTANT NUMBER 42 IS DRESSED AS SPRINGFIELD'S RESIDENT MASKED VIGILANTE, BARTMAN!
HOW HUMILIATING! I DON'T KNOW WHAT'S WORSE, GETTING NABBED BY WIGGUM OR THIS!
WELL, AT LEAST THIS CAN'T GET ANY WORSE.
JUDGES, HAVE YOU PICKED A WINNER?
YES, AND THE DECISION IS UNANIMOUS.

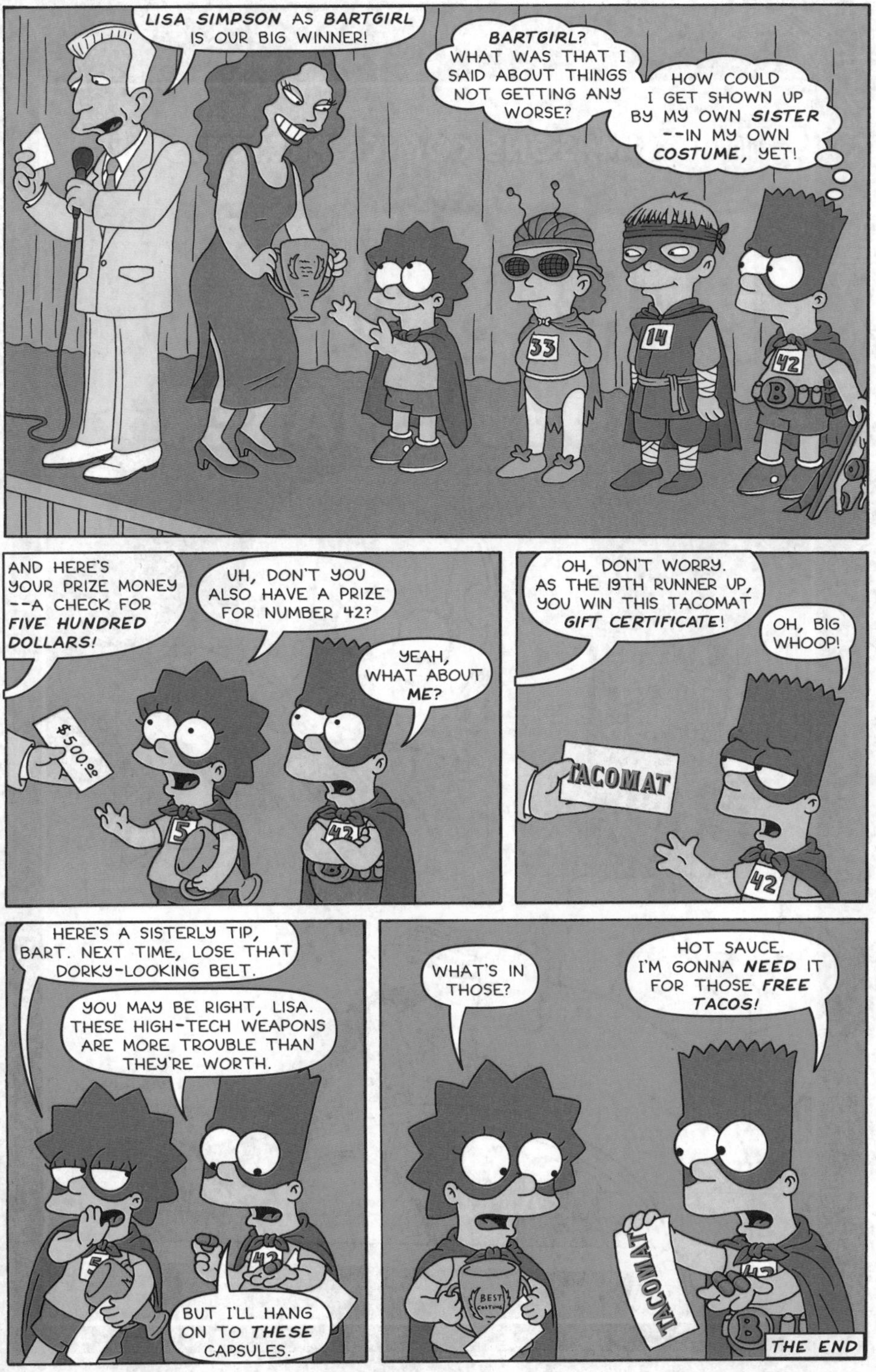
LISA SIMPSON AS BARTGIRL IS OUR BIG WINNER!
BARTGIRL? WHAT WAS THAT I SAID ABOUT THINGS NOT GETTING ANY WORSE?
HOW COULD I GET SHOWN UP BY MY OWN SISTER --IN MY OWN COSTUME, YET!
33
14
42
AND HERE'S YOUR PRIZE MONEY --A CHECK FOR FIVE HUNDRED DOLLARS!
UH, DON'T YOU ALSO HAVE A PRIZE FOR NUMBER 42?
YEAH, WHAT ABOUT ME?
$500.00
OH, DON'T WORRY. AS THE 19TH RUNNER UP, YOU WIN THIS TACOMAT GIFT CERTIFICATE!
OH, BIG WHOOP!
TACOMAT
HERE'S A SISTERLY TIP, BART. NEXT TIME, LOSE THAT DORKY-LOOKING BELT.
YOU MAY BE RIGHT, LISA. THESE HIGH-TECH WEAPONS ARE MORE TROUBLE THAN THEY'RE WORTH.
BUT I'LL HANG ON TO THESE CAPSULES.
WHAT'S IN THOSE?
HOT SAUCE. I'M GONNA NEED IT FOR THOSE FREE TACOS!
TACOMAT
THE END

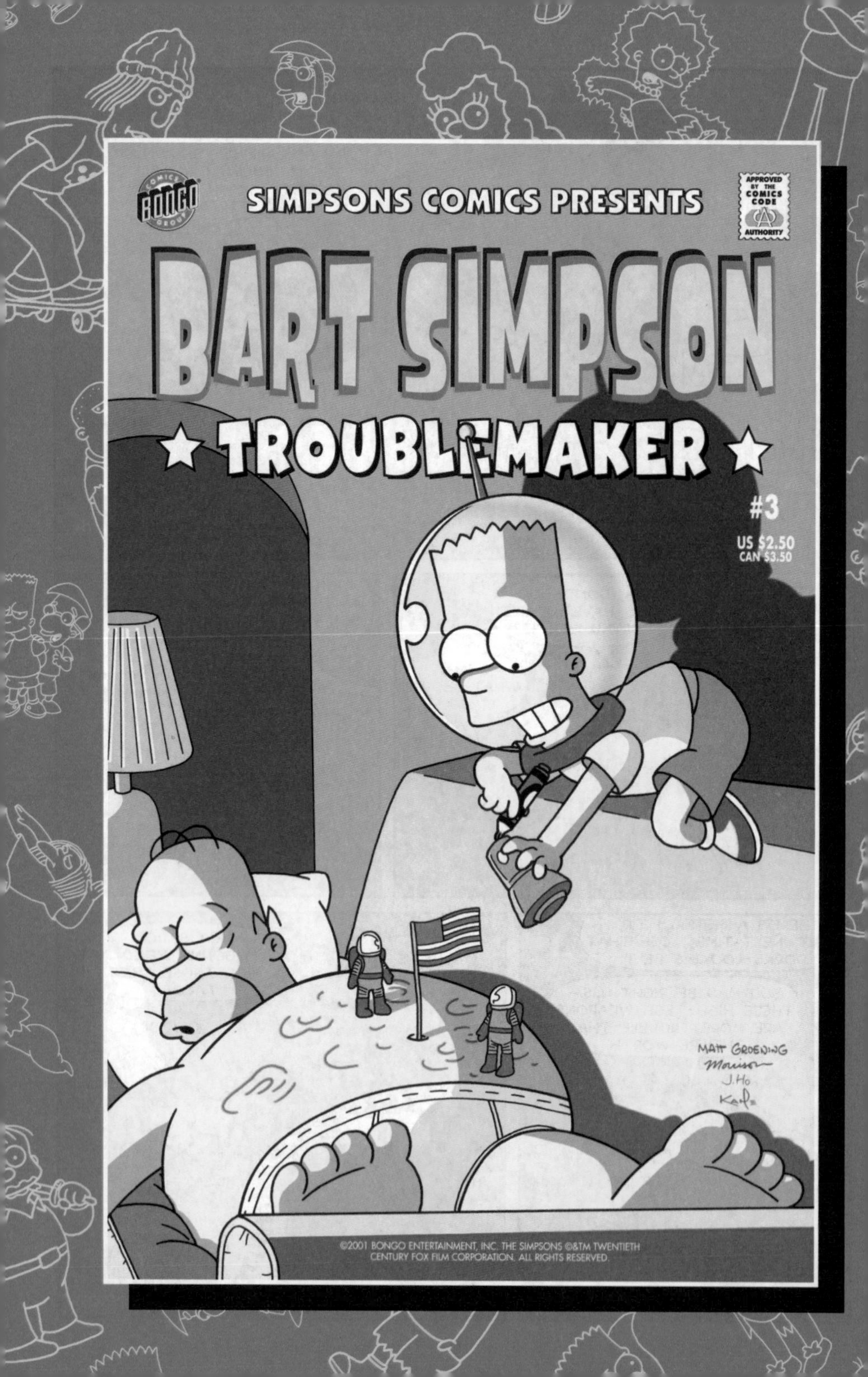
BONGO COMICS GROUP
SIMPSONS COMICS PRESENTS
APPROVED BY THE COMICS CODE AUTHORITY
BART SIMPSON
TROUBLEMAKER
#3
US $2.50
CAN $3.50
MATT GROENING
J.Ho
©2001 BONGO ENTERTAINMENT, INC. THE SIMPSONS ©&TM TWENTIETH CENTURY FOX FILM CORPORATION. ALL RIGHTS RESERVED.

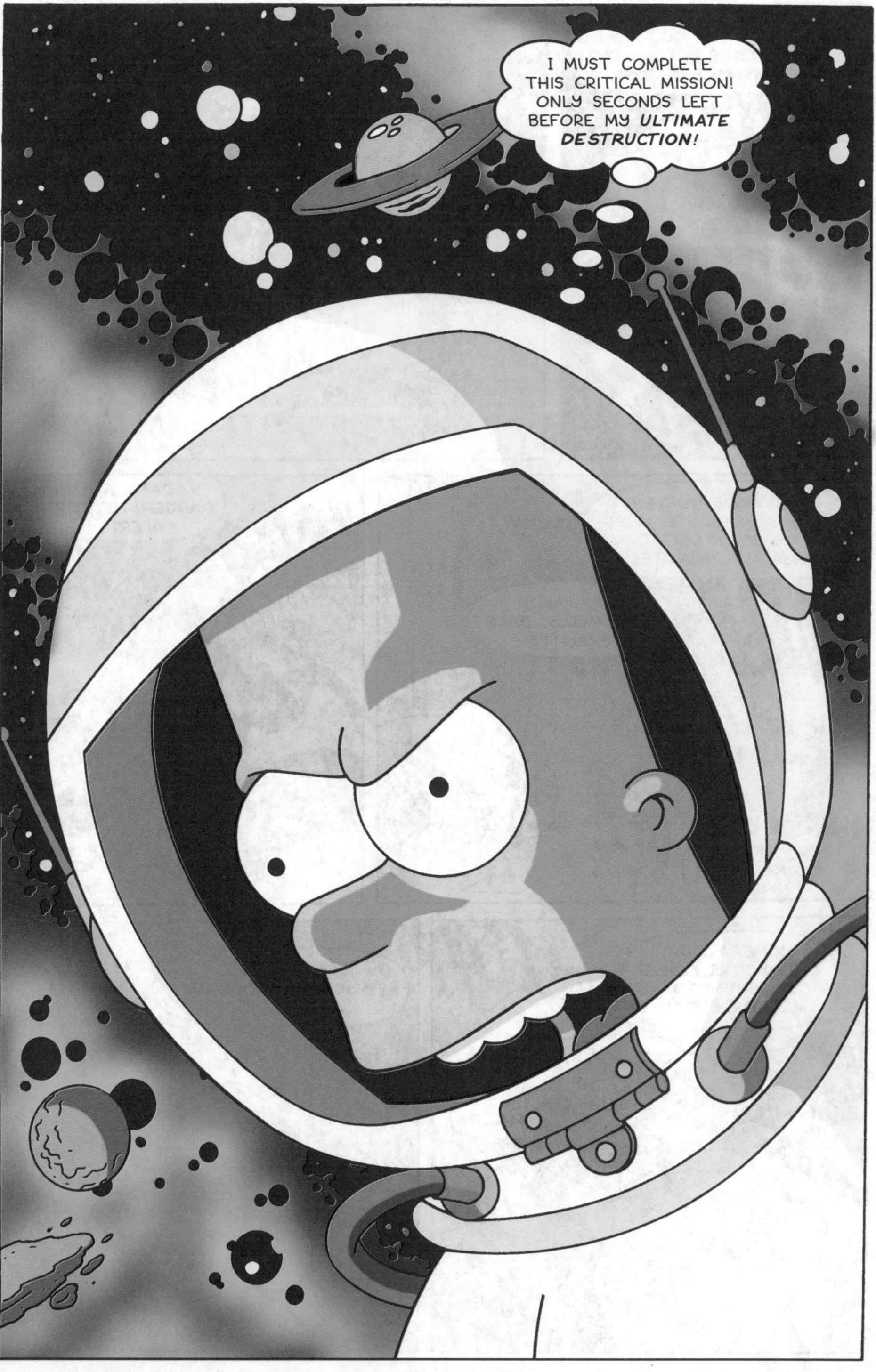
I MUST COMPLETE THIS CRITICAL MISSION! ONLY SECONDS LEFT BEFORE MY *ULTIMATE DESTRUCTION!*

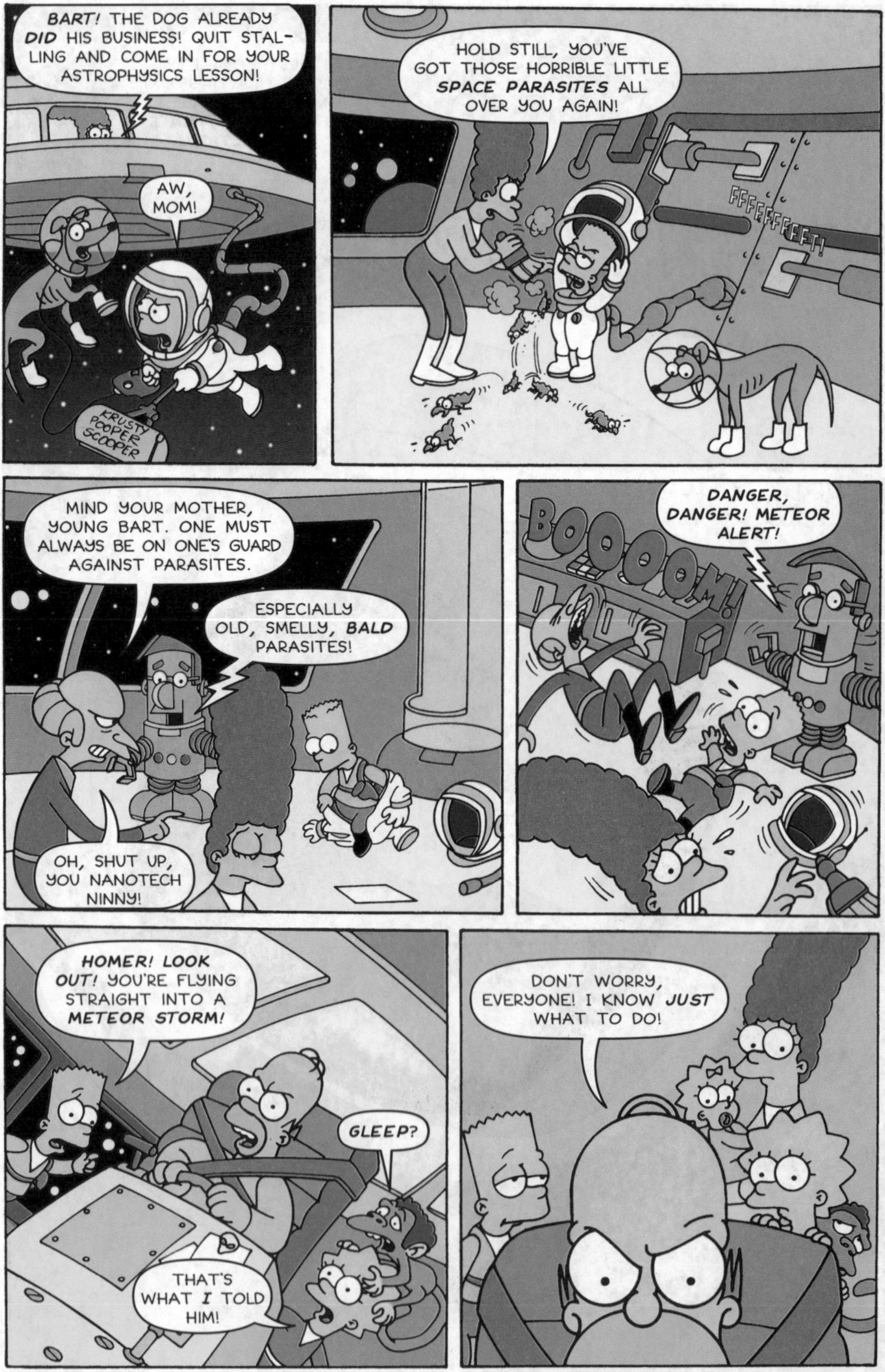
BART! THE DOG ALREADY DID HIS BUSINESS! QUIT STALLING AND COME IN FOR YOUR ASTROPHYSICS LESSON!
AW, MOM!
KRUSTY POOPER SCOOPER
HOLD STILL, YOU'VE GOT THOSE HORRIBLE LITTLE SPACE PARASITES ALL OVER YOU AGAIN!
FFFFFFFFFT!
MIND YOUR MOTHER, YOUNG BART. ONE MUST ALWAYS BE ON ONE'S GUARD AGAINST PARASITES.
ESPECIALLY OLD, SMELLY, BALD PARASITES!
OH, SHUT UP, YOU NANOTECH NINNY!
BOOOOOM!
DANGER, DANGER! METEOR ALERT!
HOMER! LOOK OUT! YOU'RE FLYING STRAIGHT INTO A METEOR STORM!
GLEEP?
THAT'S WHAT I TOLD HIM!
DON'T WORRY, EVERYONE! I KNOW JUST WHAT TO DO!

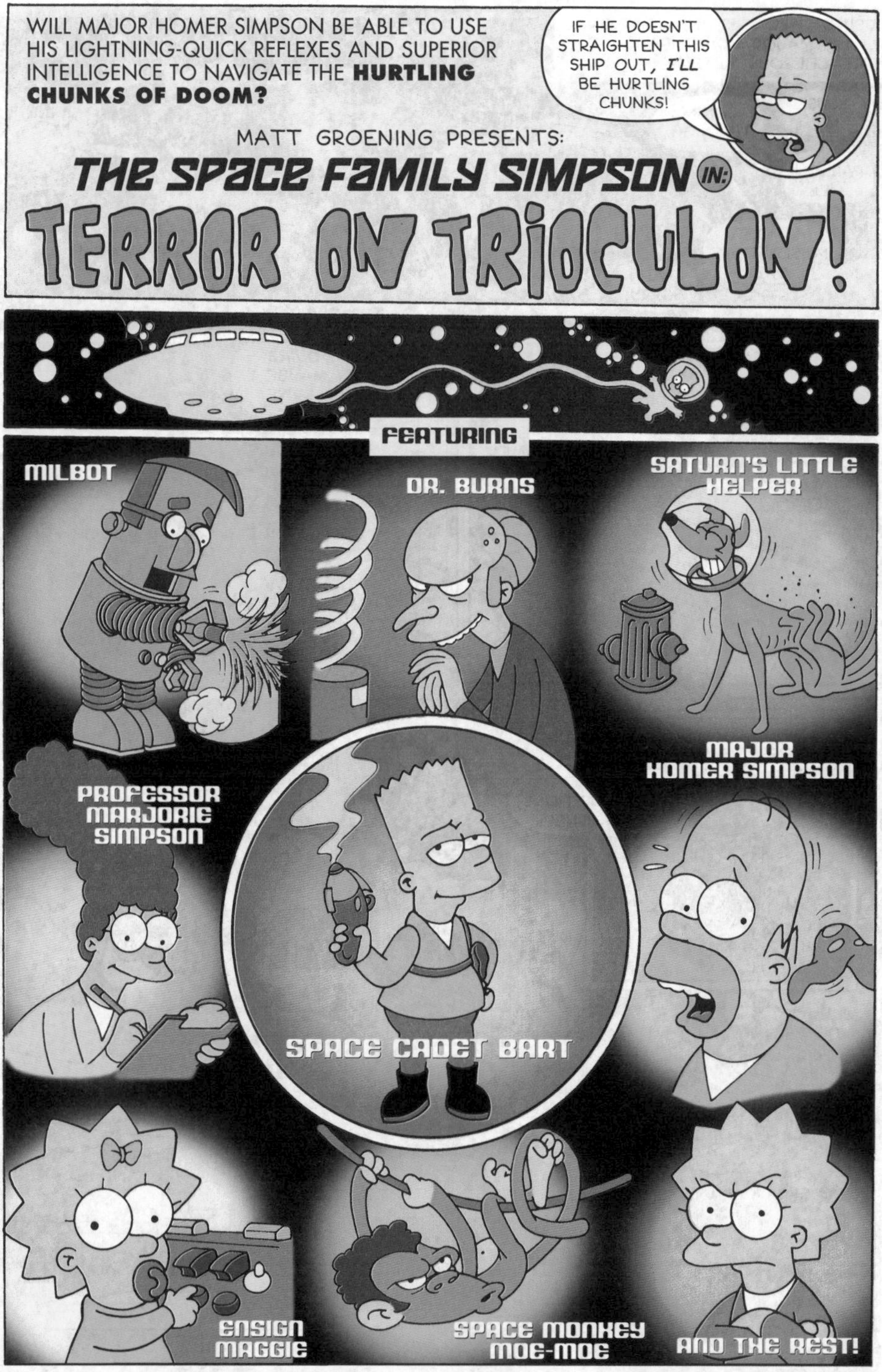
WILL MAJOR HOMER SIMPSON BE ABLE TO USE HIS LIGHTNING-QUICK REFLEXES AND SUPERIOR INTELLIGENCE TO NAVIGATE THE **HURTLING CHUNKS OF DOOM?**
IF HE DOESN'T STRAIGHTEN THIS SHIP OUT, *I'LL* BE HURTLING CHUNKS!
MATT GROENING PRESENTS:
THE SPACE FAMILY SIMPSON IN:
TERROR ON TRIOCULON!
FEATURING
MILBOT
DR. BURNS
SATURN'S LITTLE HELPER
MAJOR HOMER SIMPSON
PROFESSOR MARJORIE SIMPSON
SPACE CADET BART
ENSIGN MAGGIE
SPACE MONKEY MOE-MOE
AND THE REST!

GAIL SIMONE
SPACE COMMUNICATIONS

JOHN COSTANZA
ASTRO-PENCILS & BLACK HOLE INKS

ART VILLANUEVA
COSMIC COLORS

KAREN BATES
LIGHTSPEED LETTERS

BILL MORRISON
HYPER-EDITS

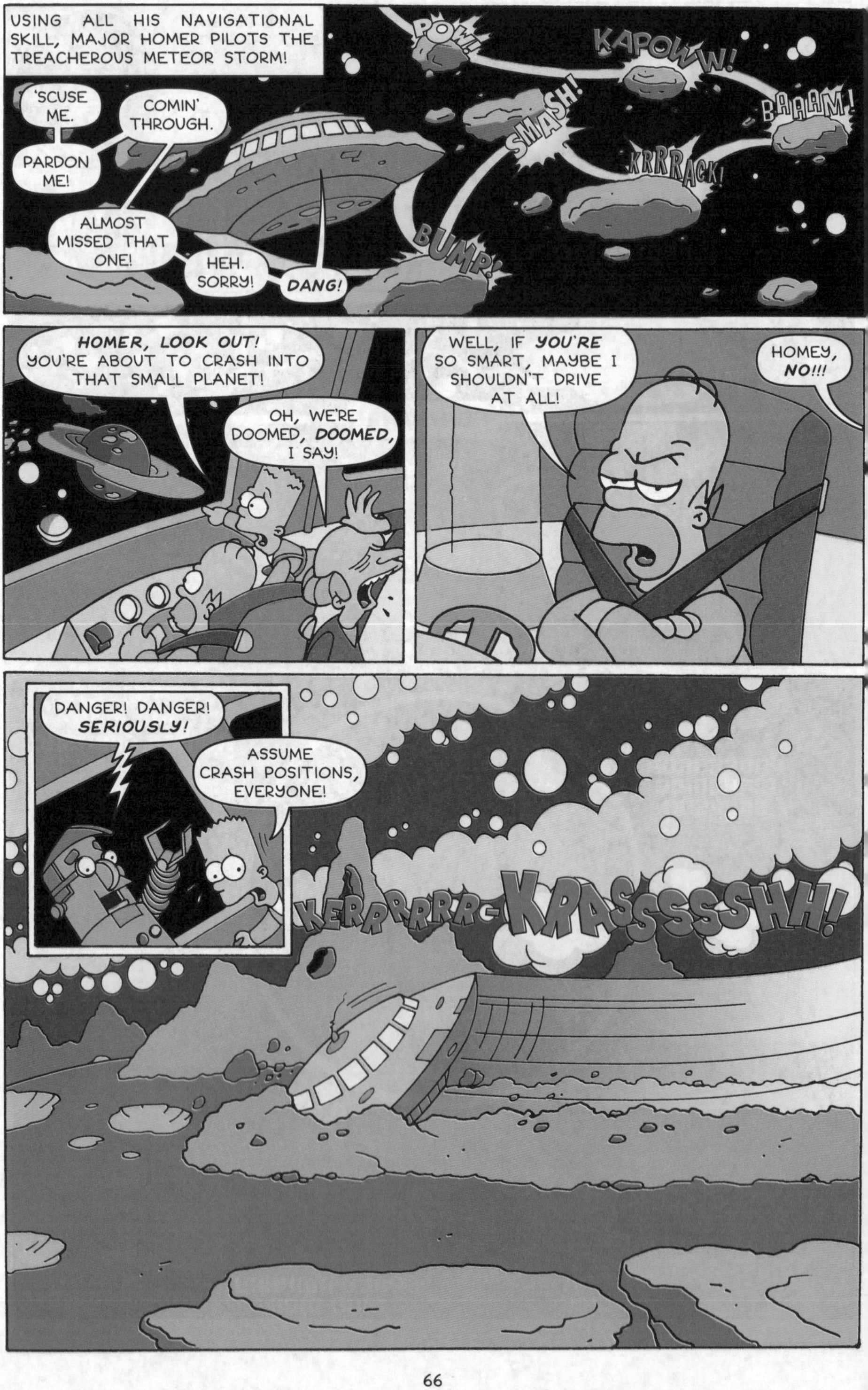
USING ALL HIS NAVIGATIONAL SKILL, MAJOR HOMER PILOTS THE TREACHEROUS METEOR STORM!
'SCUSE ME.
PARDON ME!
COMIN' THROUGH.
ALMOST MISSED THAT ONE!
HEH. SORRY!
DANG!
POW!
KAPOWWW!
SMASH!
BAAAAM!
KRRRACK!
BUMP!
HOMER, LOOK OUT! YOU'RE ABOUT TO CRASH INTO THAT SMALL PLANET!
OH, WE'RE DOOMED, DOOMED, I SAY!
WELL, IF YOU'RE SO SMART, MAYBE I SHOULDN'T DRIVE AT ALL!
HOMEY, NO!!!
DANGER! DANGER! SERIOUSLY!
ASSUME CRASH POSITIONS, EVERYONE!
KERRRRRRR-KRASSSSSSHH!

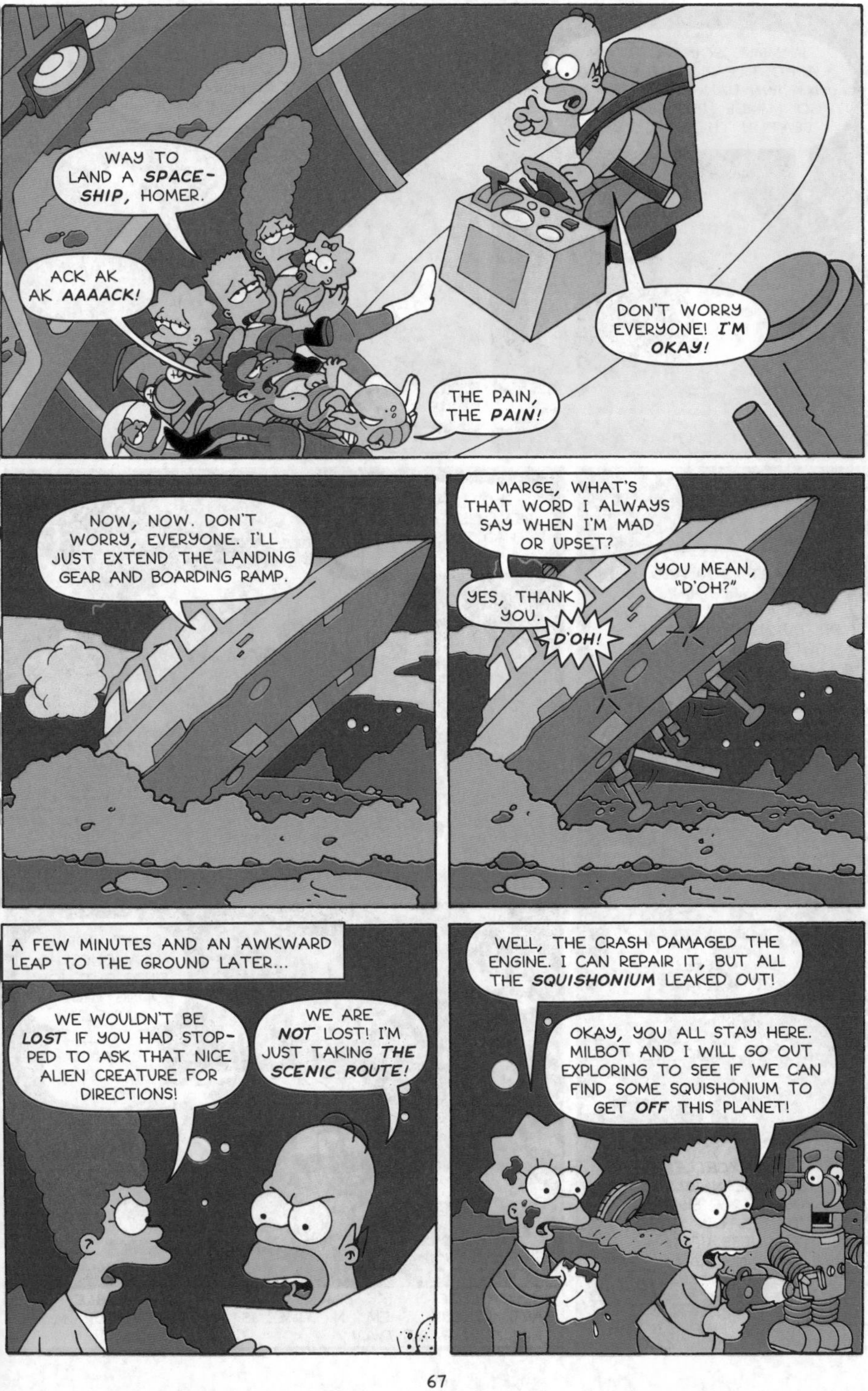

WAY TO LAND A SPACE-SHIP, HOMER.
ACK AK AK AAAACK!
DON'T WORRY EVERYONE! I'M OKAY!
THE PAIN, THE PAIN!
NOW, NOW. DON'T WORRY, EVERYONE. I'LL JUST EXTEND THE LANDING GEAR AND BOARDING RAMP.
MARGE, WHAT'S THAT WORD I ALWAYS SAY WHEN I'M MAD OR UPSET?
YOU MEAN, "D'OH?"
YES, THANK YOU.
D'OH!
A FEW MINUTES AND AN AWKWARD LEAP TO THE GROUND LATER...
WE WOULDN'T BE LOST IF YOU HAD STOP-PED TO ASK THAT NICE ALIEN CREATURE FOR DIRECTIONS!
WE ARE NOT LOST! I'M JUST TAKING THE SCENIC ROUTE!
WELL, THE CRASH DAMAGED THE ENGINE. I CAN REPAIR IT, BUT ALL THE SQUISHONIUM LEAKED OUT!
OKAY, YOU ALL STAY HERE. MILBOT AND I WILL GO OUT EXPLORING TO SEE IF WE CAN FIND SOME SQUISHONIUM TO GET OFF THIS PLANET!

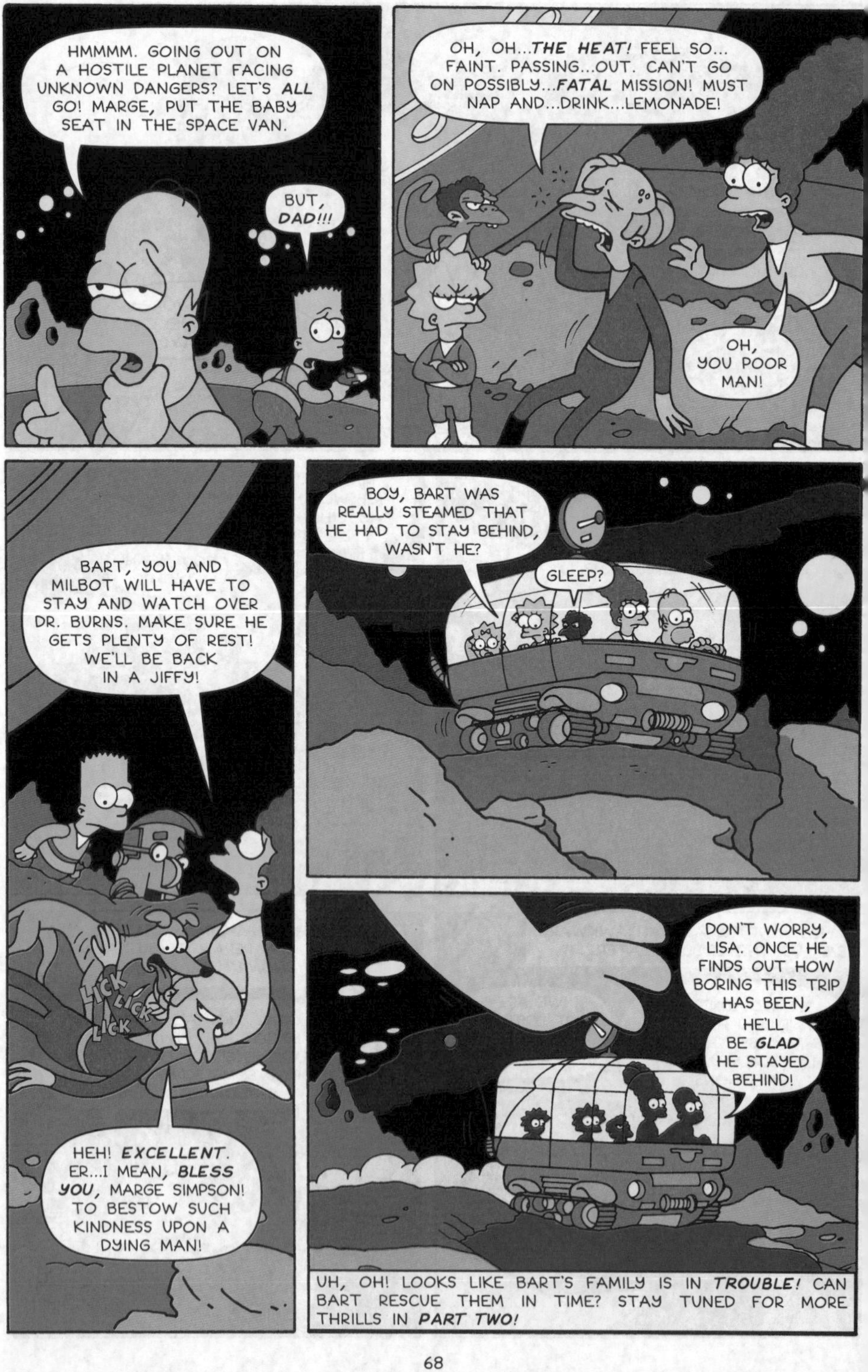
HMMMM. GOING OUT ON A HOSTILE PLANET FACING UNKNOWN DANGERS? LET'S **ALL** GO! MARGE, PUT THE BABY SEAT IN THE SPACE VAN.
BUT, **DAD!!!**
OH, OH...**THE HEAT!** FEEL SO... FAINT. PASSING...OUT. CAN'T GO ON POSSIBLY...**FATAL** MISSION! MUST NAP AND...DRINK...LEMONADE!
OH, YOU POOR MAN!
BART, YOU AND MILBOT WILL HAVE TO STAY AND WATCH OVER DR. BURNS. MAKE SURE HE GETS PLENTY OF REST! WE'LL BE BACK IN A JIFFY!
LICK LICK LICK
HEH! **EXCELLENT**. ER...I MEAN, **BLESS YOU,** MARGE SIMPSON! TO BESTOW SUCH KINDNESS UPON A DYING MAN!
BOY, BART WAS REALLY STEAMED THAT HE HAD TO STAY BEHIND, WASN'T HE?
GLEEP?
DON'T WORRY, LISA. ONCE HE FINDS OUT HOW BORING THIS TRIP HAS BEEN,
HE'LL BE **GLAD** HE STAYED BEHIND!
UH, OH! LOOKS LIKE BART'S FAMILY IS IN **TROUBLE!** CAN BART RESCUE THEM IN TIME? STAY TUNED FOR MORE THRILLS IN **PART TWO!**

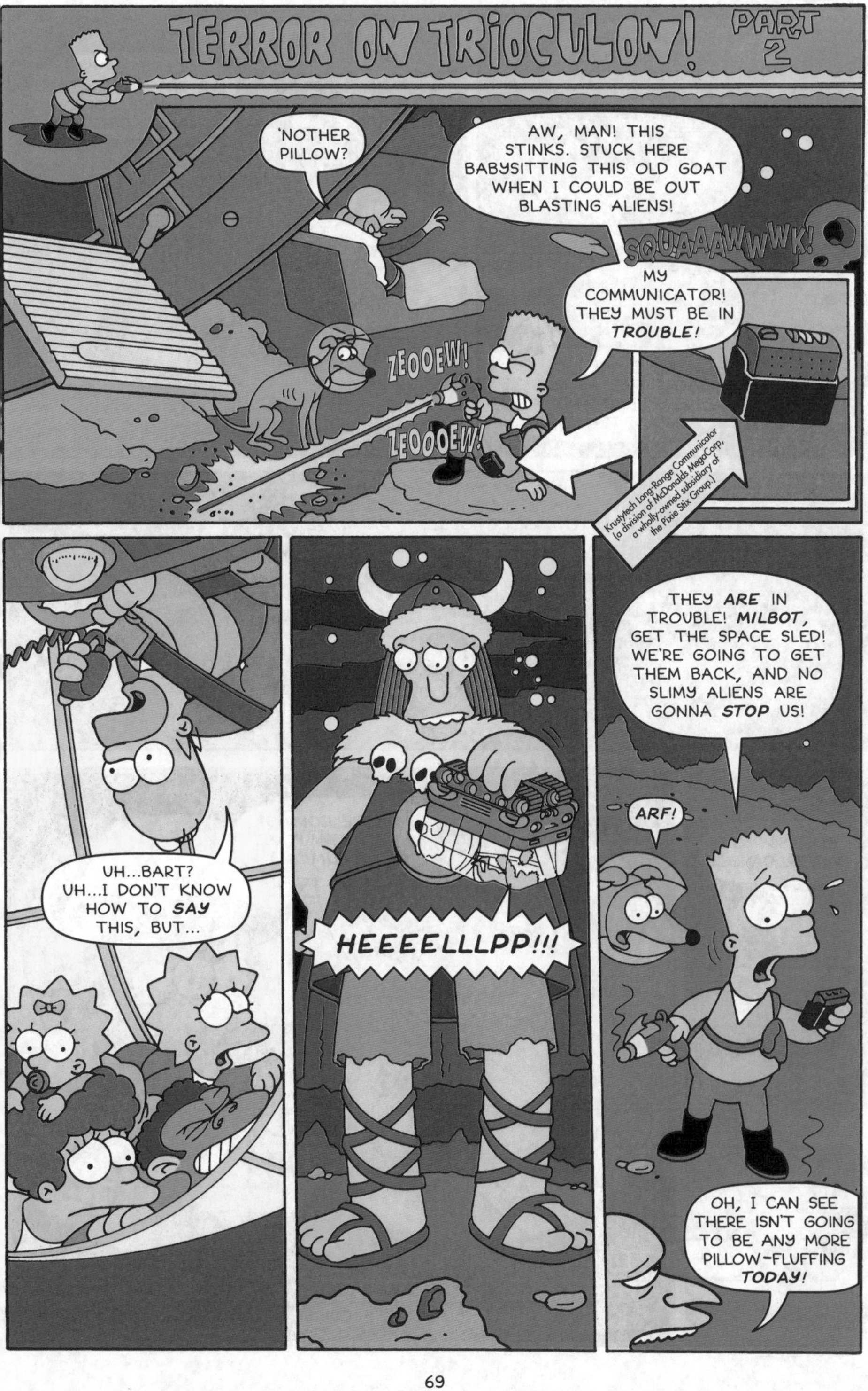
TERROR ON TRIOCULON! PART 2
'NOTHER PILLOW?
AW, MAN! THIS STINKS. STUCK HERE BABYSITTING THIS OLD GOAT WHEN I COULD BE OUT BLASTING ALIENS!
SQUAAAAWWWK!
MY COMMUNICATOR! THEY MUST BE IN TROUBLE!
ZEOOEW!
ZEOOOEW!
Krustytech Long-Range Communicator (a division of McDonalds MegaCorp, a wholly-owned subsidiary of the Pixie Stix Group.)
UH...BART? UH...I DON'T KNOW HOW TO SAY THIS, BUT...
HEEEELLLPP!!!
THEY ARE IN TROUBLE! MILBOT, GET THE SPACE SLED! WE'RE GOING TO GET THEM BACK, AND NO SLIMY ALIENS ARE GONNA STOP US!
ARF!
OH, I CAN SEE THERE ISN'T GOING TO BE ANY MORE PILLOW-FLUFFING TODAY!

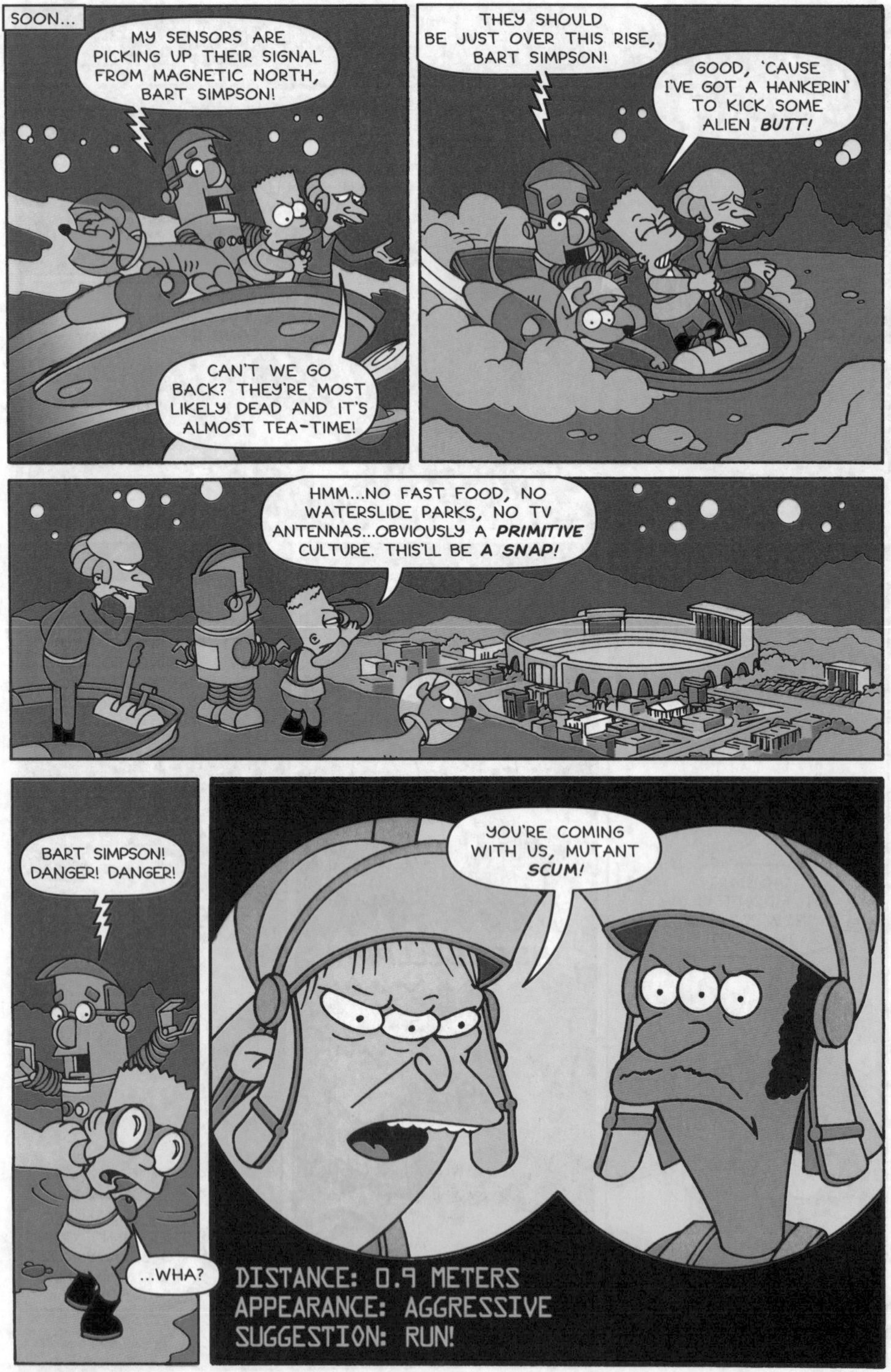
SOON...
MY SENSORS ARE PICKING UP THEIR SIGNAL FROM MAGNETIC NORTH, BART SIMPSON!
CAN'T WE GO BACK? THEY'RE MOST LIKELY DEAD AND IT'S ALMOST TEA-TIME!
THEY SHOULD BE JUST OVER THIS RISE, BART SIMPSON!
GOOD, 'CAUSE I'VE GOT A HANKERIN' TO KICK SOME ALIEN BUTT!
HMM...NO FAST FOOD, NO WATERSLIDE PARKS, NO TV ANTENNAS...OBVIOUSLY A PRIMITIVE CULTURE. THIS'LL BE A SNAP!
BART SIMPSON! DANGER! DANGER!
...WHA?
YOU'RE COMING WITH US, MUTANT SCUM!
DISTANCE: 0.9 METERS
APPEARANCE: AGGRESSIVE
SUGGESTION: RUN!

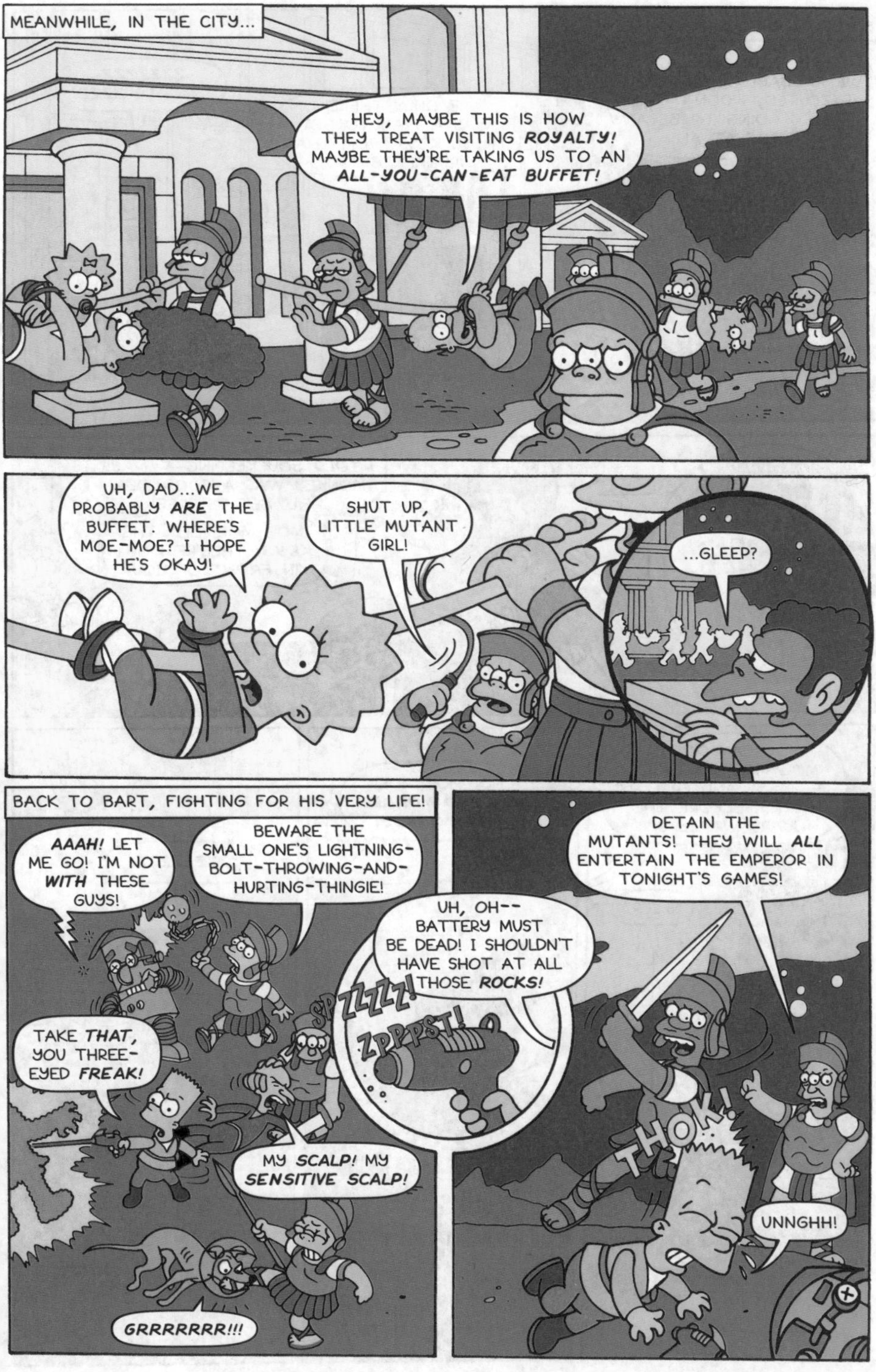
MEANWHILE, IN THE CITY...
HEY, MAYBE THIS IS HOW THEY TREAT VISITING ROYALTY! MAYBE THEY'RE TAKING US TO AN ALL-YOU-CAN-EAT BUFFET!
UH, DAD...WE PROBABLY ARE THE BUFFET. WHERE'S MOE-MOE? I HOPE HE'S OKAY!
SHUT UP, LITTLE MUTANT GIRL!
...GLEEP?
BACK TO BART, FIGHTING FOR HIS VERY LIFE!
AAAH! LET ME GO! I'M NOT WITH THESE GUYS!
BEWARE THE SMALL ONE'S LIGHTNING-BOLT-THROWING-AND-HURTING-THINGIE!
UH, OH-- BATTERY MUST BE DEAD! I SHOULDN'T HAVE SHOT AT ALL THOSE ROCKS!
SPZZZZZ!
ZPPPST!
TAKE THAT, YOU THREE-EYED FREAK!
MY SCALP! MY SENSITIVE SCALP!
GRRRRRRR!!!
DETAIN THE MUTANTS! THEY WILL ALL ENTERTAIN THE EMPEROR IN TONIGHT'S GAMES!
THOK!
UNNGHH!

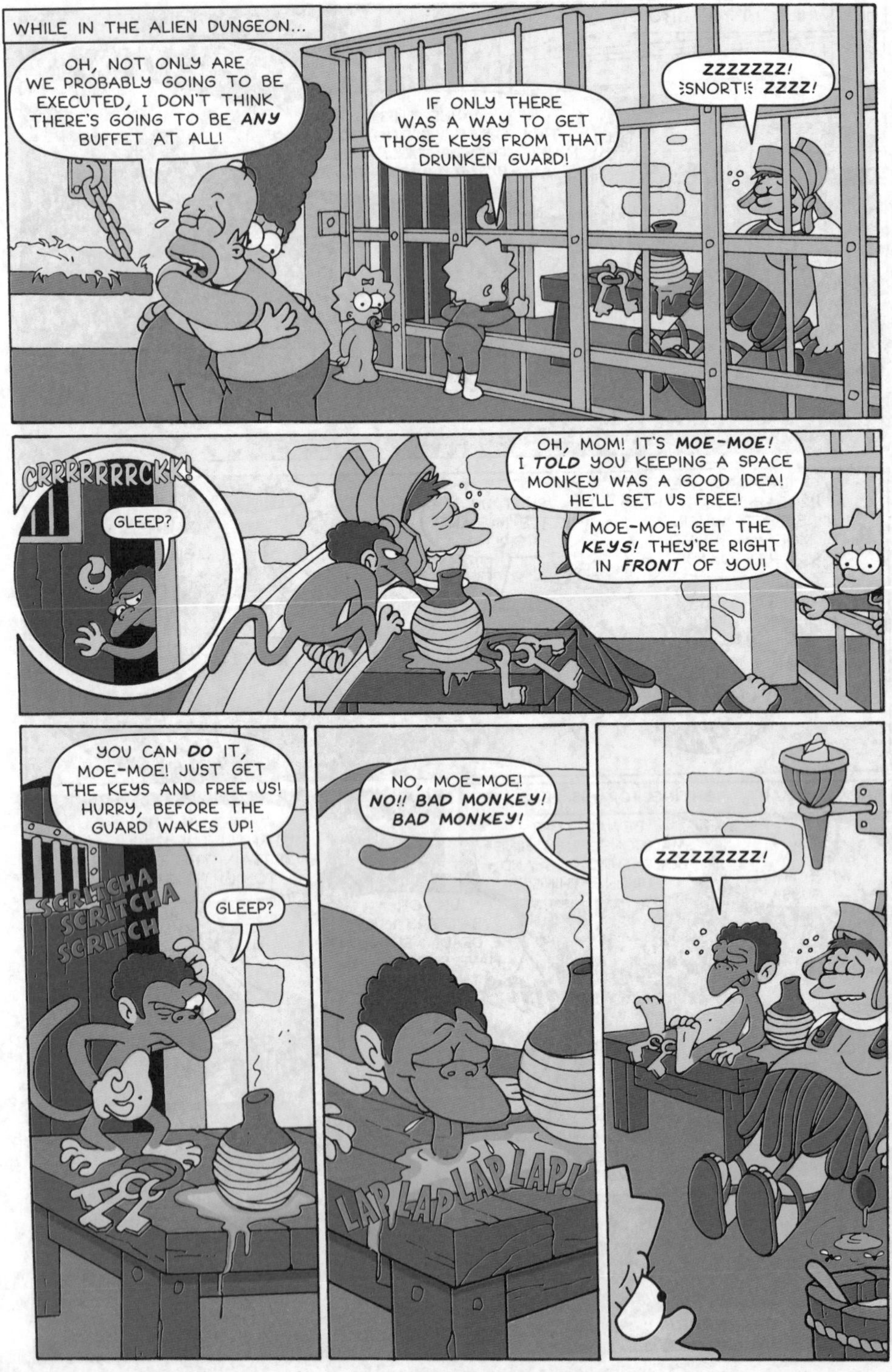
WHILE IN THE ALIEN DUNGEON...
OH, NOT ONLY ARE WE PROBABLY GOING TO BE EXECUTED, I DON'T THINK THERE'S GOING TO BE ANY BUFFET AT ALL!
IF ONLY THERE WAS A WAY TO GET THOSE KEYS FROM THAT DRUNKEN GUARD!
ZZZZZZZ! SNORT! ZZZZ!
CRRRRRRRCKK!
GLEEP?
OH, MOM! IT'S MOE-MOE! I TOLD YOU KEEPING A SPACE MONKEY WAS A GOOD IDEA! HE'LL SET US FREE!
MOE-MOE! GET THE KEYS! THEY'RE RIGHT IN FRONT OF YOU!
YOU CAN DO IT, MOE-MOE! JUST GET THE KEYS AND FREE US! HURRY, BEFORE THE GUARD WAKES UP!
SCRITCHA SCRITCHA SCRITCH
GLEEP?
NO, MOE-MOE! NO!! BAD MONKEY! BAD MONKEY!
LAP LAP LAP LAP!
ZZZZZZZZZ!

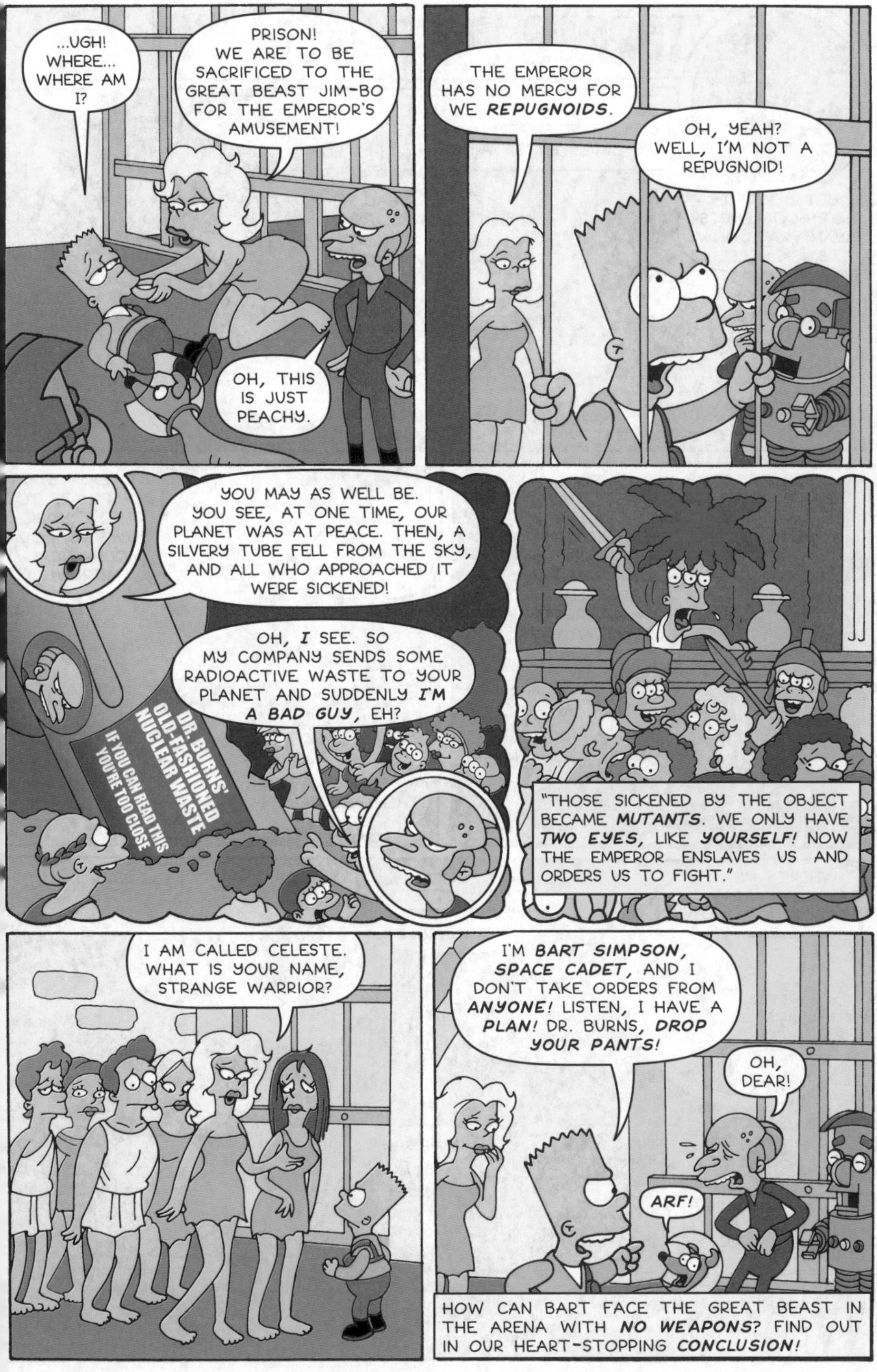

...UGH! WHERE... WHERE AM I?
PRISON! WE ARE TO BE SACRIFICED TO THE GREAT BEAST JIM-BO FOR THE EMPEROR'S AMUSEMENT!
OH, THIS IS JUST PEACHY.
THE EMPEROR HAS NO MERCY FOR WE REPUGNOIDS.
OH, YEAH? WELL, I'M NOT A REPUGNOID!
YOU MAY AS WELL BE. YOU SEE, AT ONE TIME, OUR PLANET WAS AT PEACE. THEN, A SILVERY TUBE FELL FROM THE SKY, AND ALL WHO APPROACHED IT WERE SICKENED!
OH, I SEE. SO MY COMPANY SENDS SOME RADIOACTIVE WASTE TO YOUR PLANET AND SUDDENLY I'M A BAD GUY, EH?
DR. BURNS' OLD-FASHIONED NUCLEAR WASTE
IF YOU CAN READ THIS YOU'RE TOO CLOSE
"THOSE SICKENED BY THE OBJECT BECAME MUTANTS. WE ONLY HAVE TWO EYES, LIKE YOURSELF! NOW THE EMPEROR ENSLAVES US AND ORDERS US TO FIGHT."
I AM CALLED CELESTE. WHAT IS YOUR NAME, STRANGE WARRIOR?
I'M BART SIMPSON, SPACE CADET, AND I DON'T TAKE ORDERS FROM ANYONE! LISTEN, I HAVE A PLAN! DR. BURNS, DROP YOUR PANTS!
OH, DEAR!
ARF!
HOW CAN BART FACE THE GREAT BEAST IN THE ARENA WITH NO WEAPONS? FIND OUT IN OUR HEART-STOPPING CONCLUSION!

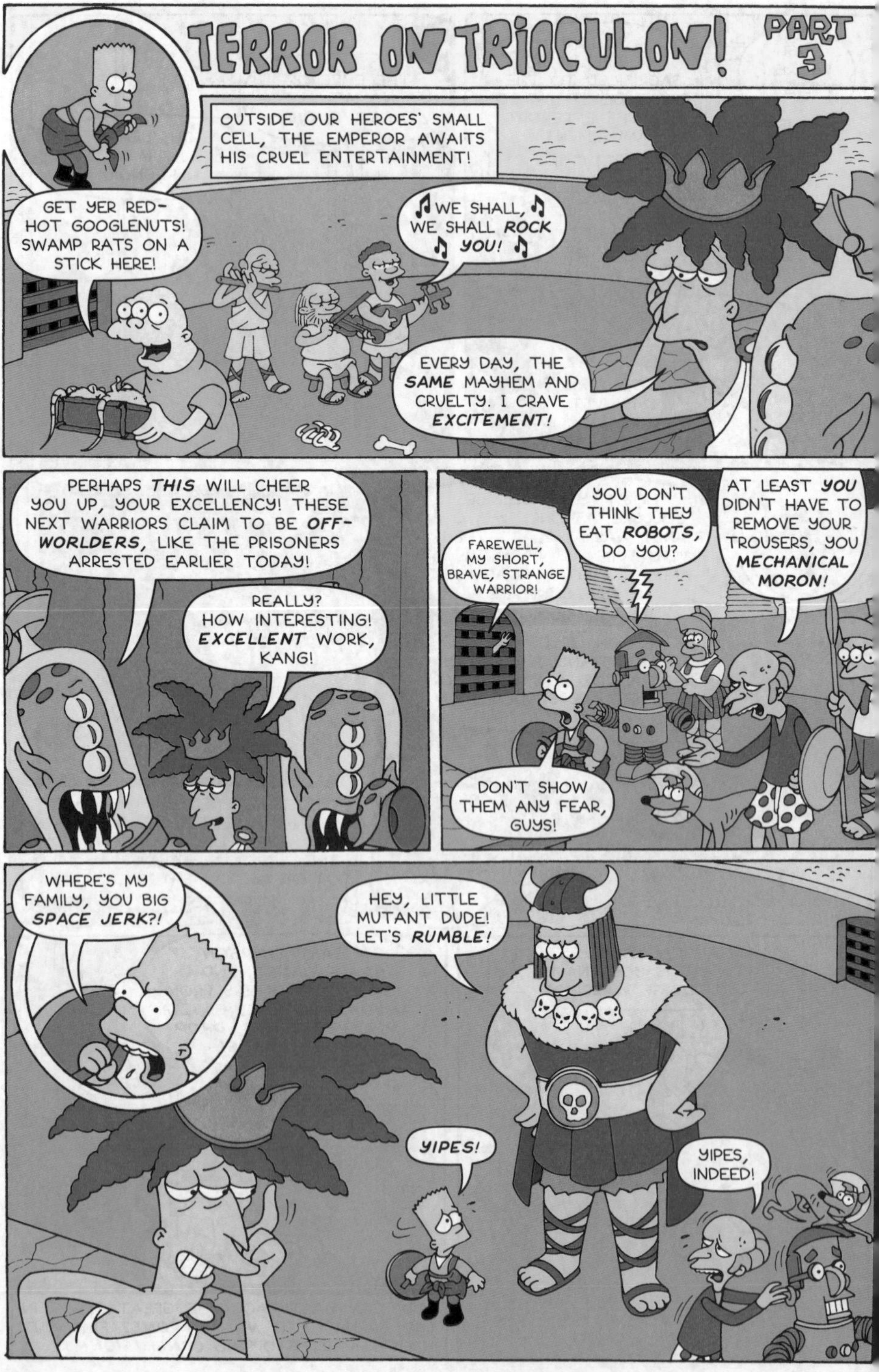
TERROR ON TRIOCULON! PART 3
OUTSIDE OUR HEROES' SMALL CELL, THE EMPEROR AWAITS HIS CRUEL ENTERTAINMENT!
GET YER RED-HOT GOOGLENUTS! SWAMP RATS ON A STICK HERE!
♫ WE SHALL, ♫ WE SHALL ROCK ♫ YOU! ♫
EVERY DAY, THE SAME MAYHEM AND CRUELTY. I CRAVE EXCITEMENT!
PERHAPS THIS WILL CHEER YOU UP, YOUR EXCELLENCY! THESE NEXT WARRIORS CLAIM TO BE OFF-WORLDERS, LIKE THE PRISONERS ARRESTED EARLIER TODAY!
REALLY? HOW INTERESTING! EXCELLENT WORK, KANG!
FAREWELL, MY SHORT, BRAVE, STRANGE WARRIOR!
YOU DON'T THINK THEY EAT ROBOTS, DO YOU?
AT LEAST YOU DIDN'T HAVE TO REMOVE YOUR TROUSERS, YOU MECHANICAL MORON!
DON'T SHOW THEM ANY FEAR, GUYS!
WHERE'S MY FAMILY, YOU BIG SPACE JERK?!
HEY, LITTLE MUTANT DUDE! LET'S RUMBLE!
YIPES!
YIPES, INDEED!

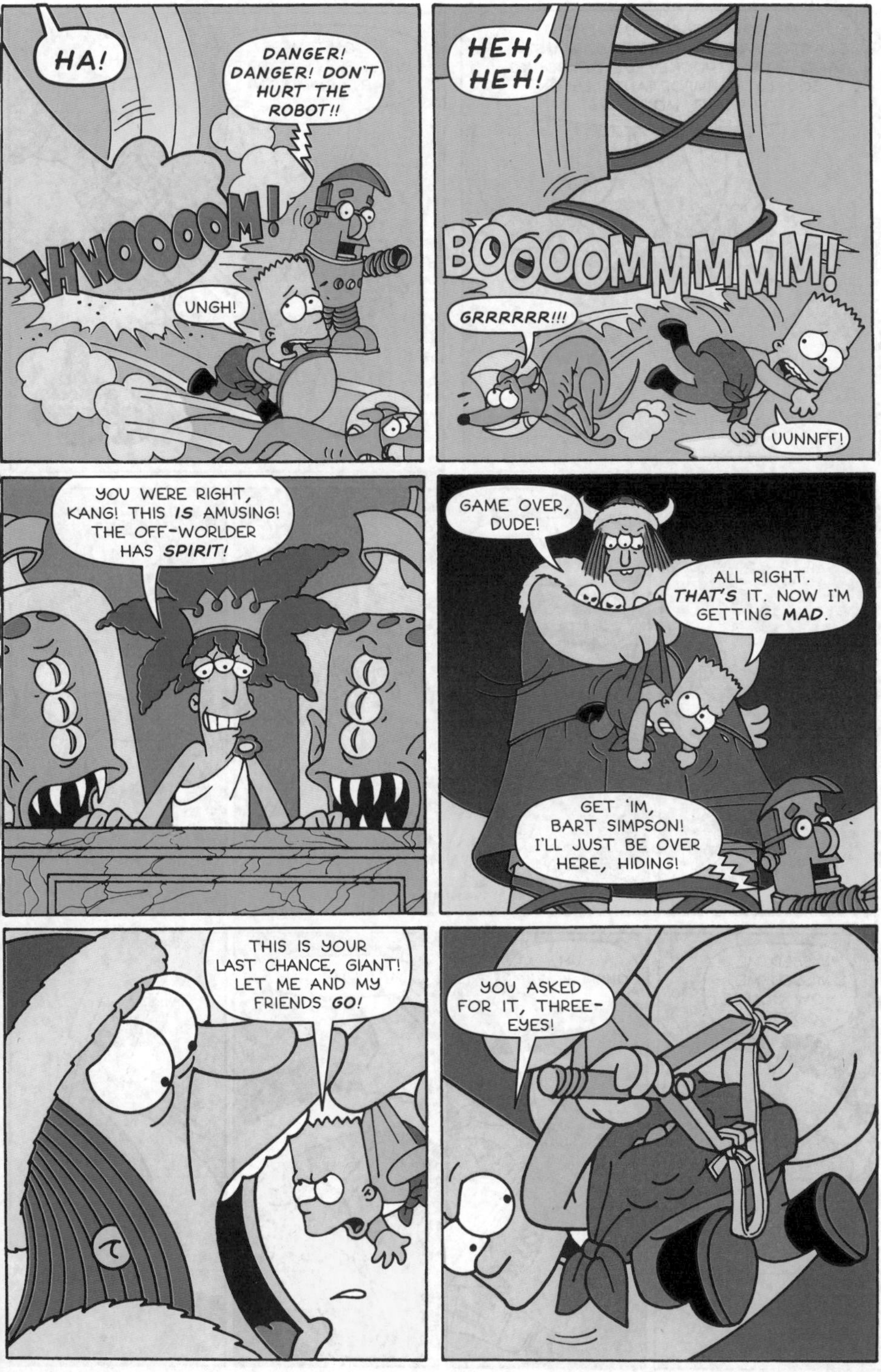
HA!
DANGER! DANGER! DON'T HURT THE ROBOT!!
THWOOOOM!
UNGH!
HEH, HEH!
BOOOOMMMMMM!
GRRRRRR!!!
UUNNFF!
YOU WERE RIGHT, KANG! THIS IS AMUSING! THE OFF-WORLDER HAS SPIRIT!
GAME OVER, DUDE!
ALL RIGHT. THAT'S IT. NOW I'M GETTING MAD.
GET 'IM, BART SIMPSON! I'LL JUST BE OVER HERE, HIDING!
THIS IS YOUR LAST CHANCE, GIANT! LET ME AND MY FRIENDS GO!
YOU ASKED FOR IT, THREE-EYES!

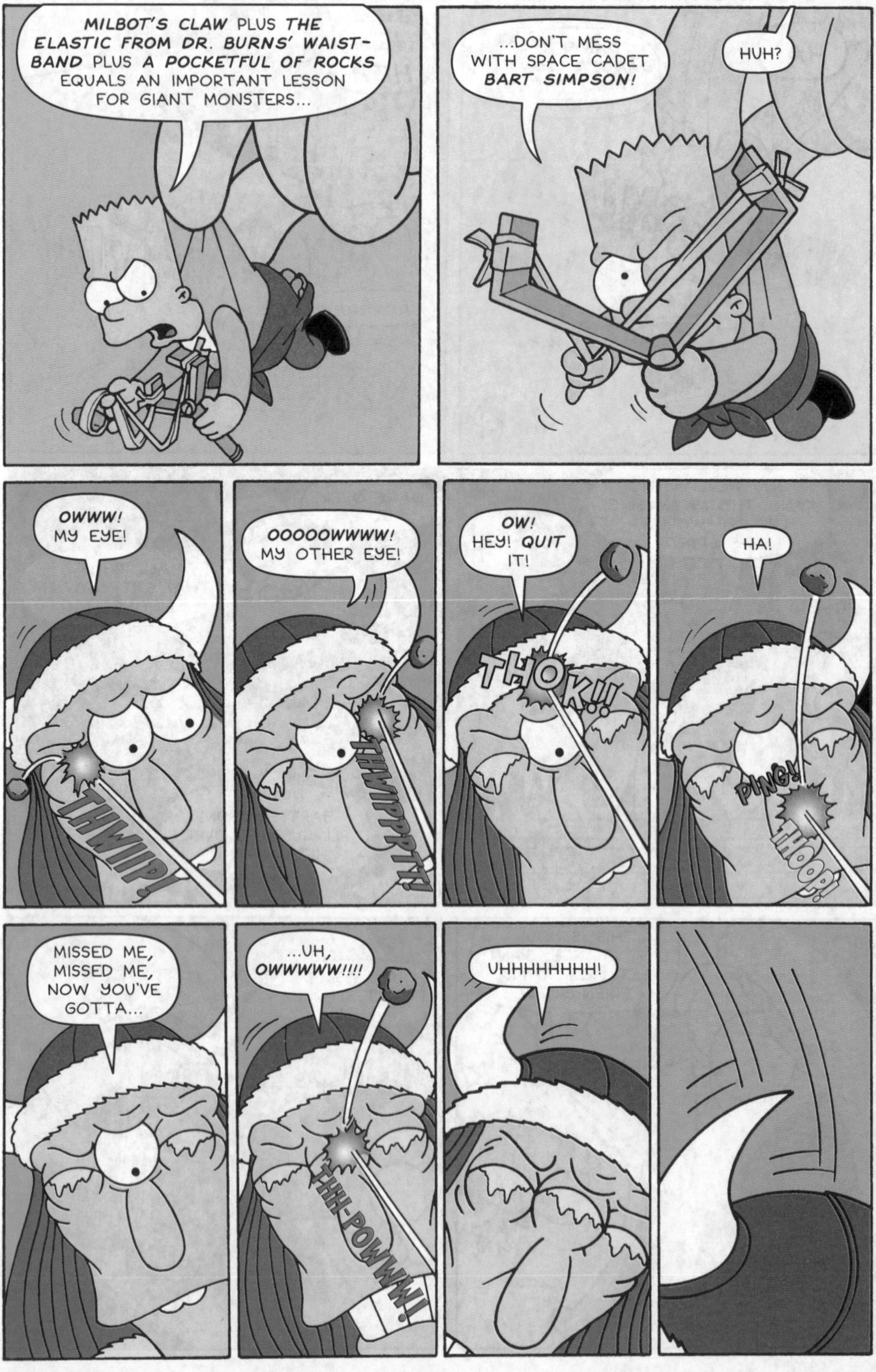
MILBOT'S CLAW PLUS THE ELASTIC FROM DR. BURNS' WAIST-BAND PLUS A POCKETFUL OF ROCKS EQUALS AN IMPORTANT LESSON FOR GIANT MONSTERS...
...DON'T MESS WITH SPACE CADET BART SIMPSON!
HUH?
OWWW! MY EYE!
THWIIP!
OOOOOWWWW! MY OTHER EYE!
THWIPPPTT!
OW! HEY! QUIT IT!
THOK!!
HA!
PING!
THOOP!
MISSED ME, MISSED ME, NOW YOU'VE GOTTA...
...UH, OWWWWW!!!!
THH-POWWW!
UHHHHHHHHH!

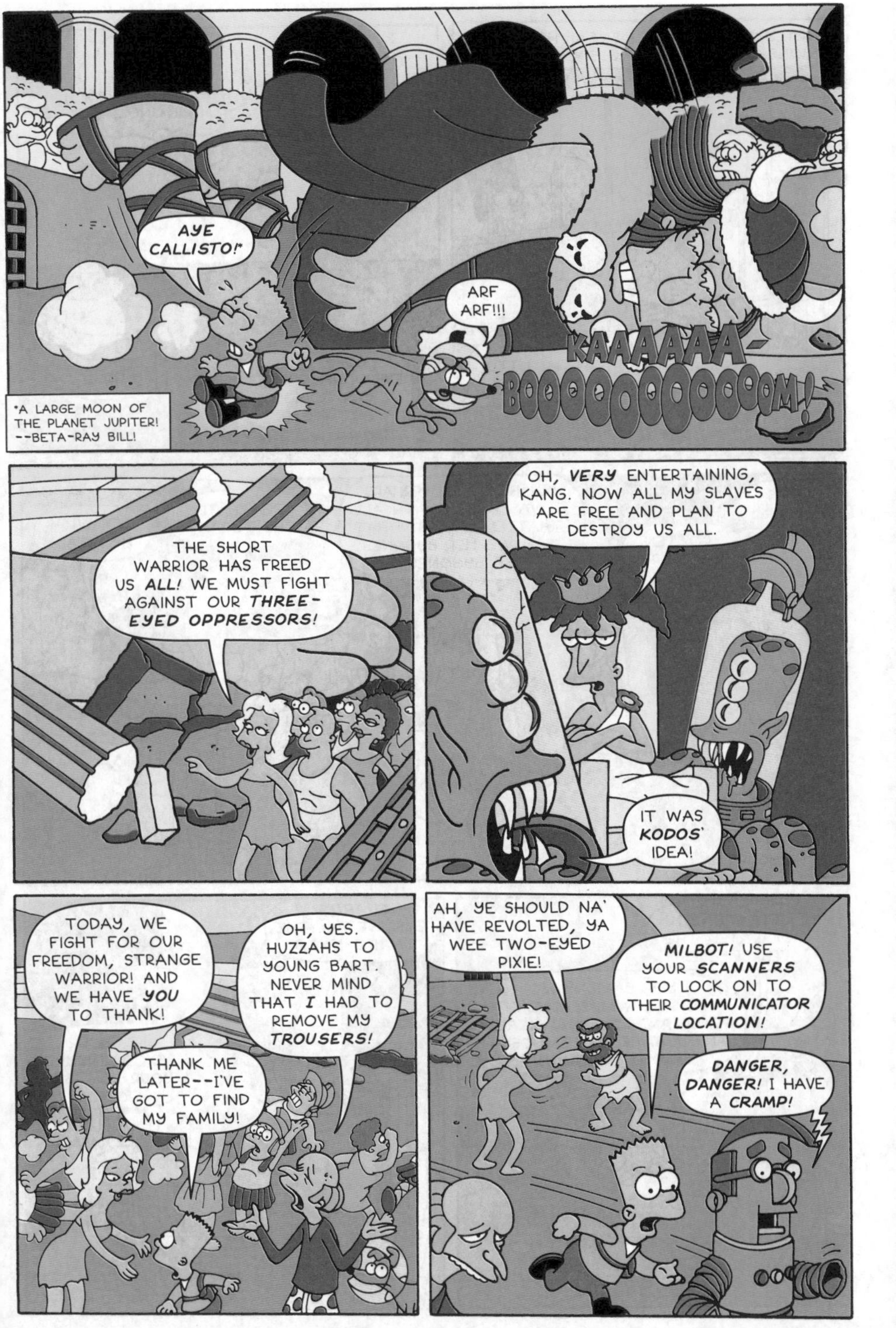
AYE CALLISTO!*
ARF ARF!!!
KAAAAAA-BOOOOOOOOOOOOM!
*A LARGE MOON OF THE PLANET JUPITER! --BETA-RAY BILL!
THE SHORT WARRIOR HAS FREED US ALL! WE MUST FIGHT AGAINST OUR THREE-EYED OPPRESSORS!
OH, VERY ENTERTAINING, KANG. NOW ALL MY SLAVES ARE FREE AND PLAN TO DESTROY US ALL.
IT WAS KODOS' IDEA!
TODAY, WE FIGHT FOR OUR FREEDOM, STRANGE WARRIOR! AND WE HAVE YOU TO THANK!
OH, YES. HUZZAHS TO YOUNG BART. NEVER MIND THAT I HAD TO REMOVE MY TROUSERS!
THANK ME LATER--I'VE GOT TO FIND MY FAMILY!
AH, YE SHOULD NA' HAVE REVOLTED, YA WEE TWO-EYED PIXIE!
MILBOT! USE YOUR SCANNERS TO LOCK ON TO THEIR COMMUNICATOR LOCATION!
DANGER, DANGER! I HAVE A CRAMP!

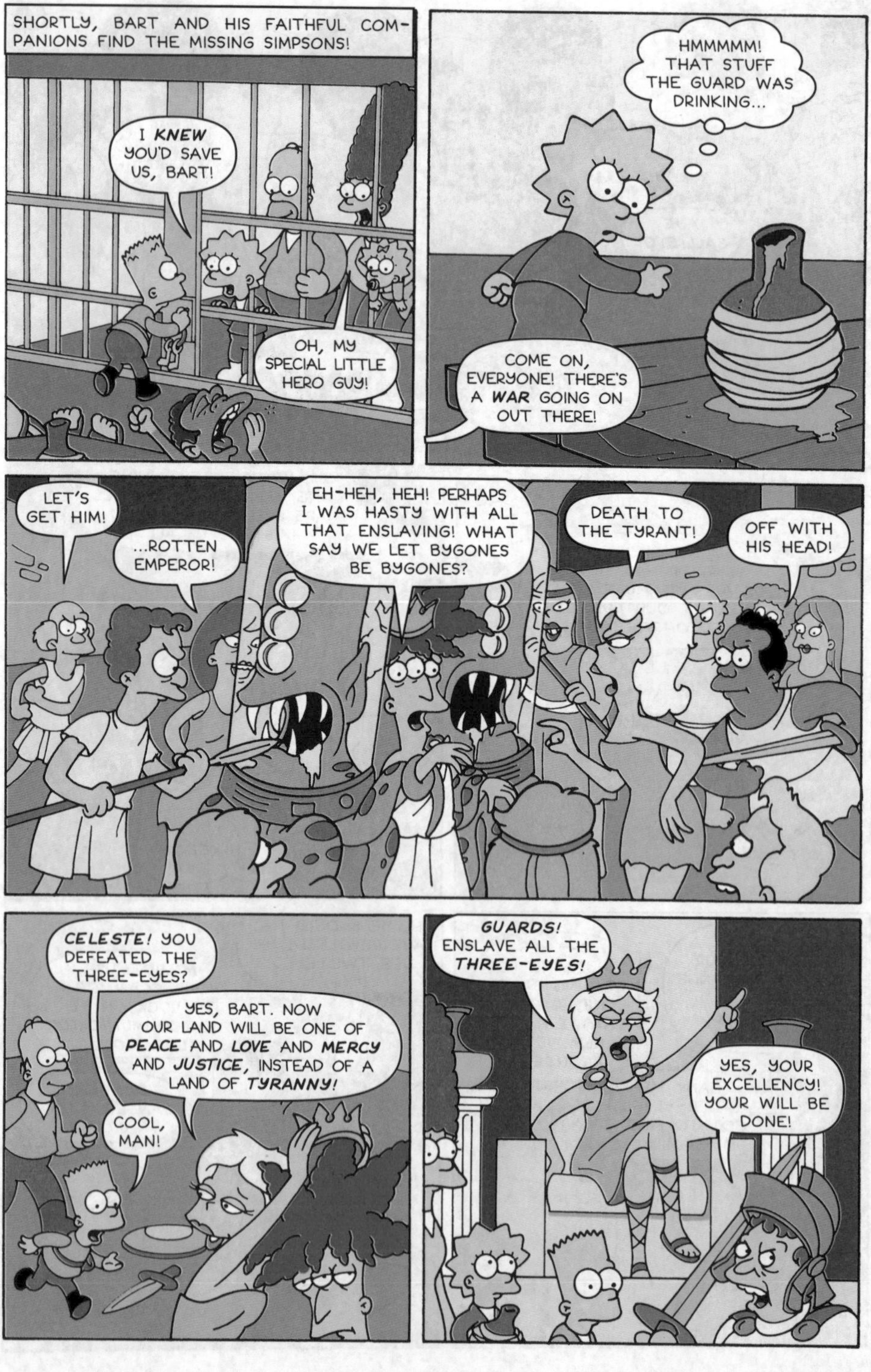

SHORTLY, BART AND HIS FAITHFUL COMPANIONS FIND THE MISSING SIMPSONS!
I KNEW YOU'D SAVE US, BART!
OH, MY SPECIAL LITTLE HERO GUY!
HMMMMM! THAT STUFF THE GUARD WAS DRINKING...
COME ON, EVERYONE! THERE'S A WAR GOING ON OUT THERE!
LET'S GET HIM!
...ROTTEN EMPEROR!
EH-HEH, HEH! PERHAPS I WAS HASTY WITH ALL THAT ENSLAVING! WHAT SAY WE LET BYGONES BE BYGONES?
DEATH TO THE TYRANT!
OFF WITH HIS HEAD!
CELESTE! YOU DEFEATED THE THREE-EYES?
YES, BART. NOW OUR LAND WILL BE ONE OF PEACE AND LOVE AND MERCY AND JUSTICE, INSTEAD OF A LAND OF TYRANNY!
COOL, MAN!
GUARDS! ENSLAVE ALL THE THREE-EYES!
YES, YOUR EXCELLENCY! YOUR WILL BE DONE!

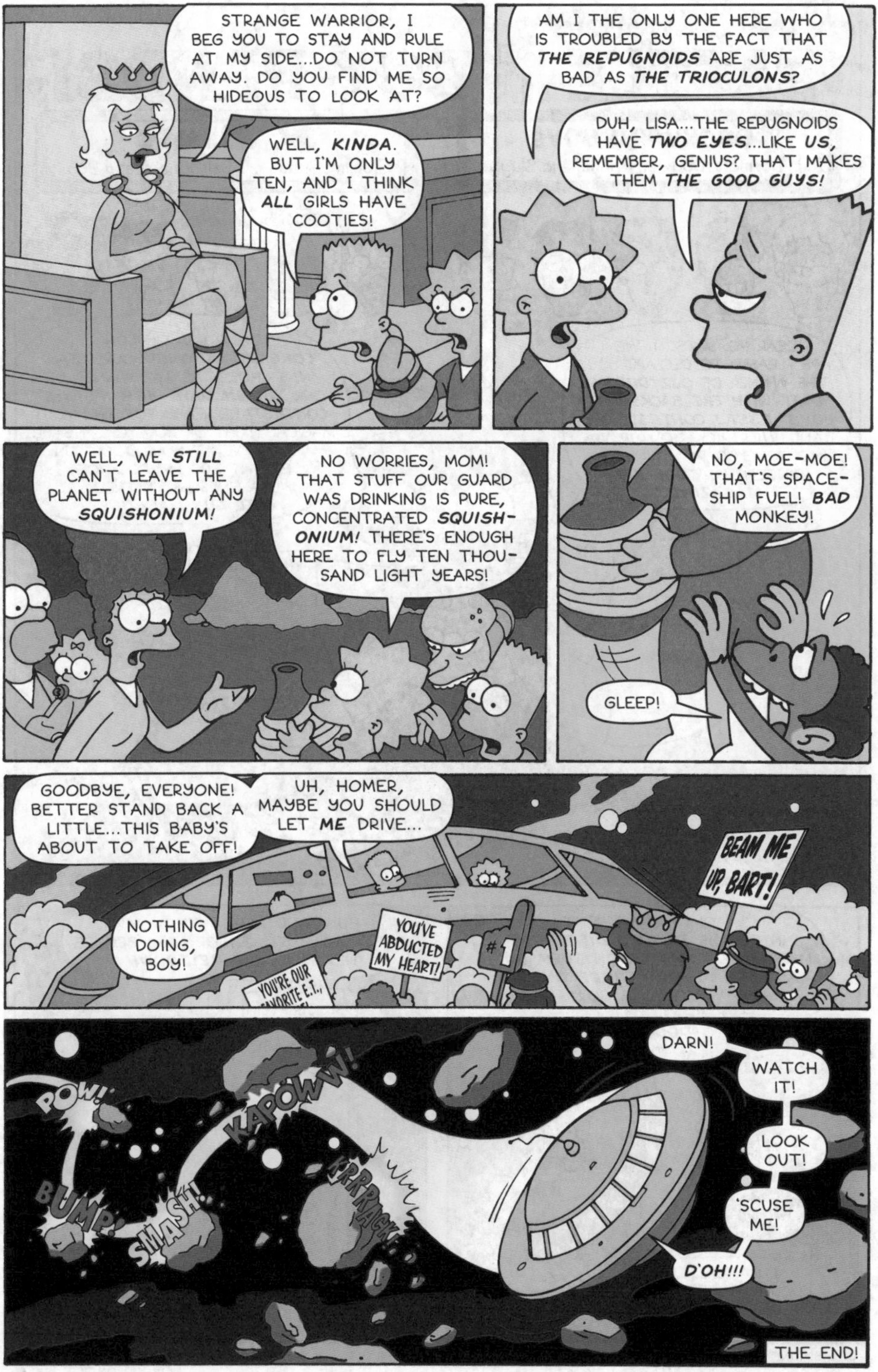
STRANGE WARRIOR, I BEG YOU TO STAY AND RULE AT MY SIDE...DO NOT TURN AWAY. DO YOU FIND ME SO HIDEOUS TO LOOK AT?
WELL, KINDA. BUT I'M ONLY TEN, AND I THINK ALL GIRLS HAVE COOTIES!
AM I THE ONLY ONE HERE WHO IS TROUBLED BY THE FACT THAT THE REPUGNOIDS ARE JUST AS BAD AS THE TRIOCULONS?
DUH, LISA...THE REPUGNOIDS HAVE TWO EYES...LIKE US, REMEMBER, GENIUS? THAT MAKES THEM THE GOOD GUYS!
WELL, WE STILL CAN'T LEAVE THE PLANET WITHOUT ANY SQUISHONIUM!
NO WORRIES, MOM! THAT STUFF OUR GUARD WAS DRINKING IS PURE, CONCENTRATED SQUISHONIUM! THERE'S ENOUGH HERE TO FLY TEN THOUSAND LIGHT YEARS!
NO, MOE-MOE! THAT'S SPACESHIP FUEL! BAD MONKEY!
GLEEP!
GOODBYE, EVERYONE! BETTER STAND BACK A LITTLE...THIS BABY'S ABOUT TO TAKE OFF!
UH, HOMER, MAYBE YOU SHOULD LET ME DRIVE...
NOTHING DOING, BOY!
BEAM ME UP, BART!
YOU'VE ABDUCTED MY HEART!
#1
YOU'RE OUR
POW!
KAPOWW!
BUMP!
SMASH!
KRRRACK!
DARN!
WATCH IT!
LOOK OUT!
'SCUSE ME!
D'OH!!!
THE END!

Lisa Simpson IN:
BATTLE OF THE BOY-BANDS!

THE BACKYARD BOYS	N'Style
R.J., Dermott, Cody B., Ryinne, and Sluggo	Tommy, Shades, T. Bell, Ignatz, and Bob

"DEAR MS. SIMPSON, WE ARE PLEASED TO DECLARE YOU THE WINNER OF OUR *"DREAM DATE WITH THE BACKYARD BOYS" ESSAY CONTEST!* THE BAND WILL PICK YOU UP VIA LIMO AT 3:00 PM, JUNE 13TH. SINCERELY, *COOL KID MAGAZINE."*

"DEAR LISA SIMPSON. *CONGRATULATIONS!* YOUR ESSAY WAS CHOSEN AS THE WINNER OF OUR *"DREAM DATE WITH N'STYLE" CONTEST!* BE READY FOR THE MOST MAGICAL NIGHT OF YOUR LIFE! N'STYLE WILL ARRIVE AT YOUR DOOR JUNE 13TH, AT 3:00 PM! ROCK ON, LISA SIMPSON! SINCERELY, *CUTE GUY MAGAZINE."*

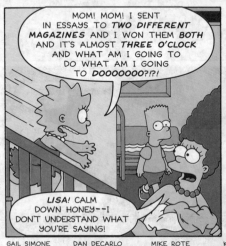

MOM! MOM! I SENT IN ESSAYS TO *TWO DIFFERENT MAGAZINES* AND I WON THEM *BOTH* AND IT'S ALMOST *THREE O'CLOCK* AND WHAT AM I GOING TO DO WHAT AM I GOING TO DOOOOOOO?!?!

LISA! CALM DOWN HONEY--I DON'T UNDERSTAND WHAT YOU'RE SAYING!

HUH. AND HERE I THOUGHT SHE'D WAIT 'TIL JUNIOR HIGH BEFORE HER FIRST BIG *MELTDOWN.*

MISS SIMPSON! CAN YOU COME OUT PLEASE?

GAIL SIMONE
SCRIPT

DAN DECARLO
LAYOUTS

MIKE ROTE
PENCILS & INKS

KAREN BATES
COLORS & LETTERS

BILL MORRISON
EDITOR

MATT GROENING
NEW KID ON THE BLOCK

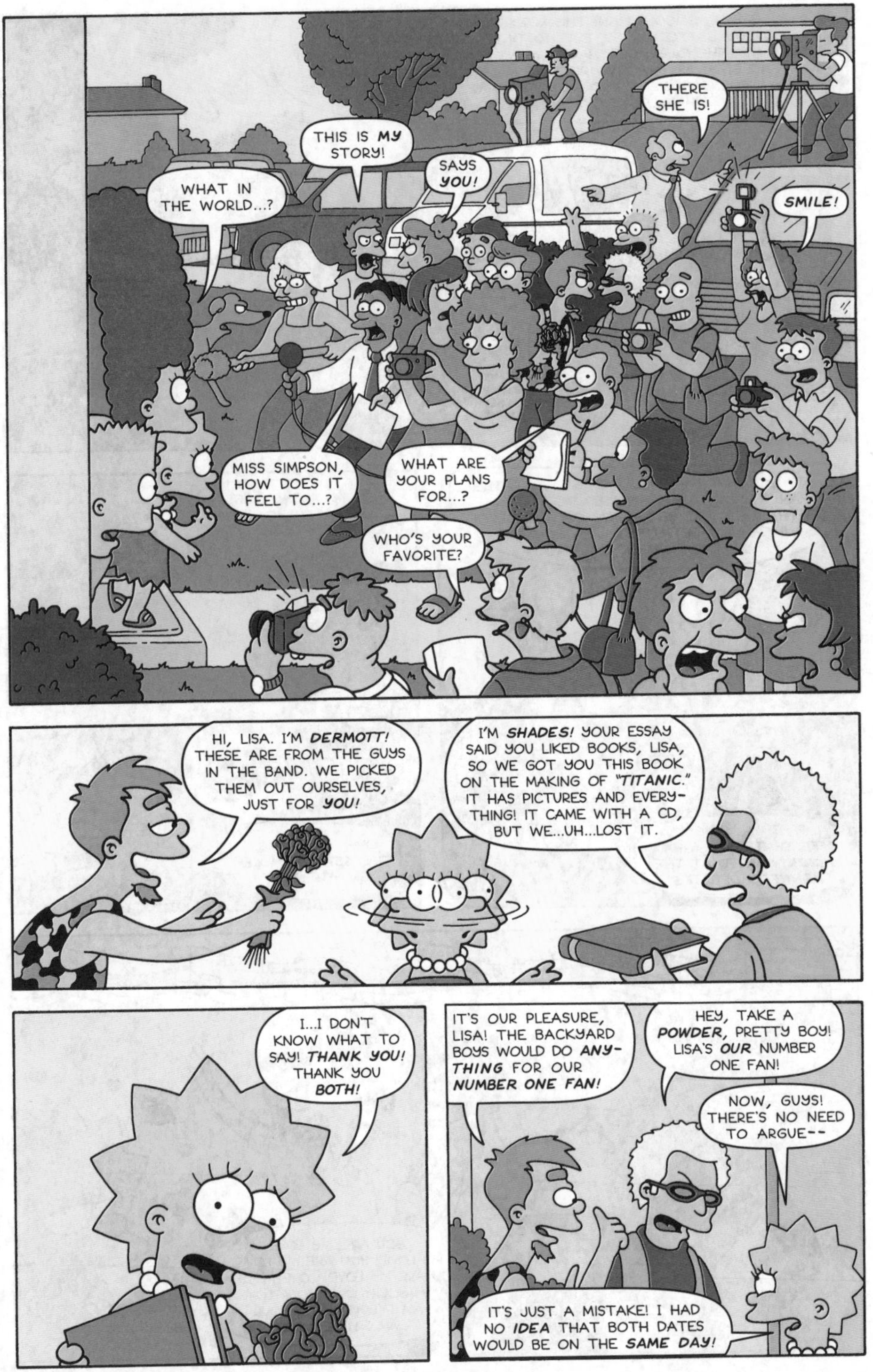
THIS IS MY STORY!
THERE SHE IS!
WHAT IN THE WORLD...?
SAYS YOU!
SMILE!
MISS SIMPSON, HOW DOES IT FEEL TO...?
WHAT ARE YOUR PLANS FOR...?
WHO'S YOUR FAVORITE?
HI, LISA. I'M DERMOTT! THESE ARE FROM THE GUYS IN THE BAND. WE PICKED THEM OUT OURSELVES, JUST FOR YOU!
I'M SHADES! YOUR ESSAY SAID YOU LIKED BOOKS, LISA, SO WE GOT YOU THIS BOOK ON THE MAKING OF "TITANIC." IT HAS PICTURES AND EVERYTHING! IT CAME WITH A CD, BUT WE...UH...LOST IT.
I...I DON'T KNOW WHAT TO SAY! THANK YOU! THANK YOU BOTH!
IT'S OUR PLEASURE, LISA! THE BACKYARD BOYS WOULD DO ANYTHING FOR OUR NUMBER ONE FAN!
HEY, TAKE A POWDER, PRETTY BOY! LISA'S OUR NUMBER ONE FAN!
NOW, GUYS! THERE'S NO NEED TO ARGUE--
IT'S JUST A MISTAKE! I HAD NO IDEA THAT BOTH DATES WOULD BE ON THE SAME DAY!

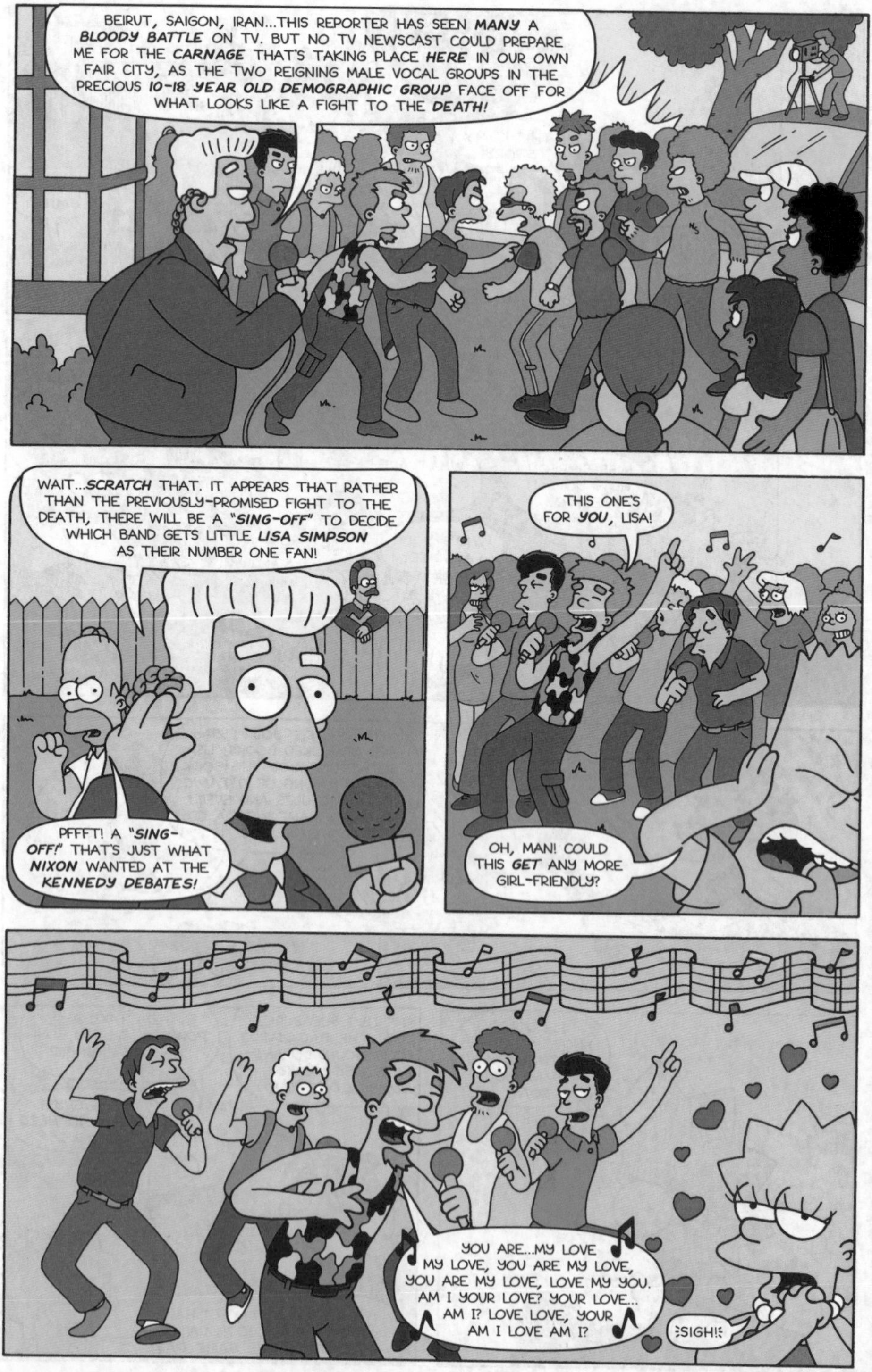
BEIRUT, SAIGON, IRAN...THIS REPORTER HAS SEEN MANY A BLOODY BATTLE ON TV. BUT NO TV NEWSCAST COULD PREPARE ME FOR THE CARNAGE THAT'S TAKING PLACE HERE IN OUR OWN FAIR CITY, AS THE TWO REIGNING MALE VOCAL GROUPS IN THE PRECIOUS 10-18 YEAR OLD DEMOGRAPHIC GROUP FACE OFF FOR WHAT LOOKS LIKE A FIGHT TO THE DEATH!
WAIT...SCRATCH THAT. IT APPEARS THAT RATHER THAN THE PREVIOUSLY-PROMISED FIGHT TO THE DEATH, THERE WILL BE A "SING-OFF" TO DECIDE WHICH BAND GETS LITTLE LISA SIMPSON AS THEIR NUMBER ONE FAN!
PFFFT! A "SING-OFF!" THAT'S JUST WHAT NIXON WANTED AT THE KENNEDY DEBATES!
THIS ONE'S FOR YOU, LISA!
OH, MAN! COULD THIS GET ANY MORE GIRL-FRIENDLY?
YOU ARE...MY LOVE MY LOVE, YOU ARE MY LOVE, YOU ARE MY LOVE, LOVE MY YOU. AM I YOUR LOVE? YOUR LOVE... AM I? LOVE LOVE, YOUR AM I LOVE AM I?
SIGH!

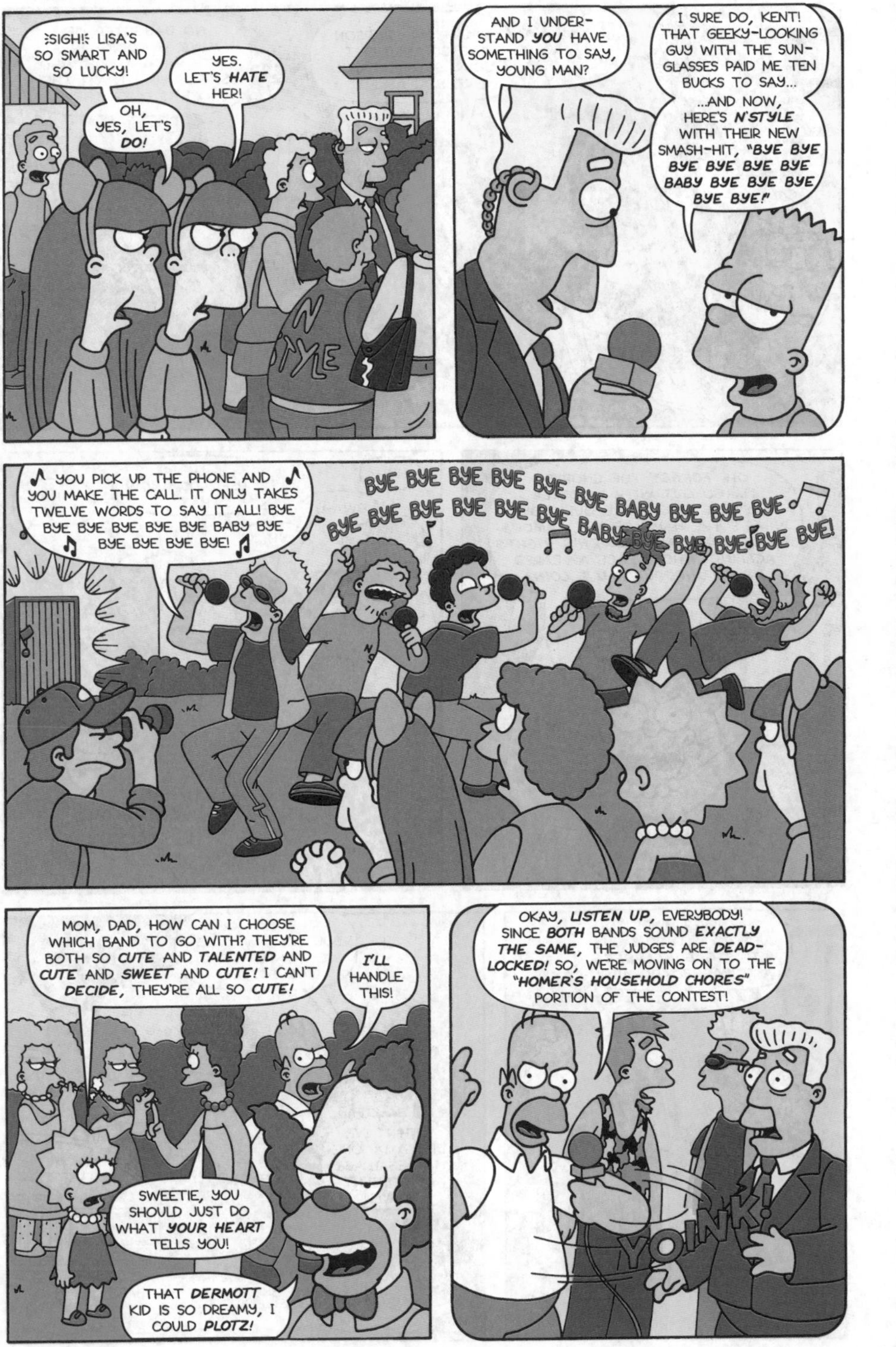
:SIGH!: LISA'S SO SMART AND SO LUCKY!
OH, YES, LET'S **DO!**
YES. LET'S **HATE** HER!
AND I UNDERSTAND **YOU** HAVE SOMETHING TO SAY, YOUNG MAN?
I SURE DO, KENT! THAT GEEKY-LOOKING GUY WITH THE SUNGLASSES PAID ME TEN BUCKS TO SAY...
...AND NOW, HERE'S **N'STYLE** WITH THEIR NEW SMASH-HIT, **"BYE BYE BYE BYE BYE BYE BABY BYE BYE BYE BYE BYE!"**
YOU PICK UP THE PHONE AND YOU MAKE THE CALL. IT ONLY TAKES TWELVE WORDS TO SAY IT ALL! BYE BYE BYE BYE BYE BYE BABY BYE BYE BYE BYE BYE!
BYE BYE BYE BYE BYE BYE BABY BYE BYE BYE
BYE BYE BYE BYE BYE BYE BABY BYE BYE BYE BYE BYE!
MOM, DAD, HOW CAN I CHOOSE WHICH BAND TO GO WITH? THEY'RE BOTH SO **CUTE** AND **TALENTED** AND **CUTE** AND **SWEET** AND **CUTE!** I CAN'T **DECIDE,** THEY'RE ALL SO **CUTE!**
I'LL HANDLE THIS!
SWEETIE, YOU SHOULD JUST DO WHAT **YOUR HEART** TELLS YOU!
THAT **DERMOTT** KID IS SO DREAMY, I COULD **PLOTZ!**
OKAY, **LISTEN UP,** EVERYBODY! SINCE **BOTH** BANDS SOUND **EXACTLY THE SAME,** THE JUDGES ARE **DEADLOCKED!** SO, WE'RE MOVING ON TO THE **"HOMER'S HOUSEHOLD CHORES"** PORTION OF THE CONTEST!
YOINK!

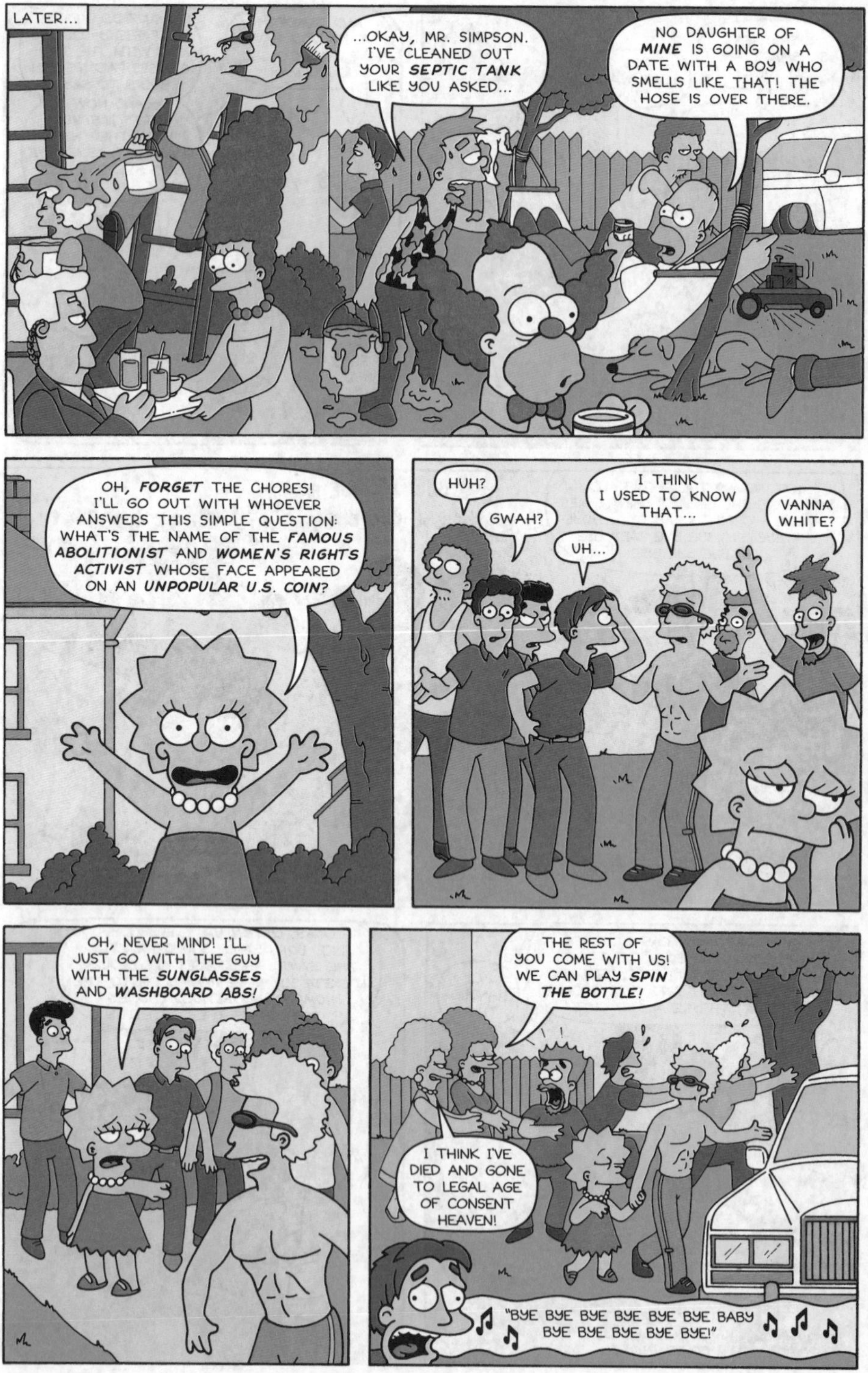
LATER...
...OKAY, MR. SIMPSON. I'VE CLEANED OUT YOUR SEPTIC TANK LIKE YOU ASKED...
NO DAUGHTER OF MINE IS GOING ON A DATE WITH A BOY WHO SMELLS LIKE THAT! THE HOSE IS OVER THERE.
OH, FORGET THE CHORES! I'LL GO OUT WITH WHOEVER ANSWERS THIS SIMPLE QUESTION: WHAT'S THE NAME OF THE FAMOUS ABOLITIONIST AND WOMEN'S RIGHTS ACTIVIST WHOSE FACE APPEARED ON AN UNPOPULAR U.S. COIN?
HUH?
GWAH?
UH...
I THINK I USED TO KNOW THAT...
VANNA WHITE?
OH, NEVER MIND! I'LL JUST GO WITH THE GUY WITH THE SUNGLASSES AND WASHBOARD ABS!
THE REST OF YOU COME WITH US! WE CAN PLAY SPIN THE BOTTLE!
I THINK I'VE DIED AND GONE TO LEGAL AGE OF CONSENT HEAVEN!
"BYE BYE BYE BYE BYE BYE BABY BYE BYE BYE BYE BYE!"

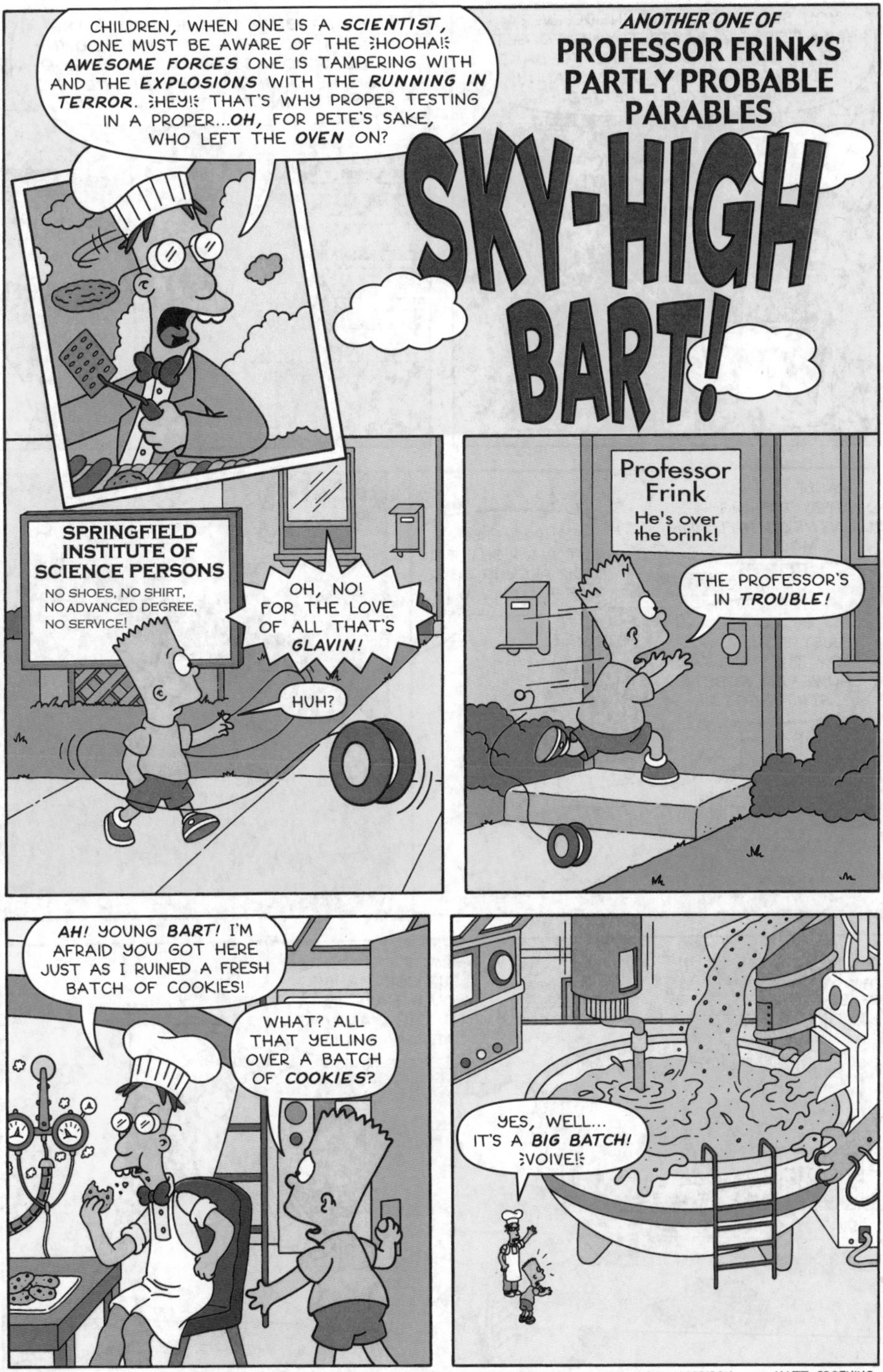
CHILDREN, WHEN ONE IS A SCIENTIST, ONE MUST BE AWARE OF THE ;HOOHA!; AWESOME FORCES ONE IS TAMPERING WITH AND THE EXPLOSIONS WITH THE RUNNING IN TERROR. ;HEY!; THAT'S WHY PROPER TESTING IN A PROPER...OH, FOR PETE'S SAKE, WHO LEFT THE OVEN ON?
ANOTHER ONE OF
PROFESSOR FRINK'S PARTLY PROBABLE PARABLES
SKY-HIGH BART!
SPRINGFIELD INSTITUTE OF SCIENCE PERSONS
NO SHOES, NO SHIRT, NO ADVANCED DEGREE, NO SERVICE!
OH, NO! FOR THE LOVE OF ALL THAT'S GLAVIN!
HUH?
Professor Frink
He's over the brink!
THE PROFESSOR'S IN TROUBLE!
AH! YOUNG BART! I'M AFRAID YOU GOT HERE JUST AS I RUINED A FRESH BATCH OF COOKIES!
WHAT? ALL THAT YELLING OVER A BATCH OF COOKIES?
YES, WELL... IT'S A BIG BATCH! ;VOIVE!;

GAIL SIMONE
RECIPE

DAN DECARLO
LUSCIOUS LAYOUTS

MIKE ROTE
ALL-PURPOSE ART

KAREN BATES
CREAMY COLORS/LUMPY LETTERS

BILL MORRISON
HEAD CHEF

MATT GROENING
TOP NUT

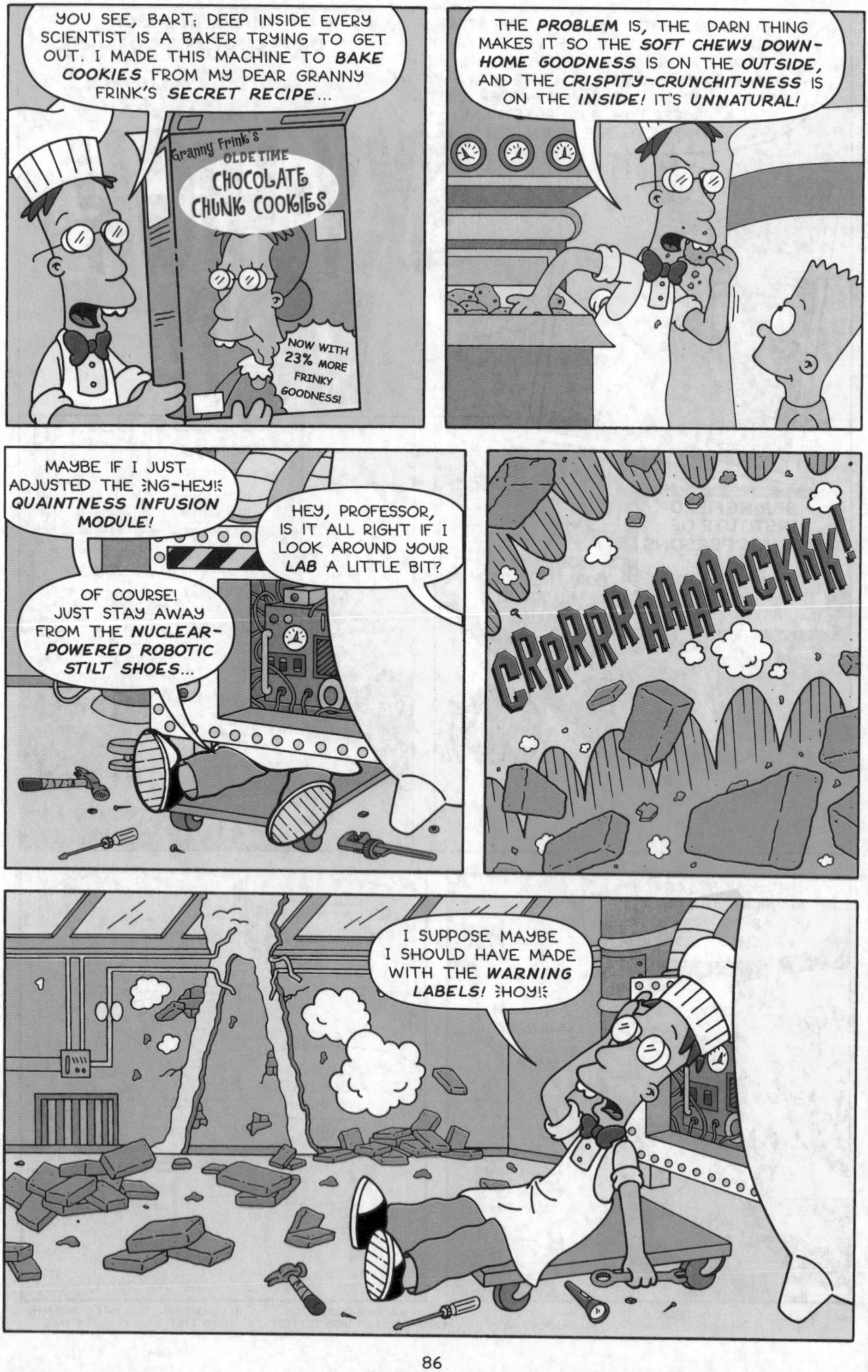
YOU SEE, BART; DEEP INSIDE EVERY SCIENTIST IS A BAKER TRYING TO GET OUT. I MADE THIS MACHINE TO BAKE COOKIES FROM MY DEAR GRANNY FRINK'S SECRET RECIPE...
Granny Frink's OLDE TIME CHOCOLATE CHUNK COOKIES
NOW WITH 23% MORE FRINKY GOODNESS!
THE PROBLEM IS, THE DARN THING MAKES IT SO THE SOFT CHEWY DOWN-HOME GOODNESS IS ON THE OUTSIDE, AND THE CRISPITY-CRUNCHITYNESS IS ON THE INSIDE! IT'S UNNATURAL!
MAYBE IF I JUST ADJUSTED THE NG-HEY! QUAINTNESS INFUSION MODULE!
HEY, PROFESSOR, IS IT ALL RIGHT IF I LOOK AROUND YOUR LAB A LITTLE BIT?
OF COURSE! JUST STAY AWAY FROM THE NUCLEAR-POWERED ROBOTIC STILT SHOES...
CRRRRAAAACCKKK!
I SUPPOSE MAYBE I SHOULD HAVE MADE WITH THE WARNING LABELS! HOY!

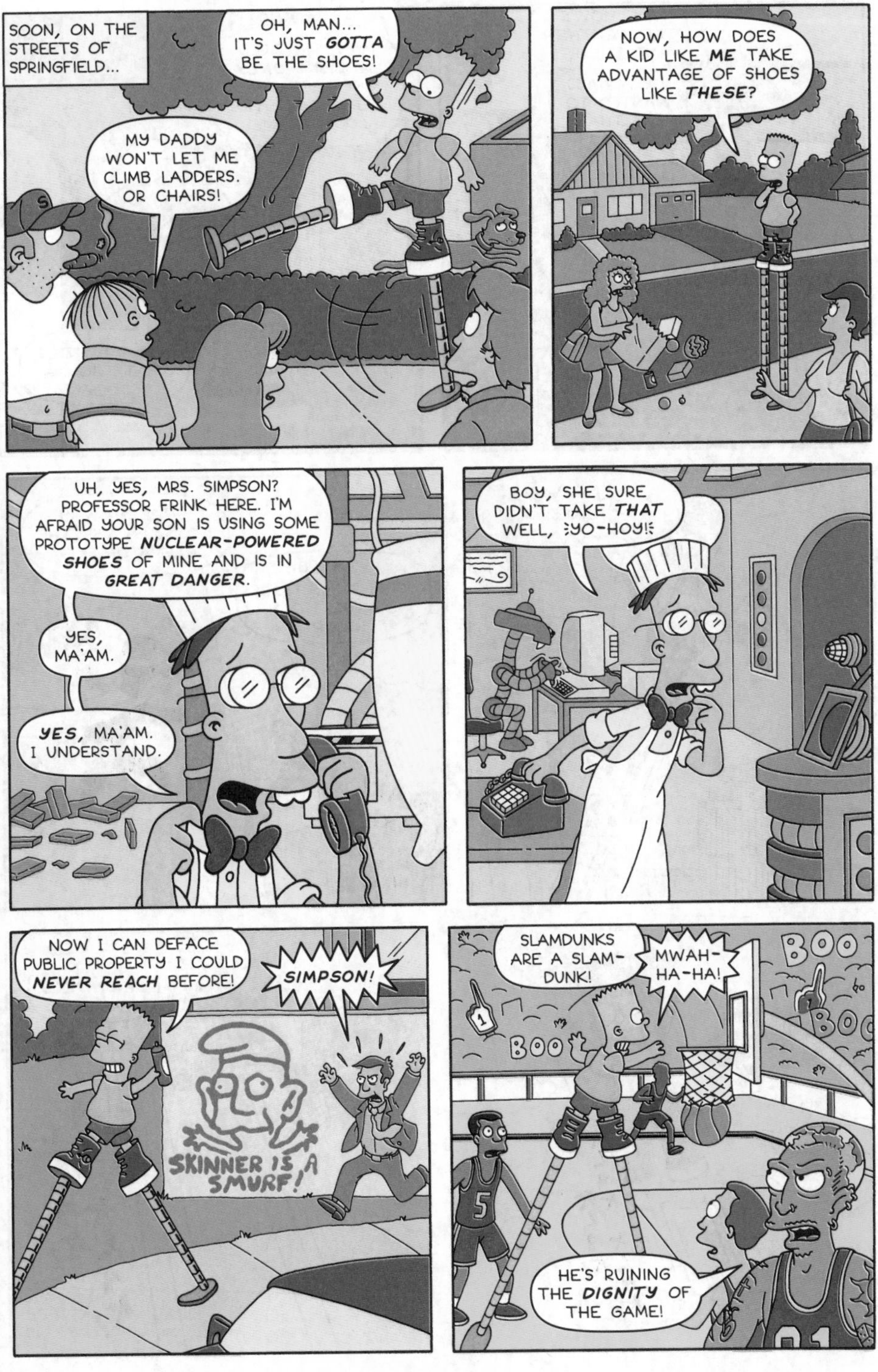

SOON, ON THE STREETS OF SPRINGFIELD...
OH, MAN... IT'S JUST GOTTA BE THE SHOES!
MY DADDY WON'T LET ME CLIMB LADDERS. OR CHAIRS!
NOW, HOW DOES A KID LIKE ME TAKE ADVANTAGE OF SHOES LIKE THESE?
UH, YES, MRS. SIMPSON? PROFESSOR FRINK HERE. I'M AFRAID YOUR SON IS USING SOME PROTOTYPE NUCLEAR-POWERED SHOES OF MINE AND IS IN GREAT DANGER.
YES, MA'AM.
YES, MA'AM. I UNDERSTAND.
BOY, SHE SURE DIDN'T TAKE THAT WELL, YO-HOY!
NOW I CAN DEFACE PUBLIC PROPERTY I COULD NEVER REACH BEFORE!
SIMPSON!
SKINNER IS A SMURF!
SLAMDUNKS ARE A SLAM-DUNK!
MWAH-HA-HA!
BOO
BOO
BOO
HE'S RUINING THE DIGNITY OF THE GAME!

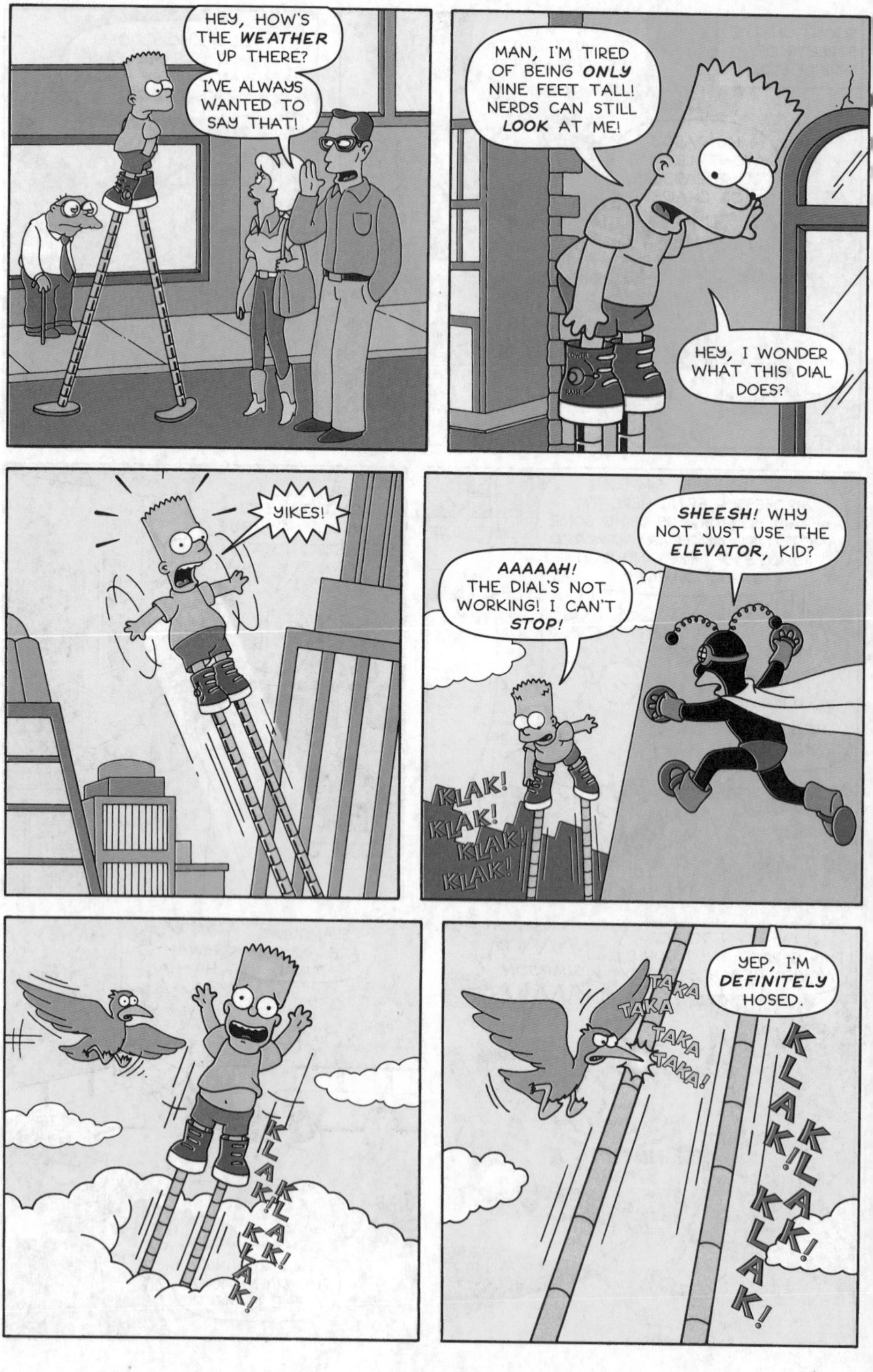
HEY, HOW'S THE WEATHER UP THERE?
I'VE ALWAYS WANTED TO SAY THAT!
MAN, I'M TIRED OF BEING ONLY NINE FEET TALL! NERDS CAN STILL LOOK AT ME!
LOWER
RAISE
HEY, I WONDER WHAT THIS DIAL DOES?
YIKES!
SHEESH! WHY NOT JUST USE THE ELEVATOR, KID?
AAAAAH! THE DIAL'S NOT WORKING! I CAN'T STOP!
KLAK! KLAK! KLAK! KLAK!
KLAK! KLAK! KLAK! KLAK!
TAKA TAKA TAKA TAKA!
YEP, I'M DEFINITELY HOSED.
KLAK! KLAK! KLAK! KLAK!

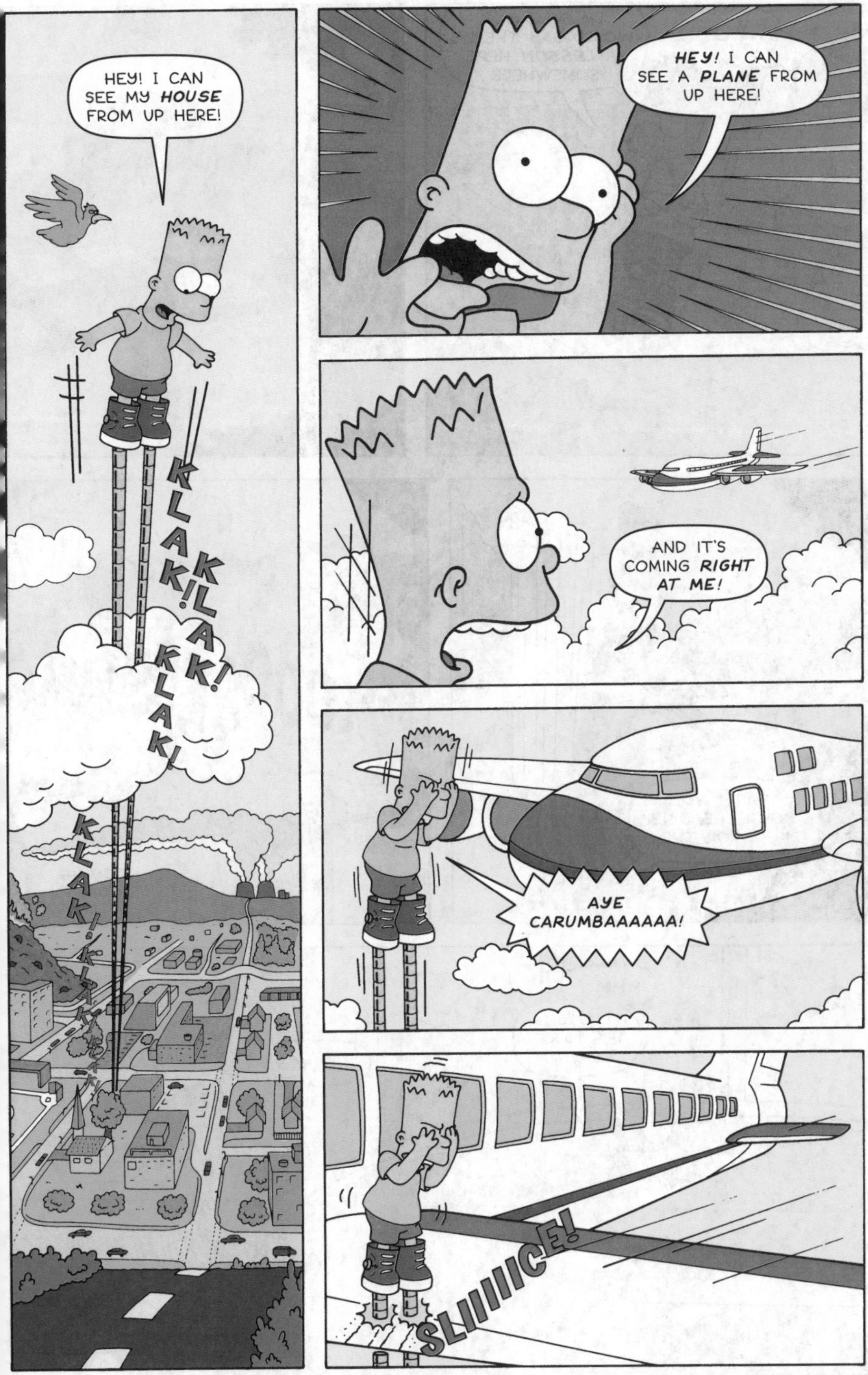
HEY! I CAN SEE MY HOUSE FROM UP HERE!
KLAK! KLAK! KLAK! KLAK!
HEY! I CAN SEE A PLANE FROM UP HERE!
AND IT'S COMING RIGHT AT ME!
AYE CARUMBAAAAAA!
SLIIIIICE!

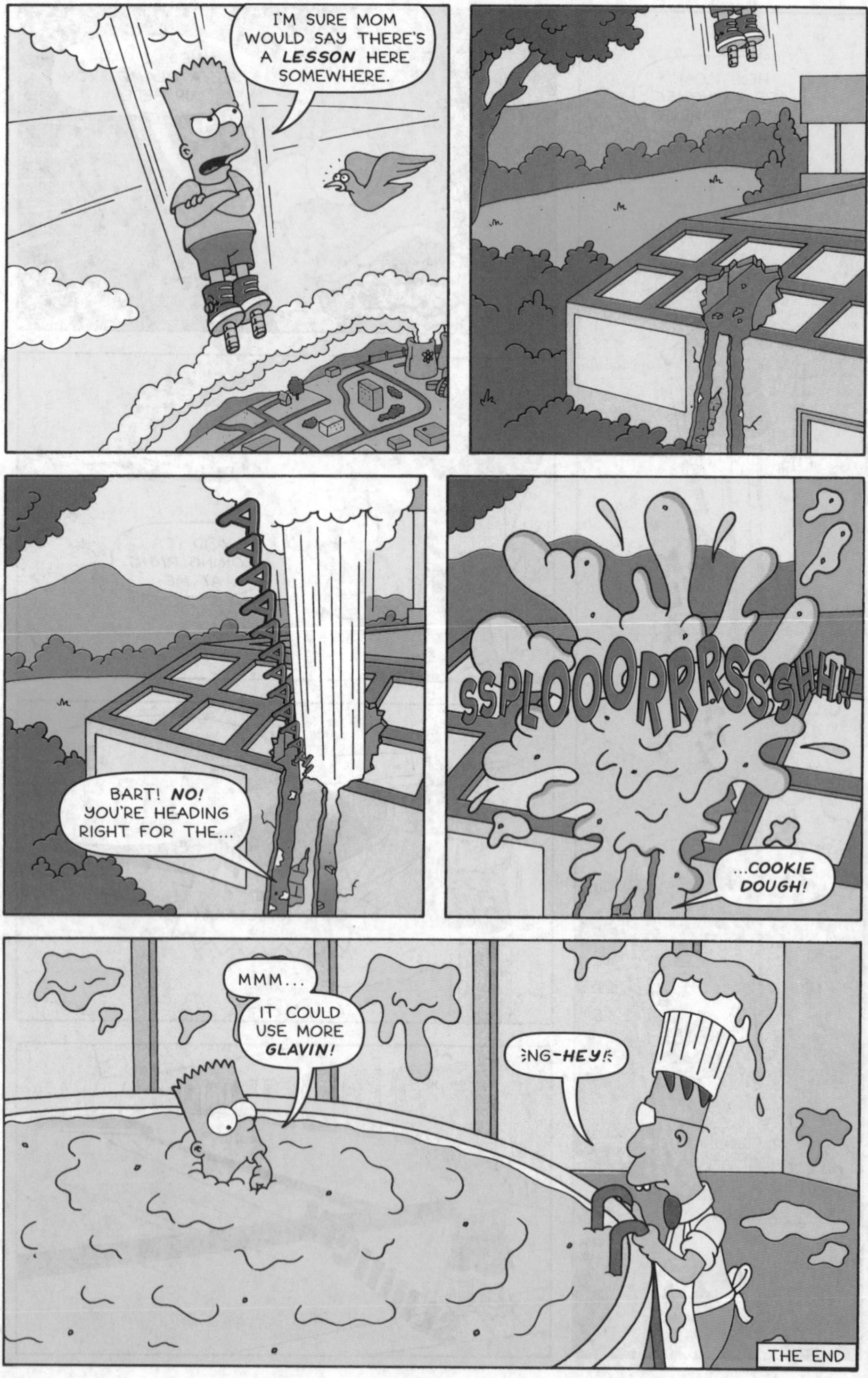

I'M SURE MOM WOULD SAY THERE'S A **LESSON** HERE SOMEWHERE.
AAAAAAAAAAAH!
BART! **NO!** YOU'RE HEADING RIGHT FOR THE...
SSPLOOORRRSSSHH!!
...COOKIE DOUGH!
MMM...
IT COULD USE MORE **GLAVIN!**
NG-**HEY!**
THE END

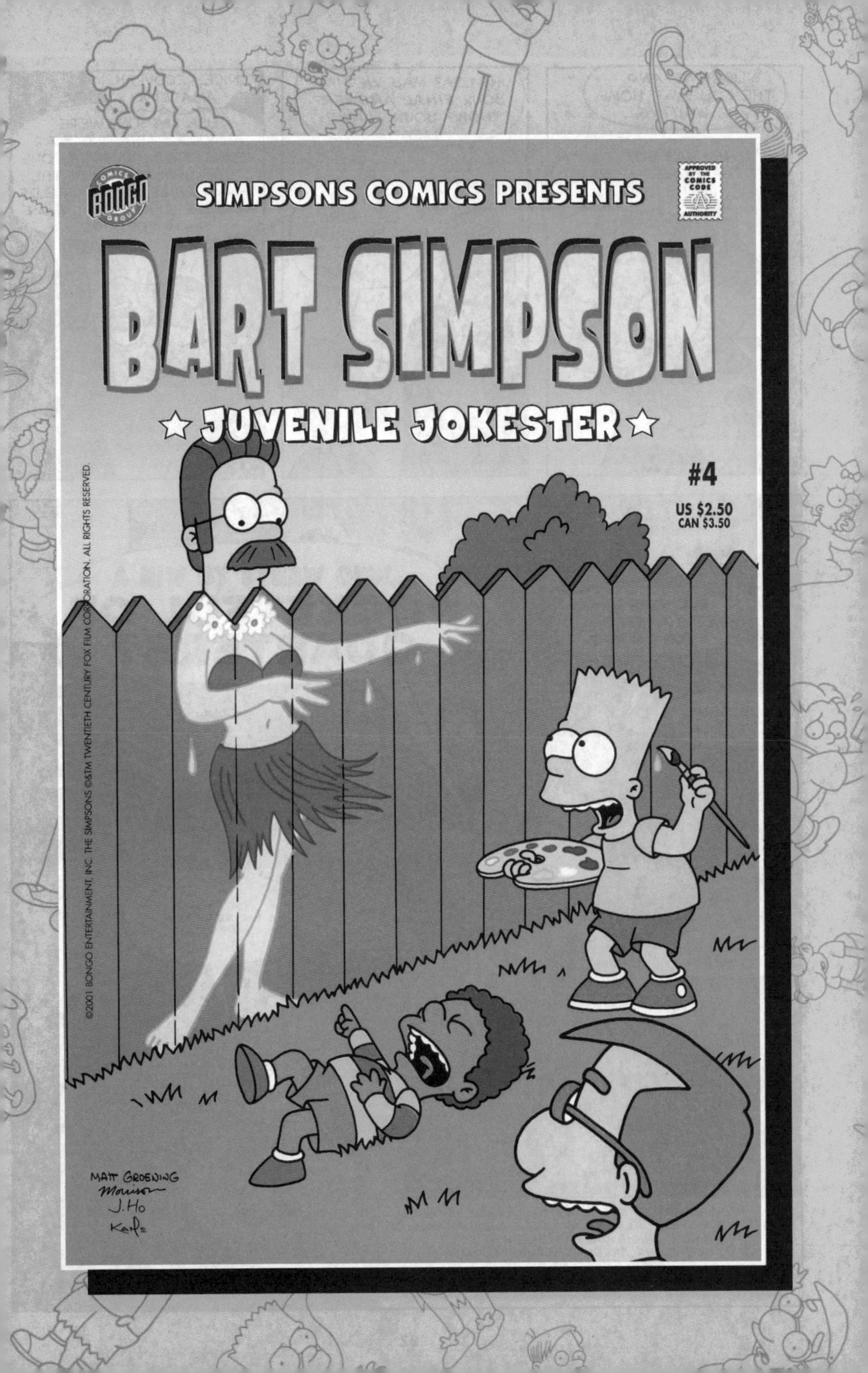
BONGO COMICS GROUP
SIMPSONS COMICS PRESENTS
APPROVED BY THE COMICS CODE AUTHORITY
BART SIMPSON
JUVENILE JOKESTER
#4
US $2.50
CAN $3.50
©2001 BONGO ENTERTAINMENT, INC. THE SIMPSONS ©&TM TWENTIETH CENTURY FOX FILM CORPORATION. ALL RIGHTS RESERVED.
MATT GROENING
J. Ho

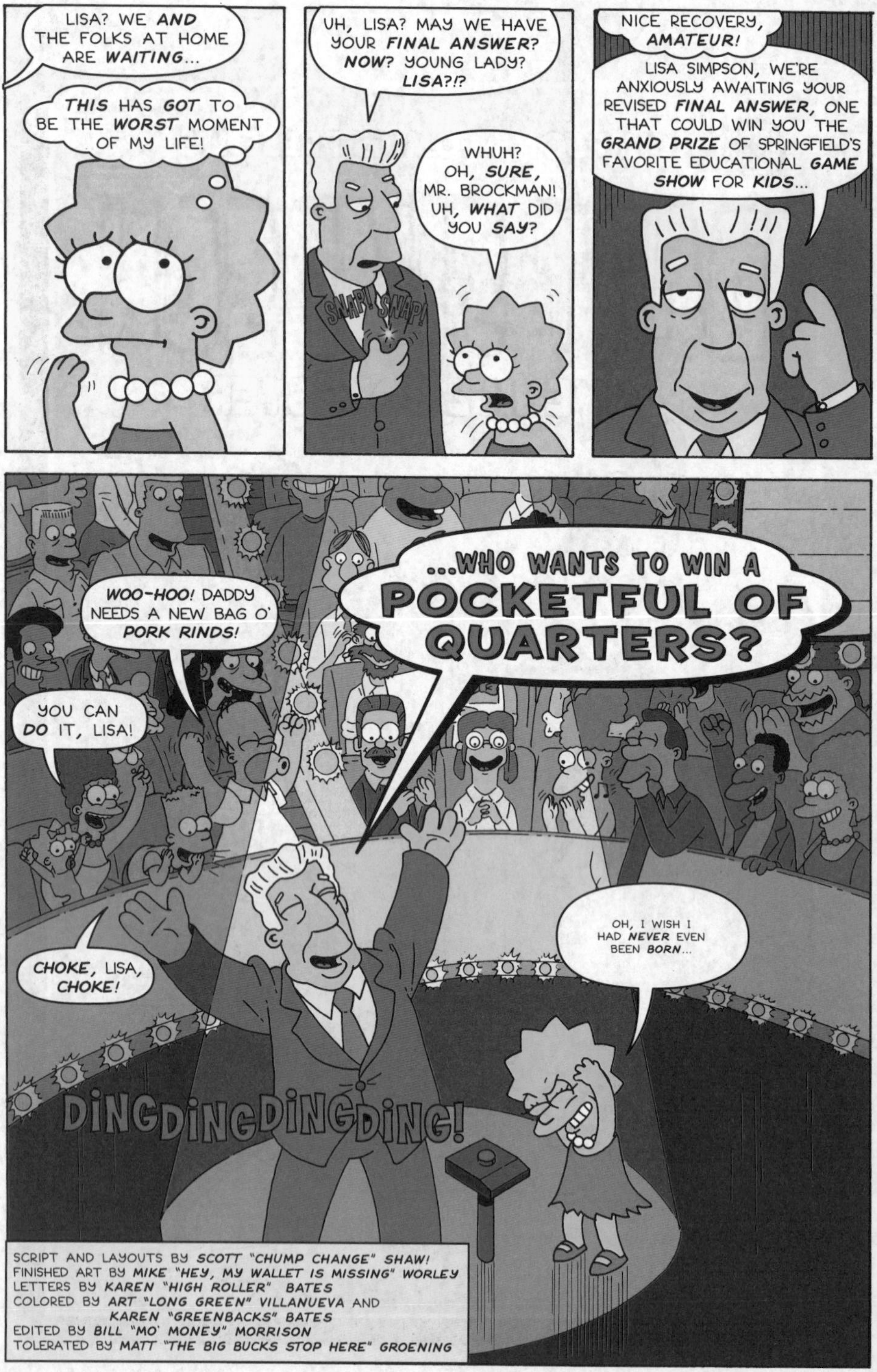
LISA? WE AND THE FOLKS AT HOME ARE WAITING...
THIS HAS GOT TO BE THE WORST MOMENT OF MY LIFE!
UH, LISA? MAY WE HAVE YOUR FINAL ANSWER? NOW? YOUNG LADY? LISA?!?
SNAP! SNAP!
WHUH? OH, SURE, MR. BROCKMAN! UH, WHAT DID YOU SAY?
NICE RECOVERY, AMATEUR!
LISA SIMPSON, WE'RE ANXIOUSLY AWAITING YOUR REVISED FINAL ANSWER, ONE THAT COULD WIN YOU THE GRAND PRIZE OF SPRINGFIELD'S FAVORITE EDUCATIONAL GAME SHOW FOR KIDS...
...WHO WANTS TO WIN A POCKETFUL OF QUARTERS?
WOO-HOO! DADDY NEEDS A NEW BAG O' PORK RINDS!
YOU CAN DO IT, LISA!
CHOKE, LISA, CHOKE!
OH, I WISH I HAD NEVER EVEN BEEN BORN...
DINGDINGDINGDING!
SCRIPT AND LAYOUTS BY SCOTT "CHUMP CHANGE" SHAW!
FINISHED ART BY MIKE "HEY, MY WALLET IS MISSING" WORLEY
LETTERS BY KAREN "HIGH ROLLER" BATES
COLORED BY ART "LONG GREEN" VILLANUEVA AND KAREN "GREENBACKS" BATES
EDITED BY BILL "MO' MONEY" MORRISON
TOLERATED BY MATT "THE BIG BUCKS STOP HERE" GROENING

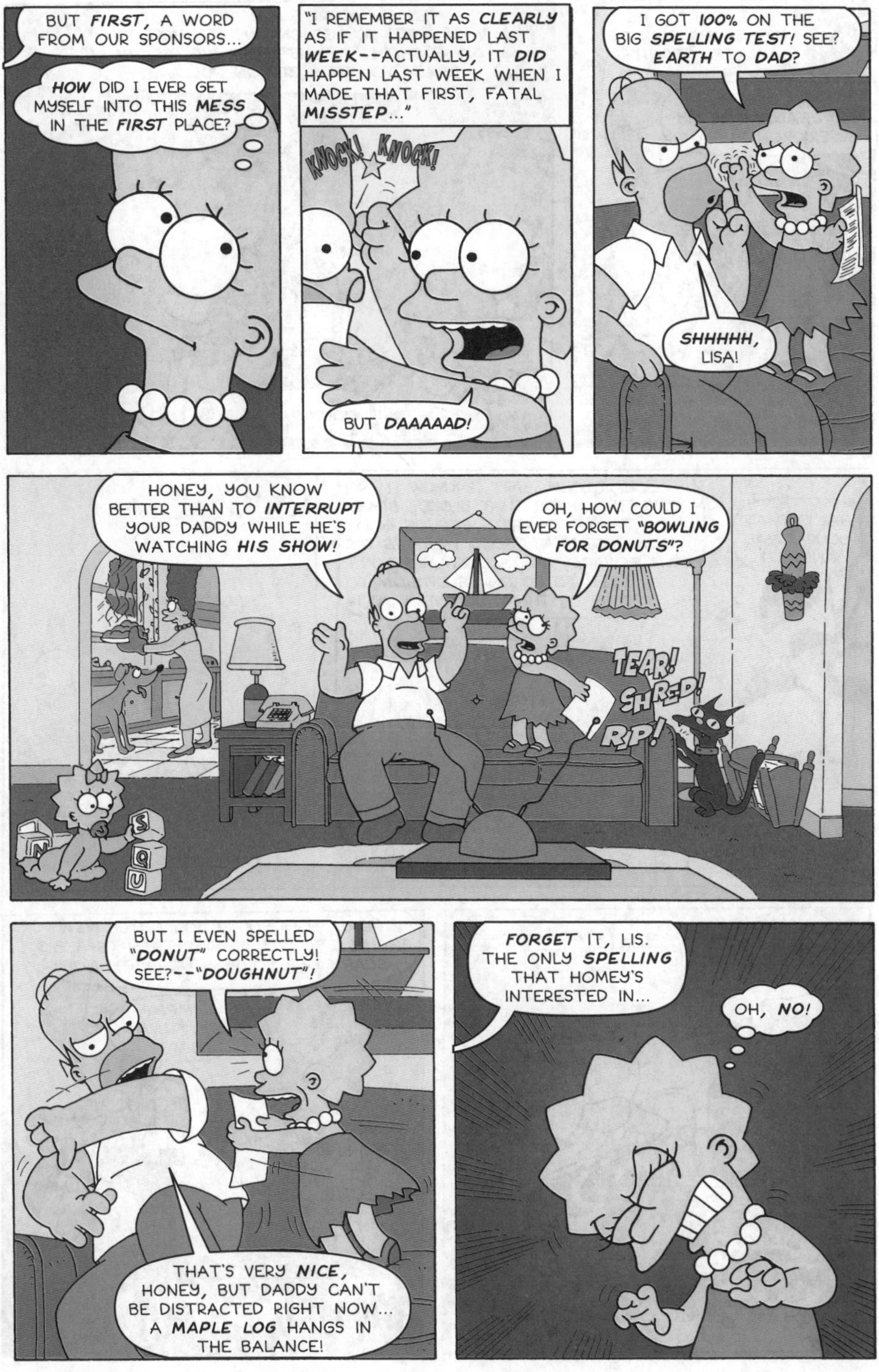

BUT FIRST, A WORD FROM OUR SPONSORS...
HOW DID I EVER GET MYSELF INTO THIS MESS IN THE FIRST PLACE?
"I REMEMBER IT AS CLEARLY AS IF IT HAPPENED LAST WEEK--ACTUALLY, IT DID HAPPEN LAST WEEK WHEN I MADE THAT FIRST, FATAL MISSTEP..."
KNOCK! KNOCK!
BUT DAAAAAD!
I GOT 100% ON THE BIG SPELLING TEST! SEE? EARTH TO DAD?
SHHHHH, LISA!
HONEY, YOU KNOW BETTER THAN TO INTERRUPT YOUR DADDY WHILE HE'S WATCHING HIS SHOW!
OH, HOW COULD I EVER FORGET "BOWLING FOR DONUTS"?
TEAR!
SHRED!
RIP!
BUT I EVEN SPELLED "DONUT" CORRECTLY! SEE?--"DOUGHNUT"!
THAT'S VERY NICE, HONEY, BUT DADDY CAN'T BE DISTRACTED RIGHT NOW... A MAPLE LOG HANGS IN THE BALANCE!
FORGET IT, LIS. THE ONLY SPELLING THAT HOMEY'S INTERESTED IN...
OH, NO!

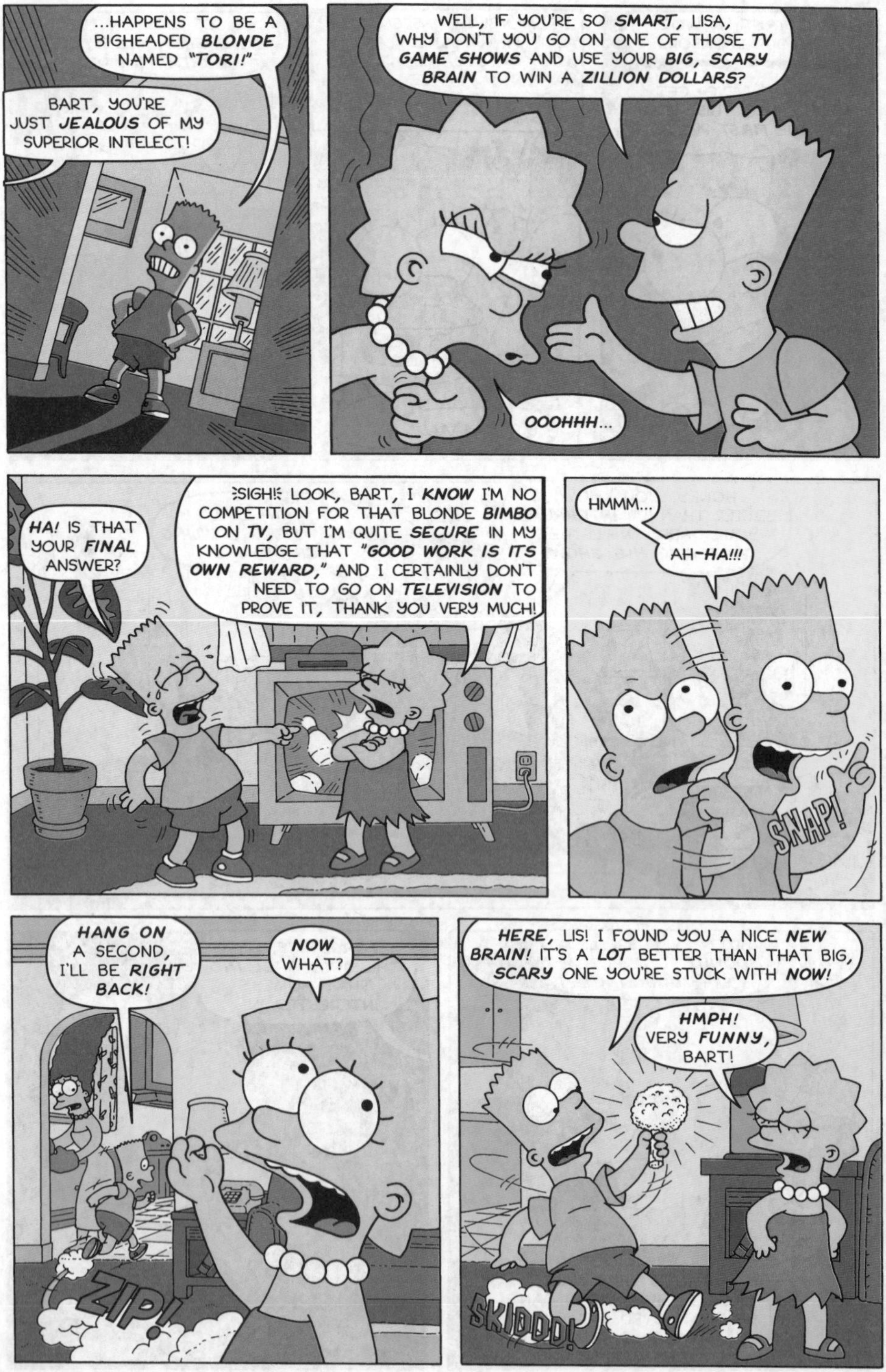
...HAPPENS TO BE A BIGHEADED BLONDE NAMED "TORI!"
BART, YOU'RE JUST JEALOUS OF MY SUPERIOR INTELECT!
WELL, IF YOU'RE SO SMART, LISA, WHY DON'T YOU GO ON ONE OF THOSE TV GAME SHOWS AND USE YOUR BIG, SCARY BRAIN TO WIN A ZILLION DOLLARS?
OOOHHH...
HA! IS THAT YOUR FINAL ANSWER?
SIGH! LOOK, BART, I KNOW I'M NO COMPETITION FOR THAT BLONDE BIMBO ON TV, BUT I'M QUITE SECURE IN MY KNOWLEDGE THAT "GOOD WORK IS ITS OWN REWARD," AND I CERTAINLY DON'T NEED TO GO ON TELEVISION TO PROVE IT, THANK YOU VERY MUCH!
HMMM...
AH-HA!!!
SNAP!
HANG ON A SECOND, I'LL BE RIGHT BACK!
NOW WHAT?
ZIP!
HERE, LIS! I FOUND YOU A NICE NEW BRAIN! IT'S A LOT BETTER THAN THAT BIG, SCARY ONE YOU'RE STUCK WITH NOW!
HMPH! VERY FUNNY, BART!
SKIDDDD!

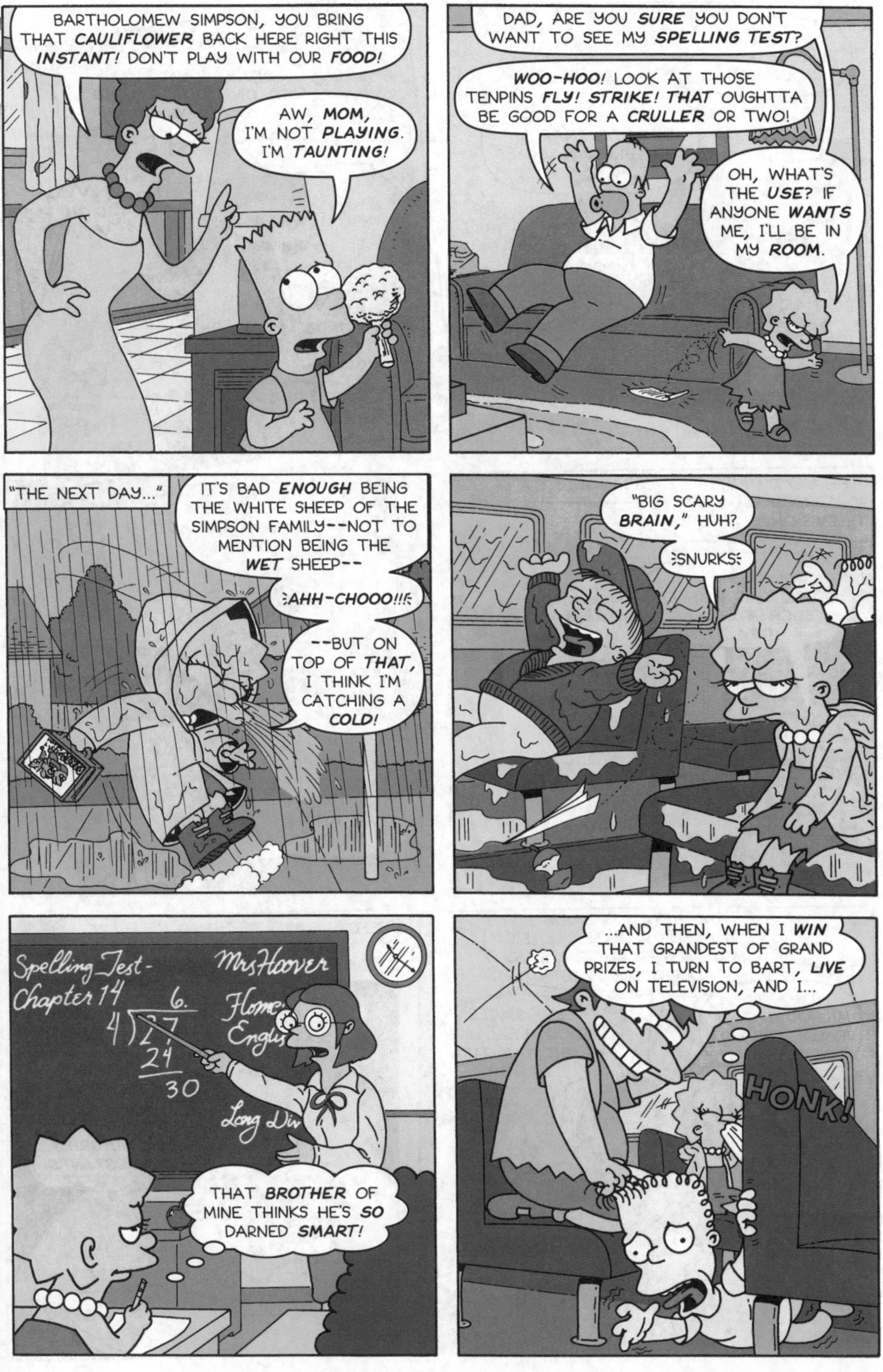
BARTHOLOMEW SIMPSON, YOU BRING THAT CAULIFLOWER BACK HERE RIGHT THIS INSTANT! DON'T PLAY WITH OUR FOOD!
AW, MOM, I'M NOT PLAYING. I'M TAUNTING!
DAD, ARE YOU SURE YOU DON'T WANT TO SEE MY SPELLING TEST?
WOO-HOO! LOOK AT THOSE TENPINS FLY! STRIKE! THAT OUGHTTA BE GOOD FOR A CRULLER OR TWO!
OH, WHAT'S THE USE? IF ANYONE WANTS ME, I'LL BE IN MY ROOM.
"THE NEXT DAY..."
IT'S BAD ENOUGH BEING THE WHITE SHEEP OF THE SIMPSON FAMILY--NOT TO MENTION BEING THE WET SHEEP--
AHH-CHOOO!!!
--BUT ON TOP OF THAT, I THINK I'M CATCHING A COLD!
"BIG SCARY BRAIN," HUH?
SNURKS
Spelling Test-
Chapter 14
Mrs Hoover
Home
English
Long Div
THAT BROTHER OF MINE THINKS HE'S SO DARNED SMART!
...AND THEN, WHEN I WIN THAT GRANDEST OF GRAND PRIZES, I TURN TO BART, LIVE ON TELEVISION, AND I...
HONK!

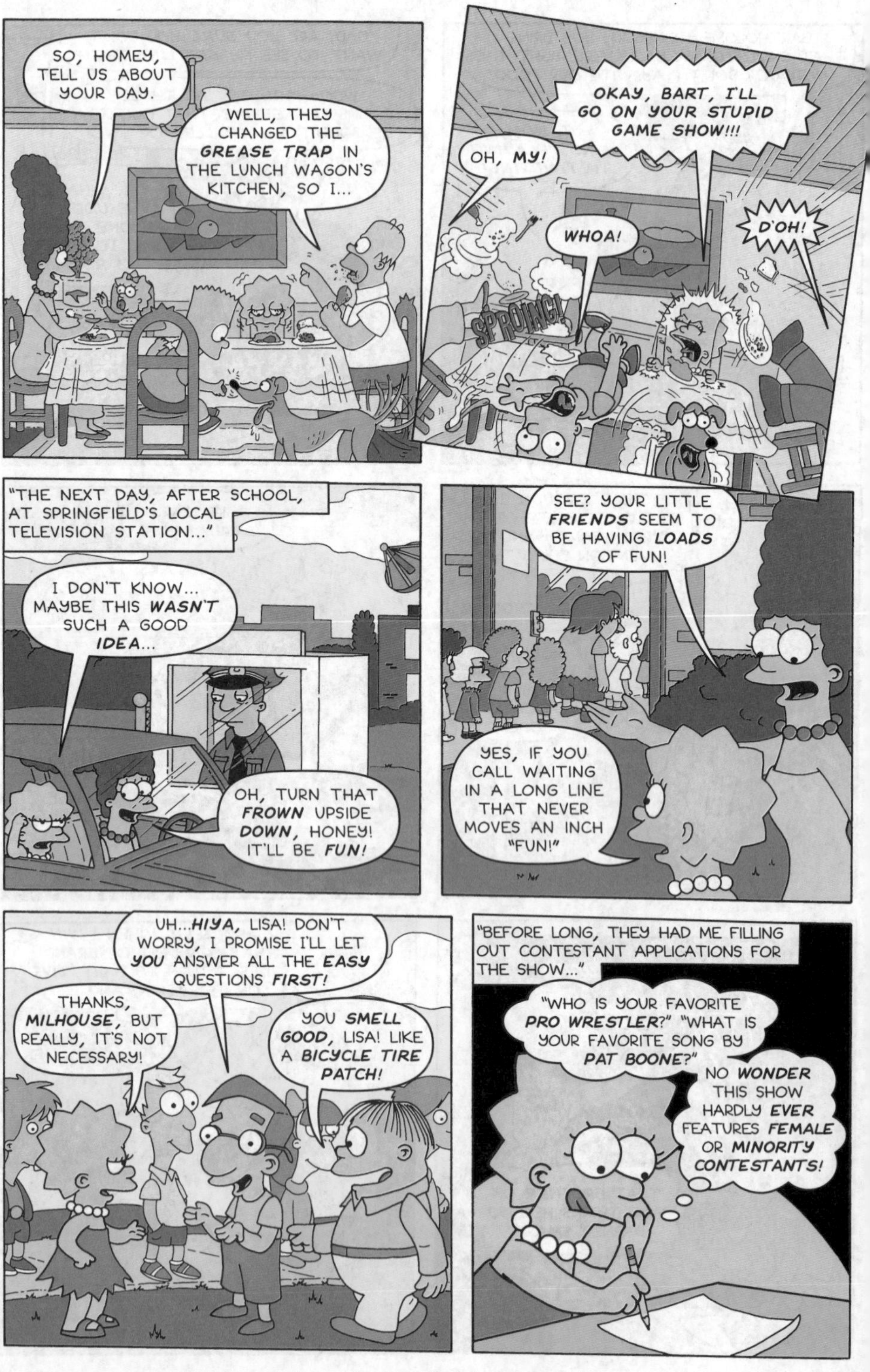
SO, HOMEY, TELL US ABOUT YOUR DAY.
WELL, THEY CHANGED THE GREASE TRAP IN THE LUNCH WAGON'S KITCHEN, SO I...
OKAY, BART, I'LL GO ON YOUR STUPID GAME SHOW!!!
OH, MY!
WHOA!
D'OH!
SPROING!
"THE NEXT DAY, AFTER SCHOOL, AT SPRINGFIELD'S LOCAL TELEVISION STATION..."
I DON'T KNOW... MAYBE THIS WASN'T SUCH A GOOD IDEA...
OH, TURN THAT FROWN UPSIDE DOWN, HONEY! IT'LL BE FUN!
SEE? YOUR LITTLE FRIENDS SEEM TO BE HAVING LOADS OF FUN!
YES, IF YOU CALL WAITING IN A LONG LINE THAT NEVER MOVES AN INCH "FUN!"
UH...HIYA, LISA! DON'T WORRY, I PROMISE I'LL LET YOU ANSWER ALL THE EASY QUESTIONS FIRST!
THANKS, MILHOUSE, BUT REALLY, IT'S NOT NECESSARY!
YOU SMELL GOOD, LISA! LIKE A BICYCLE TIRE PATCH!
"BEFORE LONG, THEY HAD ME FILLING OUT CONTESTANT APPLICATIONS FOR THE SHOW..."
"WHO IS YOUR FAVORITE PRO WRESTLER?" "WHAT IS YOUR FAVORITE SONG BY PAT BOONE?"
NO WONDER THIS SHOW HARDLY EVER FEATURES FEMALE OR MINORITY CONTESTANTS!

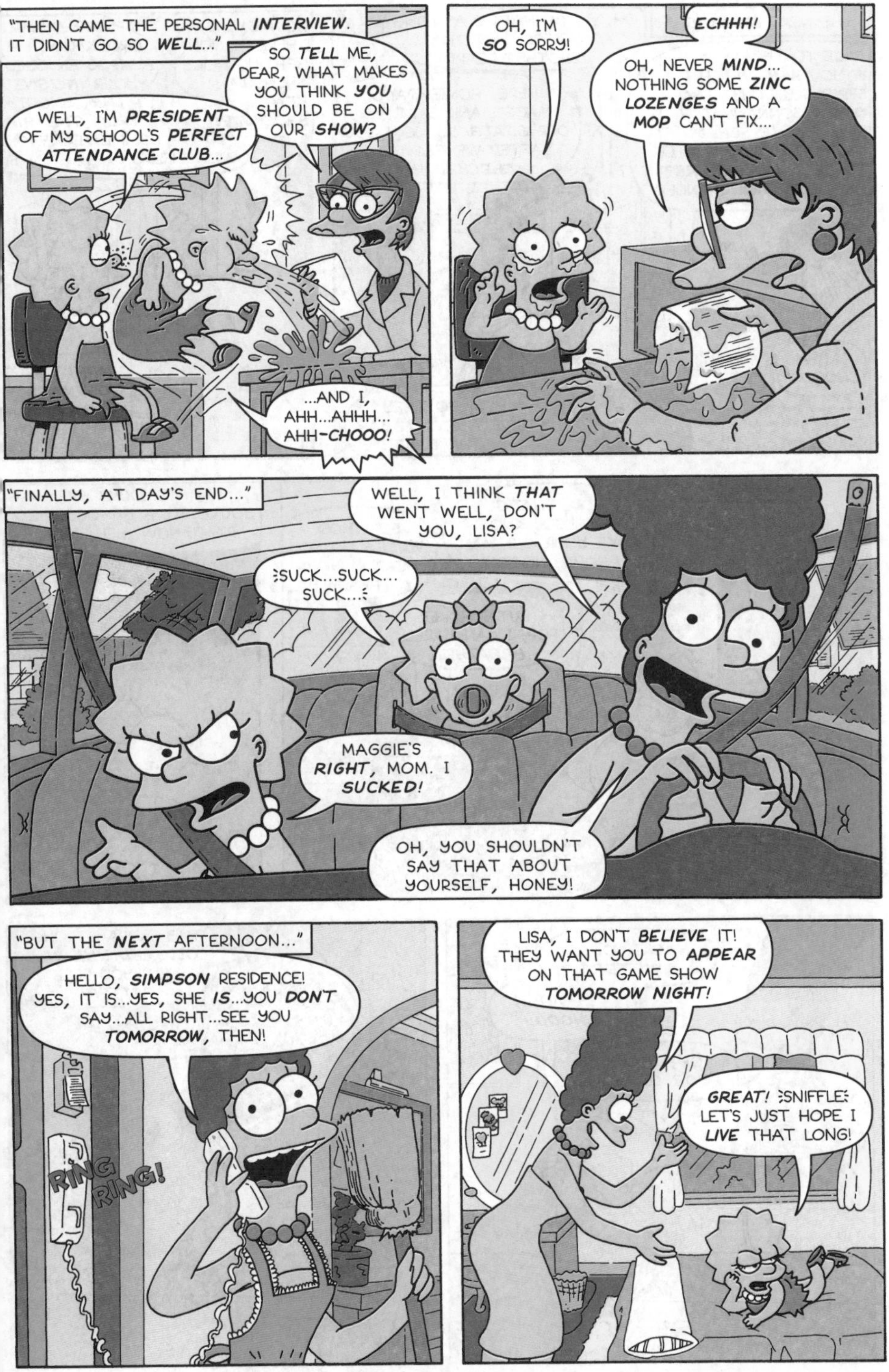
"THEN CAME THE PERSONAL INTERVIEW. IT DIDN'T GO SO WELL..."
SO TELL ME, DEAR, WHAT MAKES YOU THINK YOU SHOULD BE ON OUR SHOW?
WELL, I'M PRESIDENT OF MY SCHOOL'S PERFECT ATTENDANCE CLUB...
...AND I, AHH...AHHH... AHH-CHOOO!
OH, I'M SO SORRY!
ECHHH!
OH, NEVER MIND... NOTHING SOME ZINC LOZENGES AND A MOP CAN'T FIX...
"FINALLY, AT DAY'S END..."
WELL, I THINK THAT WENT WELL, DON'T YOU, LISA?
SUCK...SUCK... SUCK...
MAGGIE'S RIGHT, MOM. I SUCKED!
OH, YOU SHOULDN'T SAY THAT ABOUT YOURSELF, HONEY!
"BUT THE NEXT AFTERNOON..."
HELLO, SIMPSON RESIDENCE! YES, IT IS...YES, SHE IS...YOU DON'T SAY...ALL RIGHT...SEE YOU TOMORROW, THEN!
RING RING!
LISA, I DON'T BELIEVE IT! THEY WANT YOU TO APPEAR ON THAT GAME SHOW TOMORROW NIGHT!
GREAT! SNIFFLE LET'S JUST HOPE I LIVE THAT LONG!

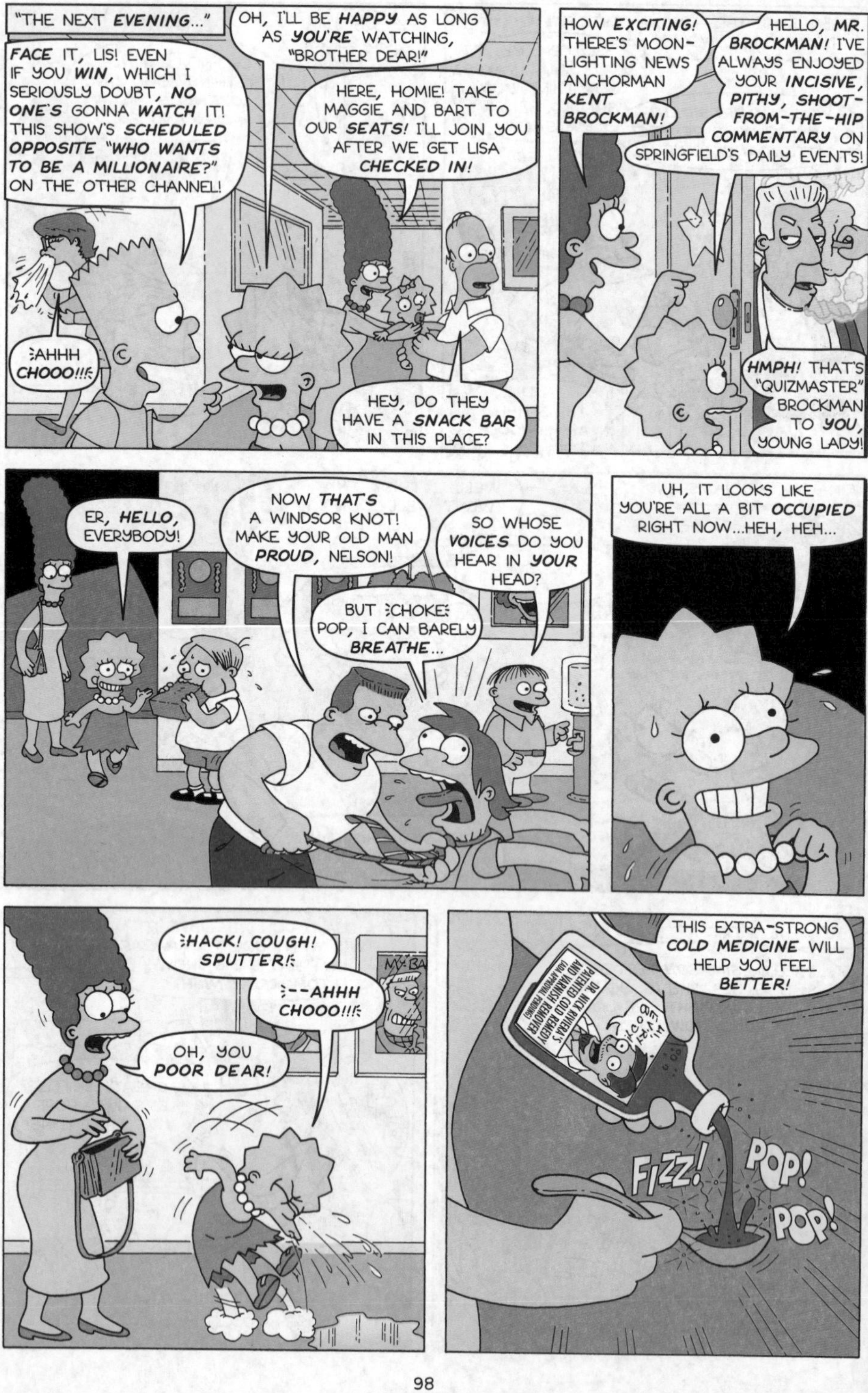
"THE NEXT EVENING..."
FACE IT, LIS! EVEN IF YOU WIN, WHICH I SERIOUSLY DOUBT, NO ONE'S GONNA WATCH IT! THIS SHOW'S SCHEDULED OPPOSITE "WHO WANTS TO BE A MILLIONAIRE?" ON THE OTHER CHANNEL!
OH, I'LL BE HAPPY AS LONG AS YOU'RE WATCHING, "BROTHER DEAR!"
HERE, HOMIE! TAKE MAGGIE AND BART TO OUR SEATS! I'LL JOIN YOU AFTER WE GET LISA CHECKED IN!
AHHH CHOOO!!!
HEY, DO THEY HAVE A SNACK BAR IN THIS PLACE?
HOW EXCITING! THERE'S MOON-LIGHTING NEWS ANCHORMAN KENT BROCKMAN!
HELLO, MR. BROCKMAN! I'VE ALWAYS ENJOYED YOUR INCISIVE, PITHY, SHOOT-FROM-THE-HIP COMMENTARY ON SPRINGFIELD'S DAILY EVENTS!
HMPH! THAT'S "QUIZMASTER" BROCKMAN TO YOU, YOUNG LADY!
ER, HELLO, EVERYBODY!
NOW THAT'S A WINDSOR KNOT! MAKE YOUR OLD MAN PROUD, NELSON!
SO WHOSE VOICES DO YOU HEAR IN YOUR HEAD?
BUT CHOKE POP, I CAN BARELY BREATHE...
UH, IT LOOKS LIKE YOU'RE ALL A BIT OCCUPIED RIGHT NOW...HEH, HEH...
HACK! COUGH! SPUTTER!
--AHHH CHOOO!!!
OH, YOU POOR DEAR!
THIS EXTRA-STRONG COLD MEDICINE WILL HELP YOU FEEL BETTER!
FIZZ!
POP!
POP!

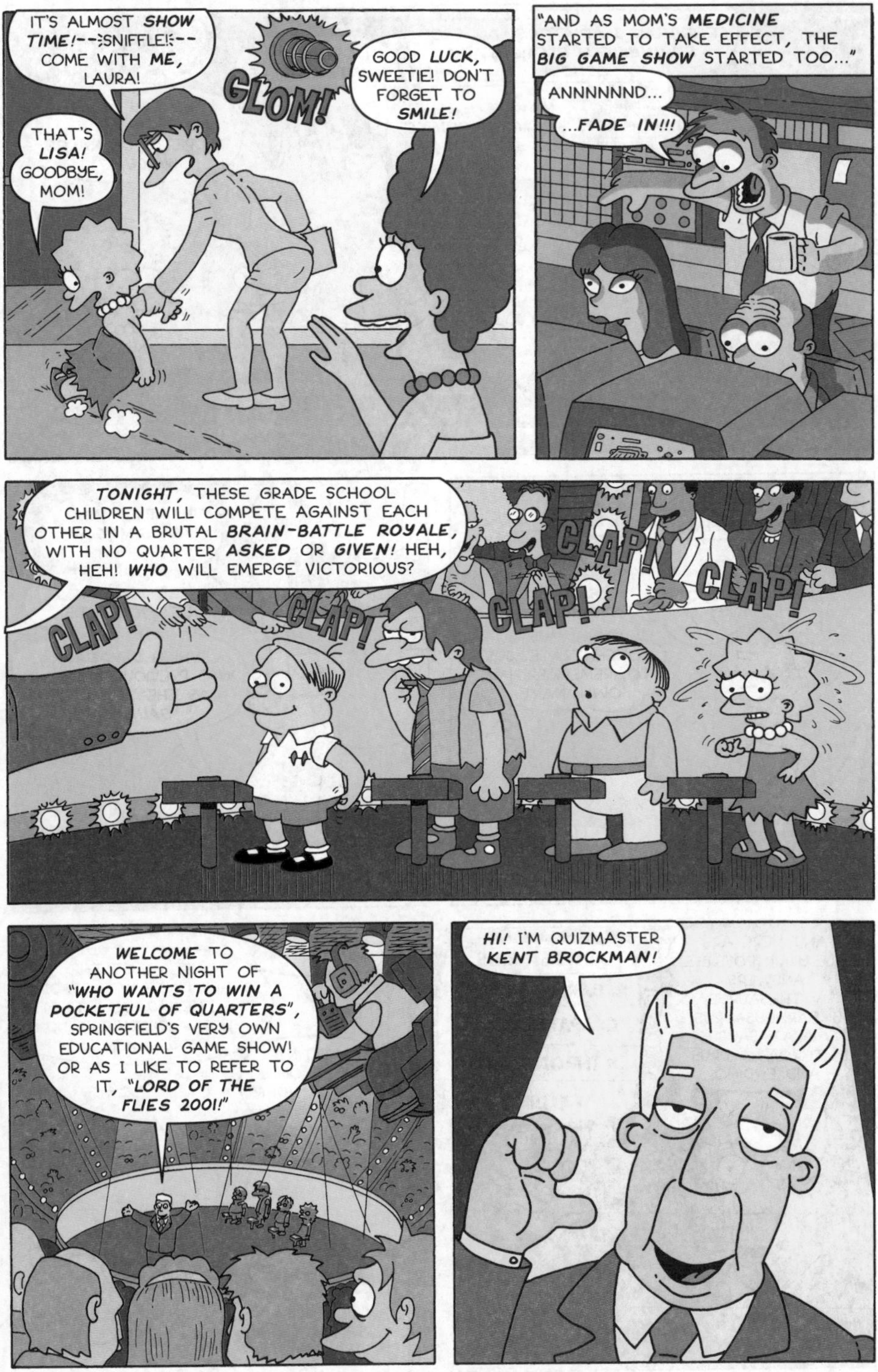
IT'S ALMOST SHOW TIME!--SNIFFLE!--COME WITH ME, LAURA!
THAT'S LISA! GOODBYE, MOM!
GLOM!
GOOD LUCK, SWEETIE! DON'T FORGET TO SMILE!
"AND AS MOM'S MEDICINE STARTED TO TAKE EFFECT, THE BIG GAME SHOW STARTED TOO..."
ANNNNNND...
...FADE IN!!!
TONIGHT, THESE GRADE SCHOOL CHILDREN WILL COMPETE AGAINST EACH OTHER IN A BRUTAL BRAIN-BATTLE ROYALE, WITH NO QUARTER ASKED OR GIVEN! HEH, HEH! WHO WILL EMERGE VICTORIOUS?
CLAP!
CLAP!
CLAP!
CLAP!
CLAP!
WELCOME TO ANOTHER NIGHT OF "WHO WANTS TO WIN A POCKETFUL OF QUARTERS", SPRINGFIELD'S VERY OWN EDUCATIONAL GAME SHOW! OR AS I LIKE TO REFER TO IT, "LORD OF THE FLIES 2001!"
HI! I'M QUIZMASTER KENT BROCKMAN!

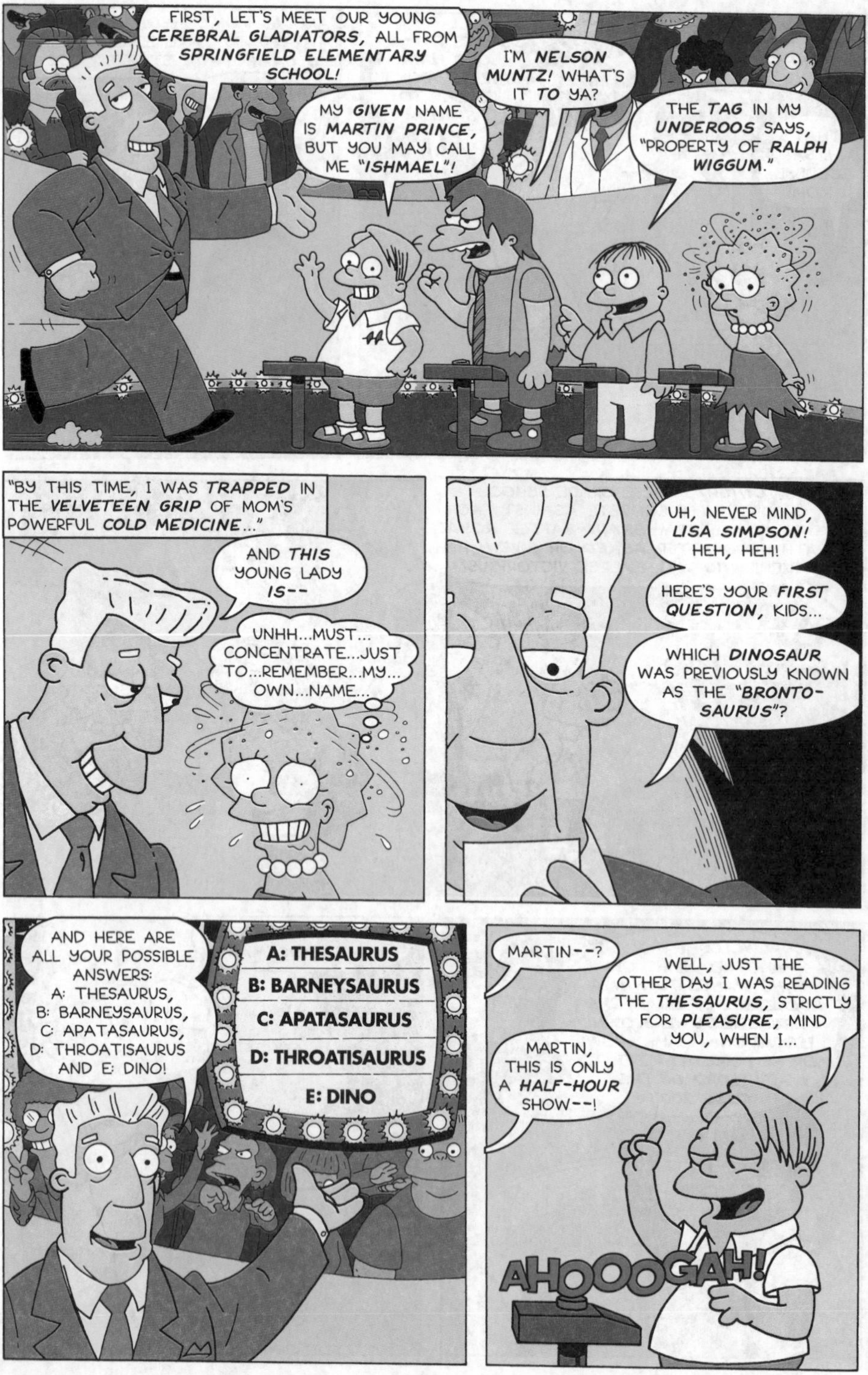
FIRST, LET'S MEET OUR YOUNG CEREBRAL GLADIATORS, ALL FROM SPRINGFIELD ELEMENTARY SCHOOL!
MY GIVEN NAME IS MARTIN PRINCE, BUT YOU MAY CALL ME "ISHMAEL"!
I'M NELSON MUNTZ! WHAT'S IT TO YA?
THE TAG IN MY UNDEROOS SAYS, "PROPERTY OF RALPH WIGGUM."
"BY THIS TIME, I WAS TRAPPED IN THE VELVETEEN GRIP OF MOM'S POWERFUL COLD MEDICINE..."
AND THIS YOUNG LADY IS--
UNHH...MUST... CONCENTRATE...JUST TO...REMEMBER...MY... OWN...NAME...
UH, NEVER MIND, LISA SIMPSON! HEH, HEH!
HERE'S YOUR FIRST QUESTION, KIDS...
WHICH DINOSAUR WAS PREVIOUSLY KNOWN AS THE "BRONTO-SAURUS"?
AND HERE ARE ALL YOUR POSSIBLE ANSWERS: A: THESAURUS, B: BARNEYSAURUS, C: APATASAURUS, D: THROATISAURUS AND E: DINO!
A: THESAURUS
B: BARNEYSAURUS
C: APATASAURUS
D: THROATISAURUS
E: DINO
MARTIN--?
WELL, JUST THE OTHER DAY I WAS READING THE THESAURUS, STRICTLY FOR PLEASURE, MIND YOU, WHEN I...
MARTIN, THIS IS ONLY A HALF-HOUR SHOW--!
AHOOOOGAH!

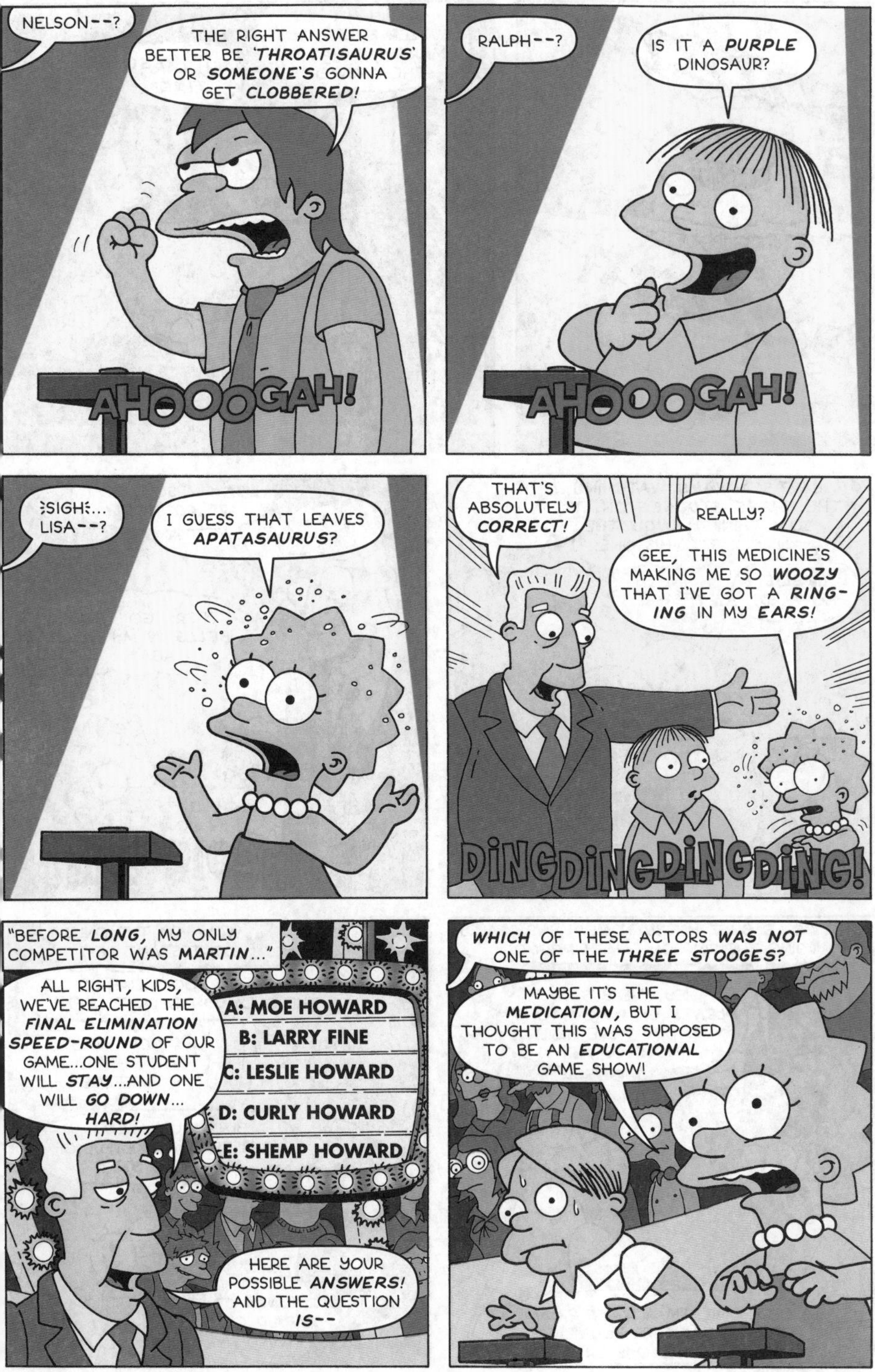
NELSON--?
THE RIGHT ANSWER BETTER BE 'THROATISAURUS' OR SOMEONE'S GONNA GET CLOBBERED!
AHOOOOGAH!
RALPH--?
IS IT A PURPLE DINOSAUR?
AHOOOOGAH!
:SIGH:... LISA--?
I GUESS THAT LEAVES APATASAURUS?
THAT'S ABSOLUTELY CORRECT!
REALLY?
GEE, THIS MEDICINE'S MAKING ME SO WOOZY THAT I'VE GOT A RINGING IN MY EARS!
DINGDINGDINGDING!
"BEFORE LONG, MY ONLY COMPETITOR WAS MARTIN..."
ALL RIGHT, KIDS, WE'VE REACHED THE FINAL ELIMINATION SPEED-ROUND OF OUR GAME...ONE STUDENT WILL STAY...AND ONE WILL GO DOWN... HARD!
A: MOE HOWARD
B: LARRY FINE
C: LESLIE HOWARD
D: CURLY HOWARD
E: SHEMP HOWARD
HERE ARE YOUR POSSIBLE ANSWERS! AND THE QUESTION IS--
WHICH OF THESE ACTORS WAS NOT ONE OF THE THREE STOOGES?
MAYBE IT'S THE MEDICATION, BUT I THOUGHT THIS WAS SUPPOSED TO BE AN EDUCATIONAL GAME SHOW!

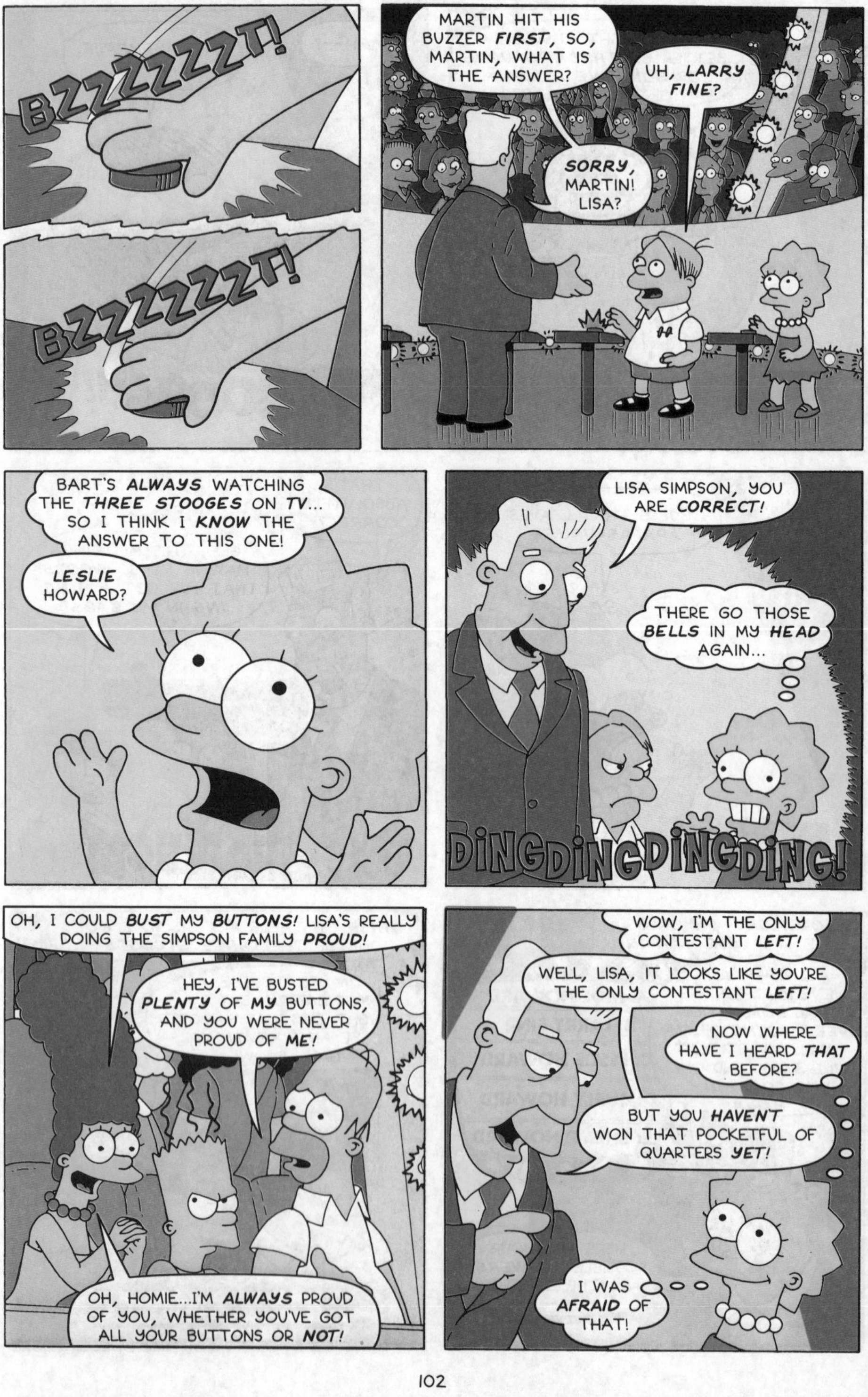
BZZZZZZZT!
BZZZZZZZT!
MARTIN HIT HIS BUZZER FIRST, SO, MARTIN, WHAT IS THE ANSWER?
UH, LARRY FINE?
SORRY, MARTIN! LISA?
BART'S ALWAYS WATCHING THE THREE STOOGES ON TV... SO I THINK I KNOW THE ANSWER TO THIS ONE!
LESLIE HOWARD?
LISA SIMPSON, YOU ARE CORRECT!
THERE GO THOSE BELLS IN MY HEAD AGAIN...
DINGDINGDINGDING!
OH, I COULD BUST MY BUTTONS! LISA'S REALLY DOING THE SIMPSON FAMILY PROUD!
HEY, I'VE BUSTED PLENTY OF MY BUTTONS, AND YOU WERE NEVER PROUD OF ME!
OH, HOMIE...I'M ALWAYS PROUD OF YOU, WHETHER YOU'VE GOT ALL YOUR BUTTONS OR NOT!
WOW, I'M THE ONLY CONTESTANT LEFT!
WELL, LISA, IT LOOKS LIKE YOU'RE THE ONLY CONTESTANT LEFT!
NOW WHERE HAVE I HEARD THAT BEFORE?
BUT YOU HAVEN'T WON THAT POCKETFUL OF QUARTERS YET!
I WAS AFRAID OF THAT!

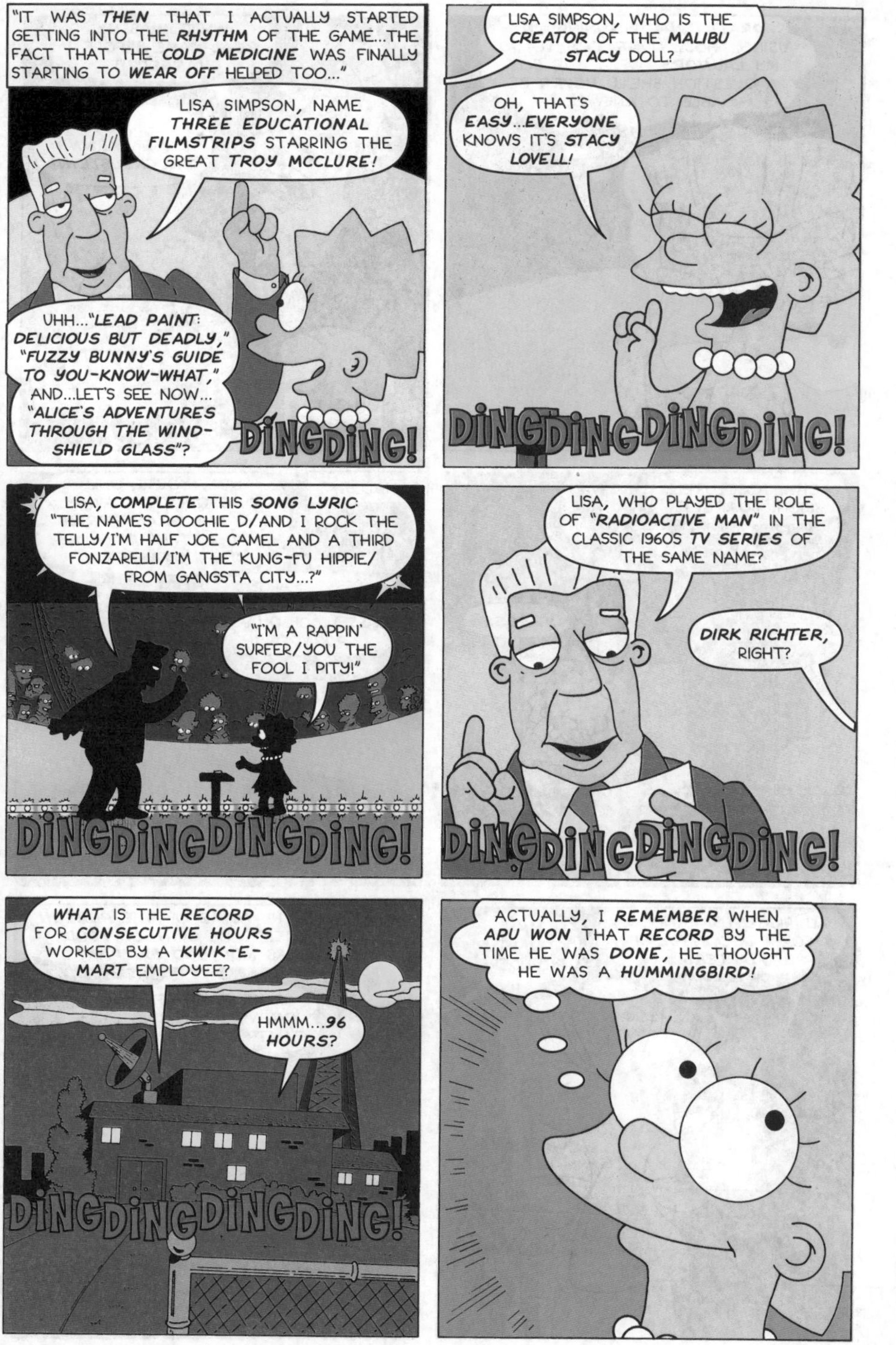
"IT WAS THEN THAT I ACTUALLY STARTED GETTING INTO THE RHYTHM OF THE GAME...THE FACT THAT THE COLD MEDICINE WAS FINALLY STARTING TO WEAR OFF HELPED TOO..."
LISA SIMPSON, NAME THREE EDUCATIONAL FILMSTRIPS STARRING THE GREAT TROY MCCLURE!
UHH..."LEAD PAINT: DELICIOUS BUT DEADLY," "FUZZY BUNNY'S GUIDE TO YOU-KNOW-WHAT," AND...LET'S SEE NOW... "ALICE'S ADVENTURES THROUGH THE WIND-SHIELD GLASS"?
DINGDING!
LISA SIMPSON, WHO IS THE CREATOR OF THE MALIBU STACY DOLL?
OH, THAT'S EASY...EVERYONE KNOWS IT'S STACY LOVELL!
DINGDINGDINGDING!
LISA, COMPLETE THIS SONG LYRIC: "THE NAME'S POOCHIE D/AND I ROCK THE TELLY/I'M HALF JOE CAMEL AND A THIRD FONZARELLI/I'M THE KUNG-FU HIPPIE/ FROM GANGSTA CITY...?"
"I'M A RAPPIN' SURFER/YOU THE FOOL I PITY!"
DINGDINGDINGDING!
LISA, WHO PLAYED THE ROLE OF "RADIOACTIVE MAN" IN THE CLASSIC 1960S TV SERIES OF THE SAME NAME?
DIRK RICHTER, RIGHT?
DINGDINGDINGDING!
WHAT IS THE RECORD FOR CONSECUTIVE HOURS WORKED BY A KWIK-E-MART EMPLOYEE?
HMMM...96 HOURS?
DINGDINGDINGDING!
ACTUALLY, I REMEMBER WHEN APU WON THAT RECORD BY THE TIME HE WAS DONE, HE THOUGHT HE WAS A HUMMINGBIRD!

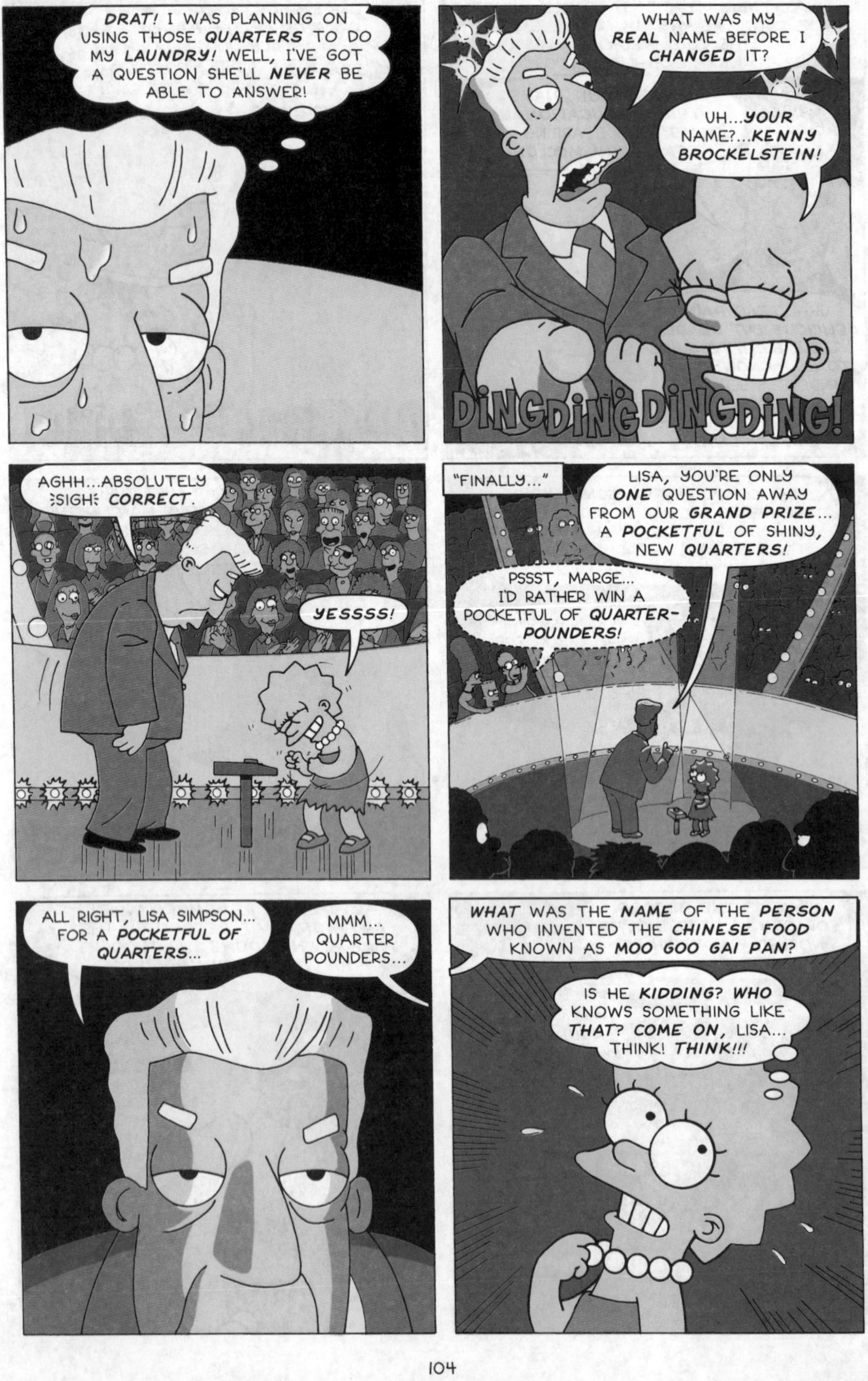
DRAT! I WAS PLANNING ON USING THOSE QUARTERS TO DO MY LAUNDRY! WELL, I'VE GOT A QUESTION SHE'LL NEVER BE ABLE TO ANSWER!
WHAT WAS MY REAL NAME BEFORE I CHANGED IT?
UH...YOUR NAME?...KENNY BROCKELSTEIN!
DINGDINGDINGDING!
AGHH...ABSOLUTELY :SIGH: CORRECT.
YESSSS!
"FINALLY..."
LISA, YOU'RE ONLY ONE QUESTION AWAY FROM OUR GRAND PRIZE... A POCKETFUL OF SHINY, NEW QUARTERS!
PSSST, MARGE... I'D RATHER WIN A POCKETFUL OF QUARTER-POUNDERS!
ALL RIGHT, LISA SIMPSON... FOR A POCKETFUL OF QUARTERS...
MMM... QUARTER POUNDERS...
WHAT WAS THE NAME OF THE PERSON WHO INVENTED THE CHINESE FOOD KNOWN AS MOO GOO GAI PAN?
IS HE KIDDING? WHO KNOWS SOMETHING LIKE THAT? COME ON, LISA... THINK! THINK!!!

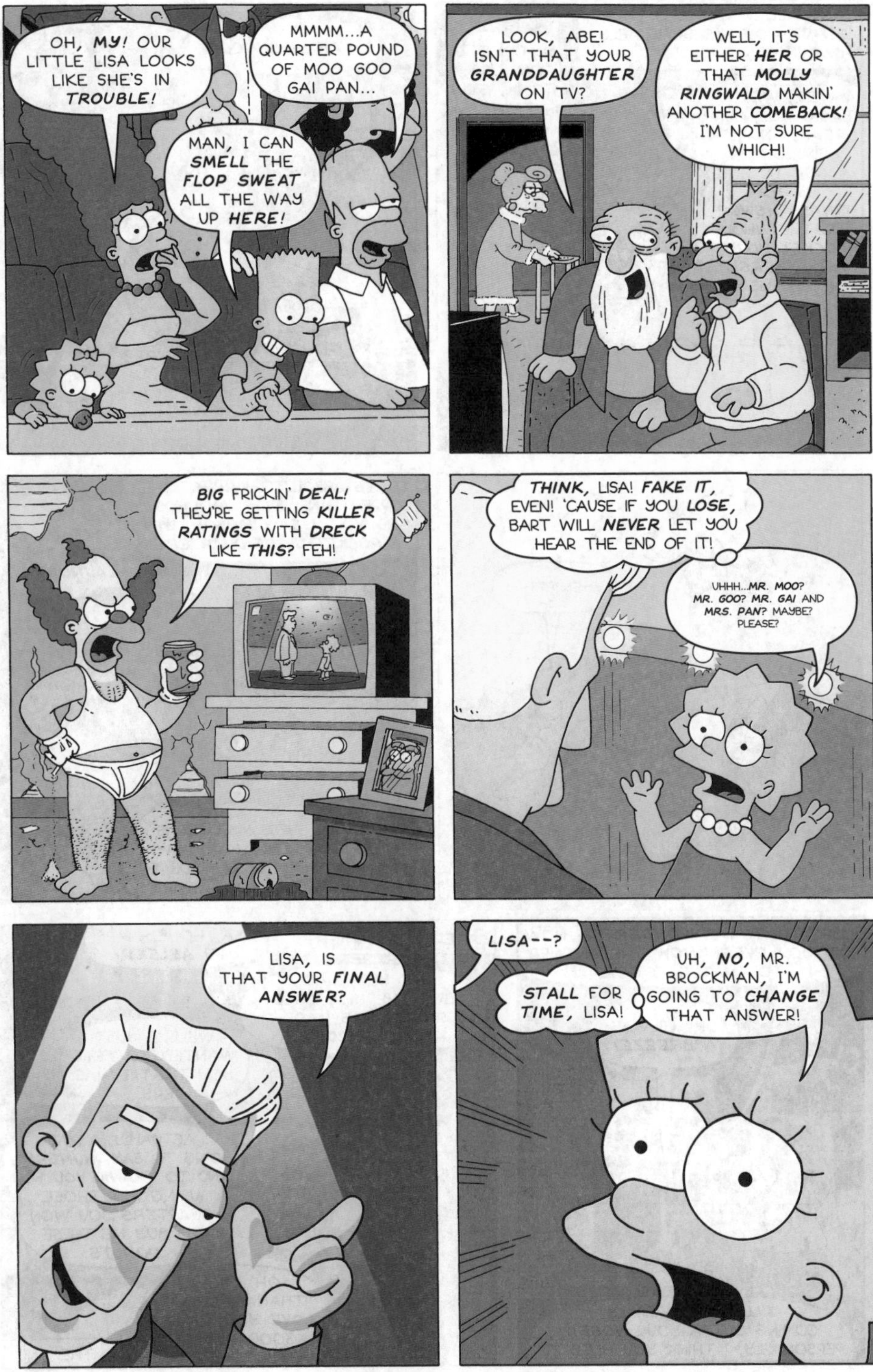
OH, MY! OUR LITTLE LISA LOOKS LIKE SHE'S IN TROUBLE!
MMMM...A QUARTER POUND OF MOO GOO GAI PAN...
MAN, I CAN SMELL THE FLOP SWEAT ALL THE WAY UP HERE!
LOOK, ABE! ISN'T THAT YOUR GRANDDAUGHTER ON TV?
WELL, IT'S EITHER HER OR THAT MOLLY RINGWALD MAKIN' ANOTHER COMEBACK! I'M NOT SURE WHICH!
BIG FRICKIN' DEAL! THEY'RE GETTING KILLER RATINGS WITH DRECK LIKE THIS? FEH!
THINK, LISA! FAKE IT, EVEN! 'CAUSE IF YOU LOSE, BART WILL NEVER LET YOU HEAR THE END OF IT!
UHHH...MR. MOO? MR. GOO? MR. GAI AND MRS. PAN? MAYBE? PLEASE?
LISA, IS THAT YOUR FINAL ANSWER?
LISA--?
STALL FOR TIME, LISA!
UH, NO, MR. BROCKMAN, I'M GOING TO CHANGE THAT ANSWER!

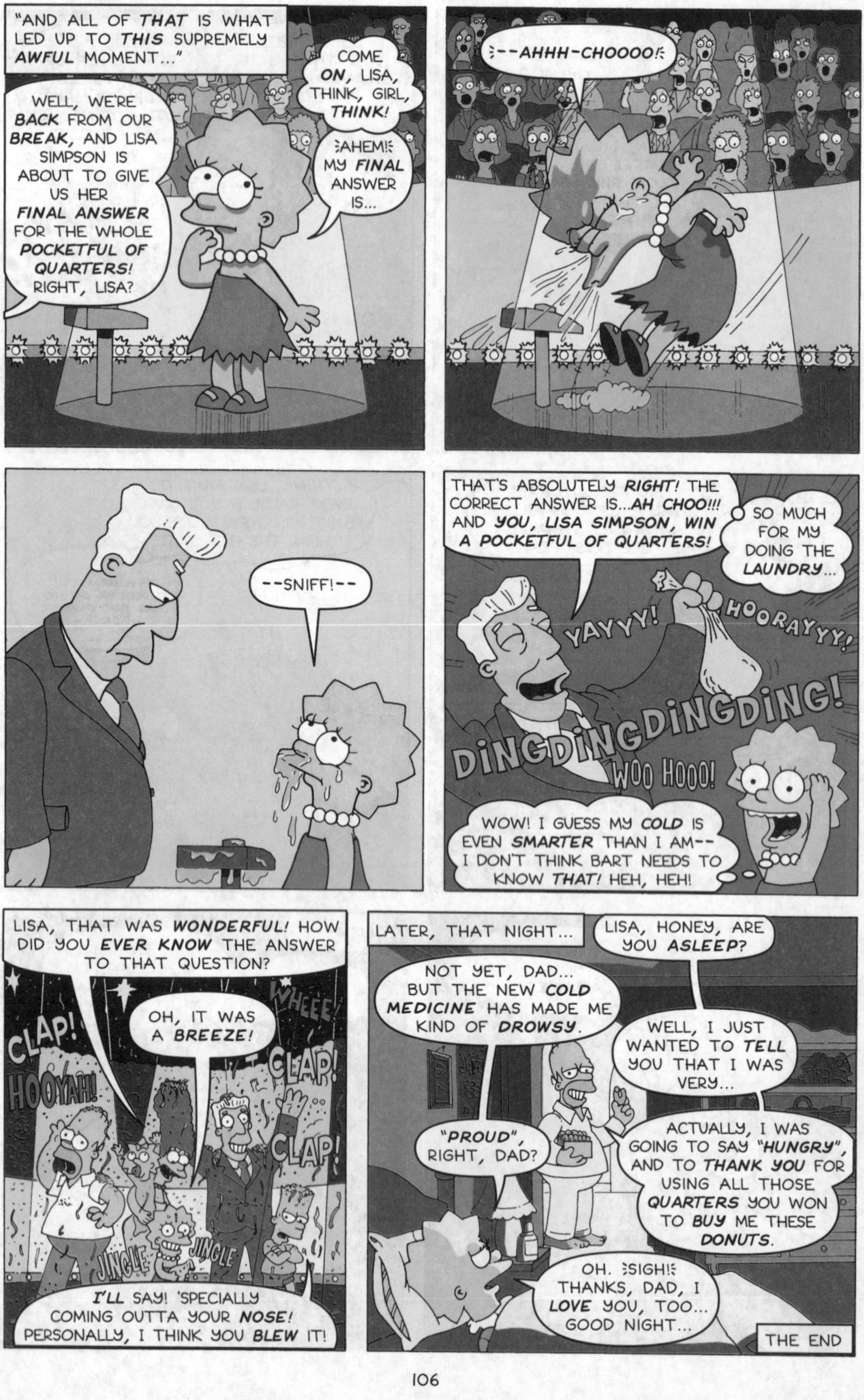
"AND ALL OF THAT IS WHAT LED UP TO THIS SUPREMELY AWFUL MOMENT..."
WELL, WE'RE BACK FROM OUR BREAK, AND LISA SIMPSON IS ABOUT TO GIVE US HER FINAL ANSWER FOR THE WHOLE POCKETFUL OF QUARTERS! RIGHT, LISA?
COME ON, LISA, THINK, GIRL, THINK!
AHEM! MY FINAL ANSWER IS...
--AHHH-CHOOOO!
--SNIFF!--
THAT'S ABSOLUTELY RIGHT! THE CORRECT ANSWER IS...AH CHOO!!! AND YOU, LISA SIMPSON, WIN A POCKETFUL OF QUARTERS!
SO MUCH FOR MY DOING THE LAUNDRY...
YAYYY!
HOORAYYY!
DINGDINGDINGDING!
WOO HOOO!
WOW! I GUESS MY COLD IS EVEN SMARTER THAN I AM-- I DON'T THINK BART NEEDS TO KNOW THAT! HEH, HEH!
LISA, THAT WAS WONDERFUL! HOW DID YOU EVER KNOW THE ANSWER TO THAT QUESTION?
OH, IT WAS A BREEZE!
CLAP!
WHEEE!
HOOYAH!
CLAP!
CLAP!
JINGLE
JINGLE
I'LL SAY! 'SPECIALLY COMING OUTTA YOUR NOSE! PERSONALLY, I THINK YOU BLEW IT!
LATER, THAT NIGHT...
LISA, HONEY, ARE YOU ASLEEP?
NOT YET, DAD... BUT THE NEW COLD MEDICINE HAS MADE ME KIND OF DROWSY.
WELL, I JUST WANTED TO TELL YOU THAT I WAS VERY...
"PROUD", RIGHT, DAD?
ACTUALLY, I WAS GOING TO SAY "HUNGRY", AND TO THANK YOU FOR USING ALL THOSE QUARTERS YOU WON TO BUY ME THESE DONUTS.
OH. SIGH! THANKS, DAD, I LOVE YOU, TOO... GOOD NIGHT...
THE END

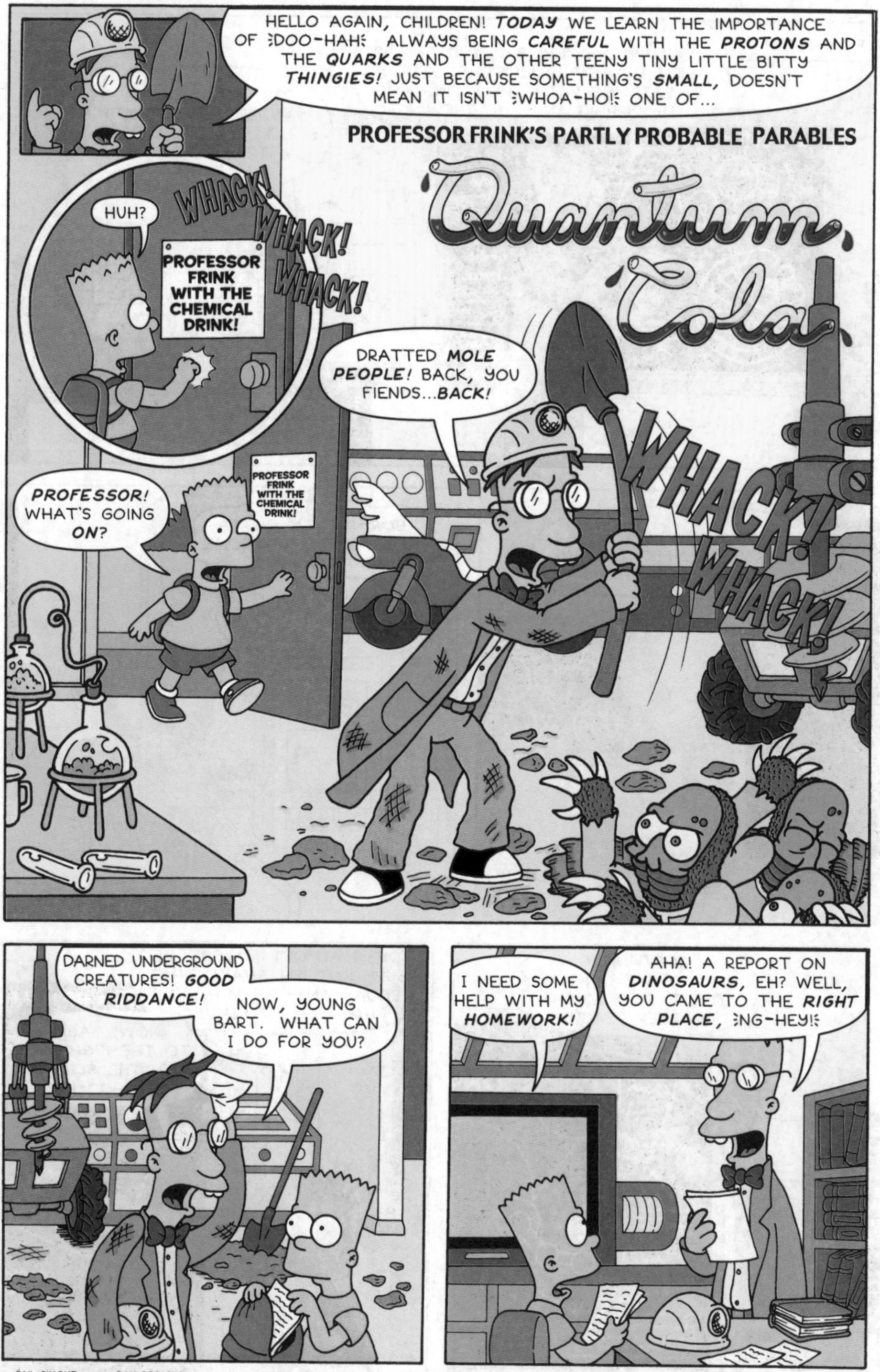
HELLO AGAIN, CHILDREN! TODAY WE LEARN THE IMPORTANCE OF ∃DOO-HAH∃ ALWAYS BEING CAREFUL WITH THE PROTONS AND THE QUARKS AND THE OTHER TEENY TINY LITTLE BITTY THINGIES! JUST BECAUSE SOMETHING'S SMALL, DOESN'T MEAN IT ISN'T ∃WHOA-HO!∃ ONE OF...
PROFESSOR FRINK'S PARTLY PROBABLE PARABLES
Quantum Cola
HUH?
WHACK! WHACK! WHACK!
PROFESSOR FRINK WITH THE CHEMICAL DRINK!
DRATTED MOLE PEOPLE! BACK, YOU FIENDS...BACK!
PROFESSOR! WHAT'S GOING ON?
PROFESSOR FRINK WITH THE CHEMICAL DRINK!
WHACK! WHACK! WHACK!
DARNED UNDERGROUND CREATURES! GOOD RIDDANCE!
NOW, YOUNG BART. WHAT CAN I DO FOR YOU?
I NEED SOME HELP WITH MY HOMEWORK!
AHA! A REPORT ON DINOSAURS, EH? WELL, YOU CAME TO THE RIGHT PLACE, ∃NG-HEY!∃

GAIL SIMONE — SODA JERK SCRIPT
DAN DECARLO — LO-CAL LAYOUTS
JASON HO — SIX-PACK PENCILS & FIZZY INKS
CHRIS UNGAR — CARBONATED COLORS
KAREN BATES — LEMON-LIME LETTERS
BILL MORRISON — ALL-NATURAL EDITS
MATT GROENING — BEST BURPS

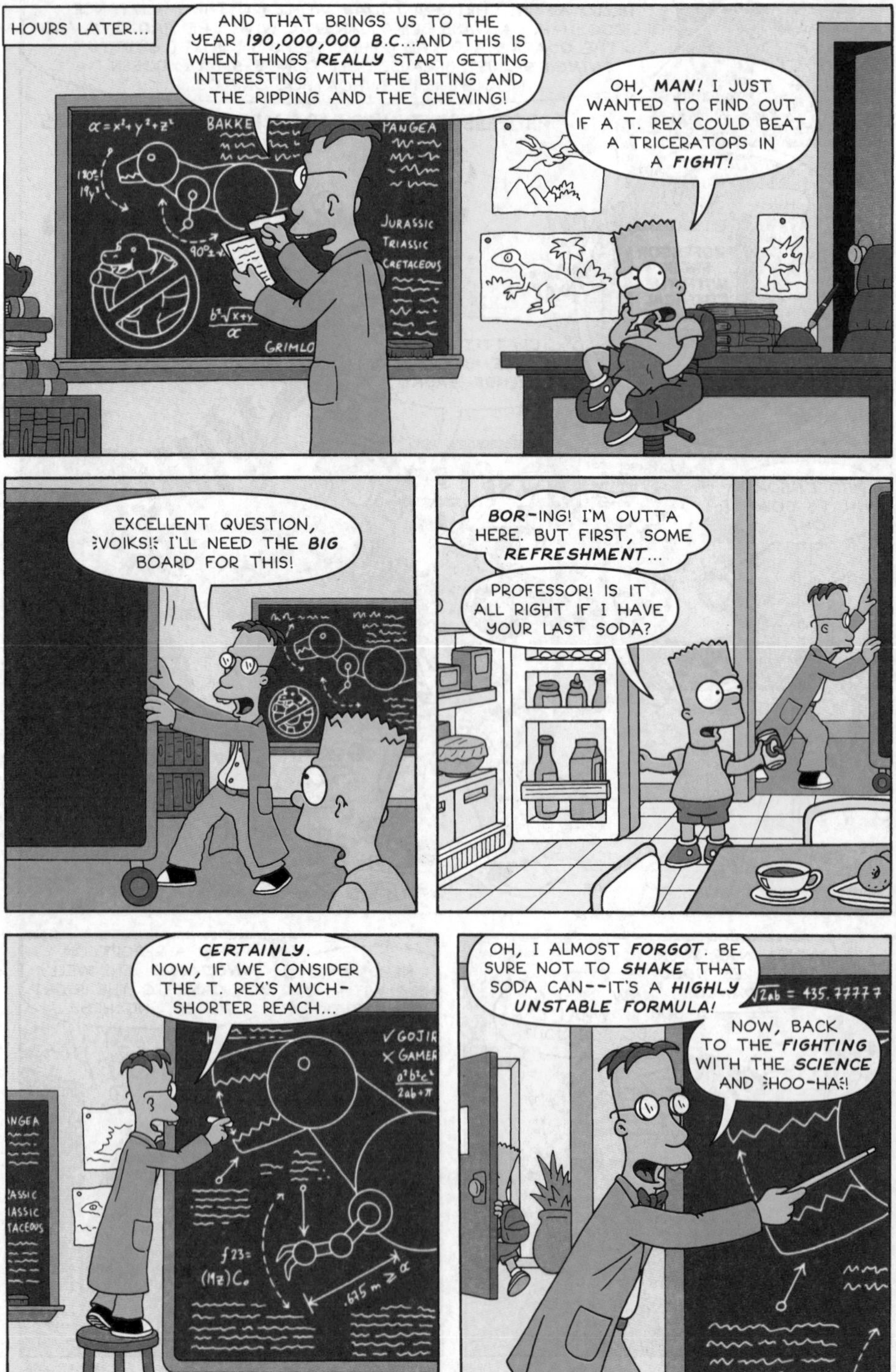
HOURS LATER...
AND THAT BRINGS US TO THE YEAR 190,000,000 B.C....AND THIS IS WHEN THINGS REALLY START GETTING INTERESTING WITH THE BITING AND THE RIPPING AND THE CHEWING!
OH, MAN! I JUST WANTED TO FIND OUT IF A T. REX COULD BEAT A TRICERATOPS IN A FIGHT!
EXCELLENT QUESTION, ⁝VOIKS!⁝ I'LL NEED THE BIG BOARD FOR THIS!
BOR-ING! I'M OUTTA HERE. BUT FIRST, SOME REFRESHMENT...
PROFESSOR! IS IT ALL RIGHT IF I HAVE YOUR LAST SODA?
CERTAINLY. NOW, IF WE CONSIDER THE T. REX'S MUCH-SHORTER REACH...
OH, I ALMOST FORGOT. BE SURE NOT TO SHAKE THAT SODA CAN--IT'S A HIGHLY UNSTABLE FORMULA!
NOW, BACK TO THE FIGHTING WITH THE SCIENCE AND ⁝HOO-HA⁝!

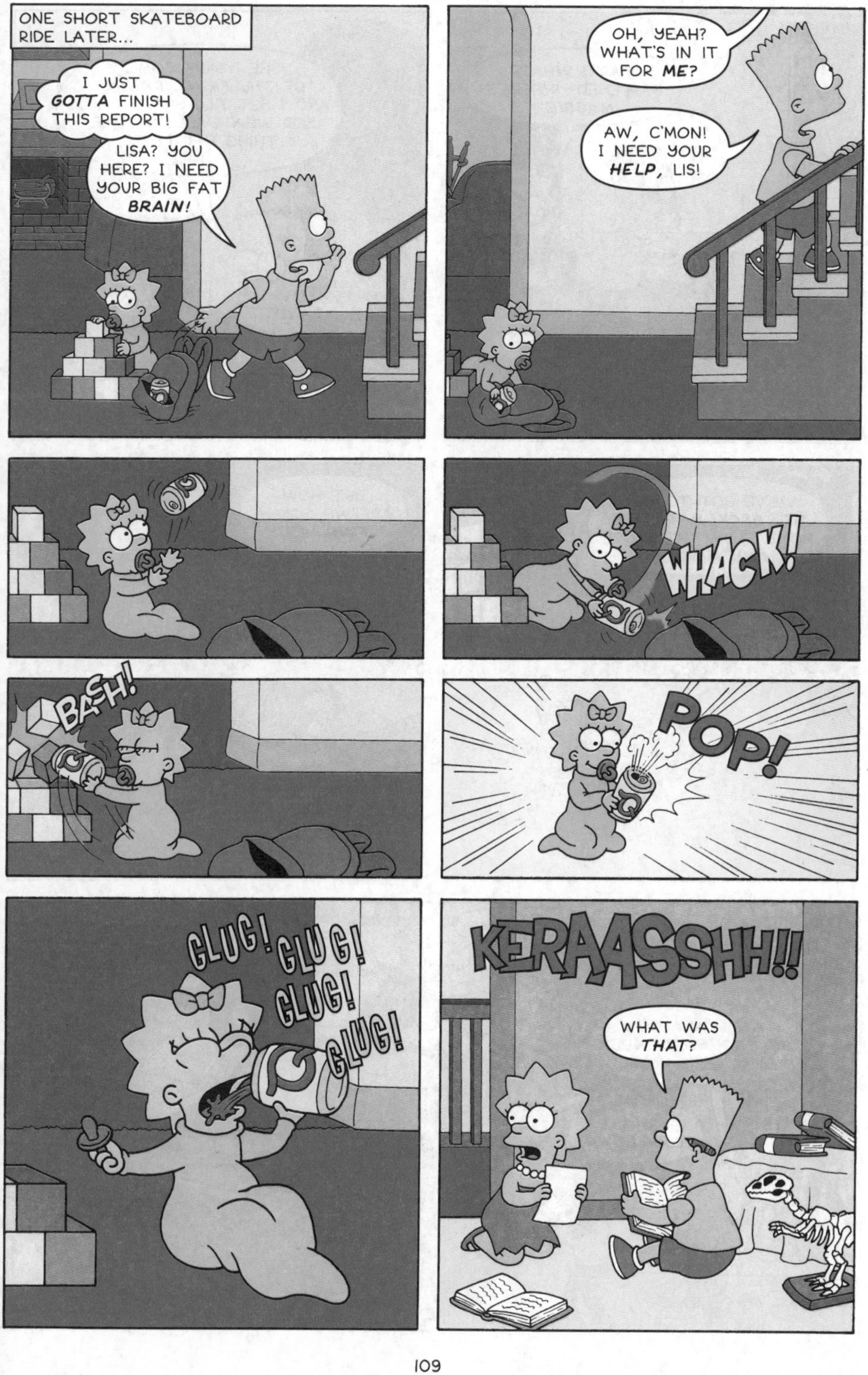
ONE SHORT SKATEBOARD RIDE LATER...
I JUST GOTTA FINISH THIS REPORT!
LISA? YOU HERE? I NEED YOUR BIG FAT BRAIN!
OH, YEAH? WHAT'S IN IT FOR ME?
AW, C'MON! I NEED YOUR HELP, LIS!
WHACK!
BASH!
POP!
GLUG! GLUG! GLUG! GLUG!
KERAASSHH!!
WHAT WAS THAT?

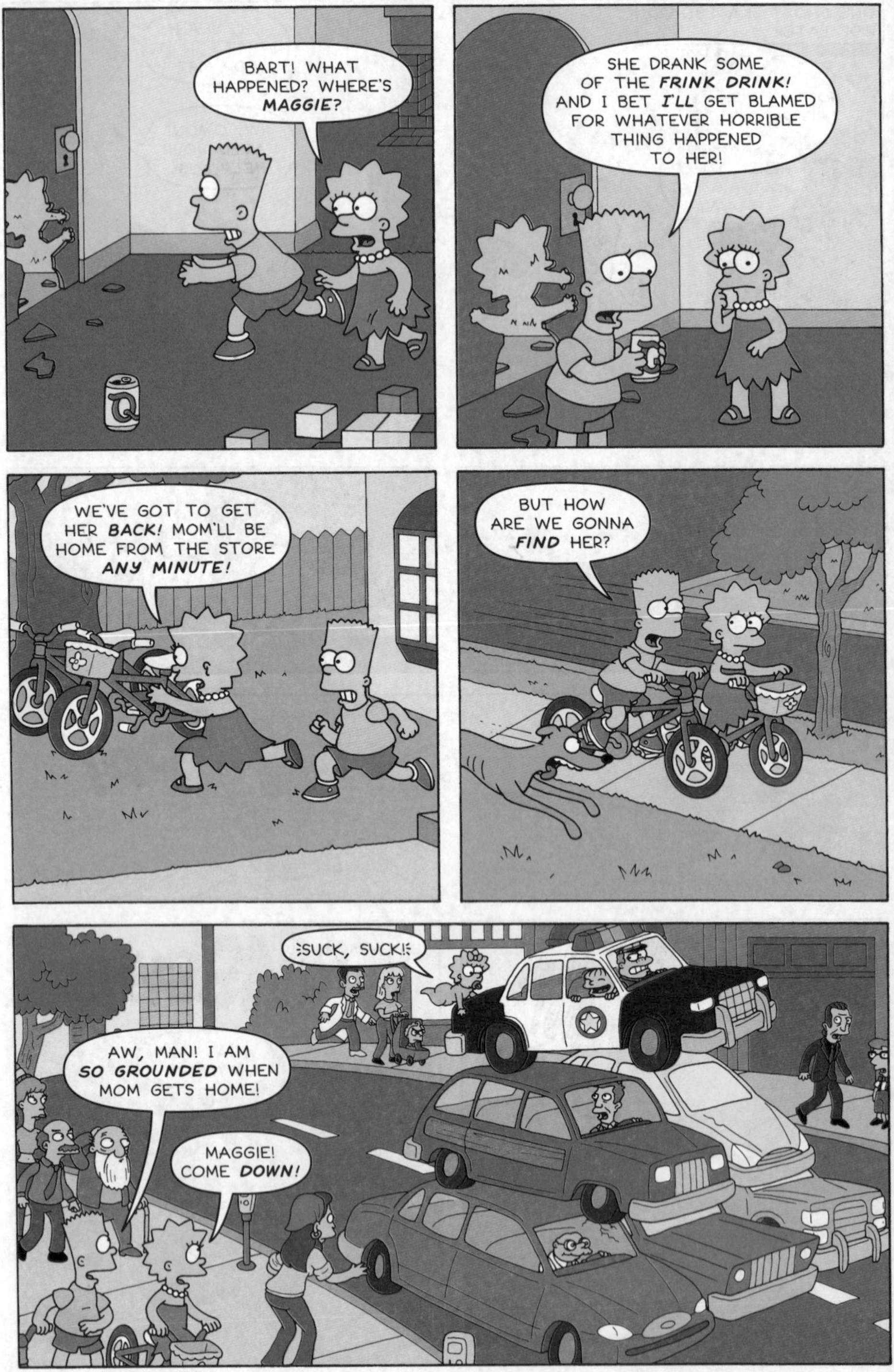
BART! WHAT HAPPENED? WHERE'S **MAGGIE**?
SHE DRANK SOME OF THE ***FRINK DRINK!*** AND I BET ***I'LL*** GET BLAMED FOR WHATEVER HORRIBLE THING HAPPENED TO HER!
WE'VE GOT TO GET HER ***BACK!*** MOM'LL BE HOME FROM THE STORE ***ANY MINUTE!***
BUT HOW ARE WE GONNA ***FIND*** HER?
SUCK, SUCK!
AW, MAN! I AM ***SO GROUNDED*** WHEN MOM GETS HOME!
MAGGIE! COME ***DOWN!***

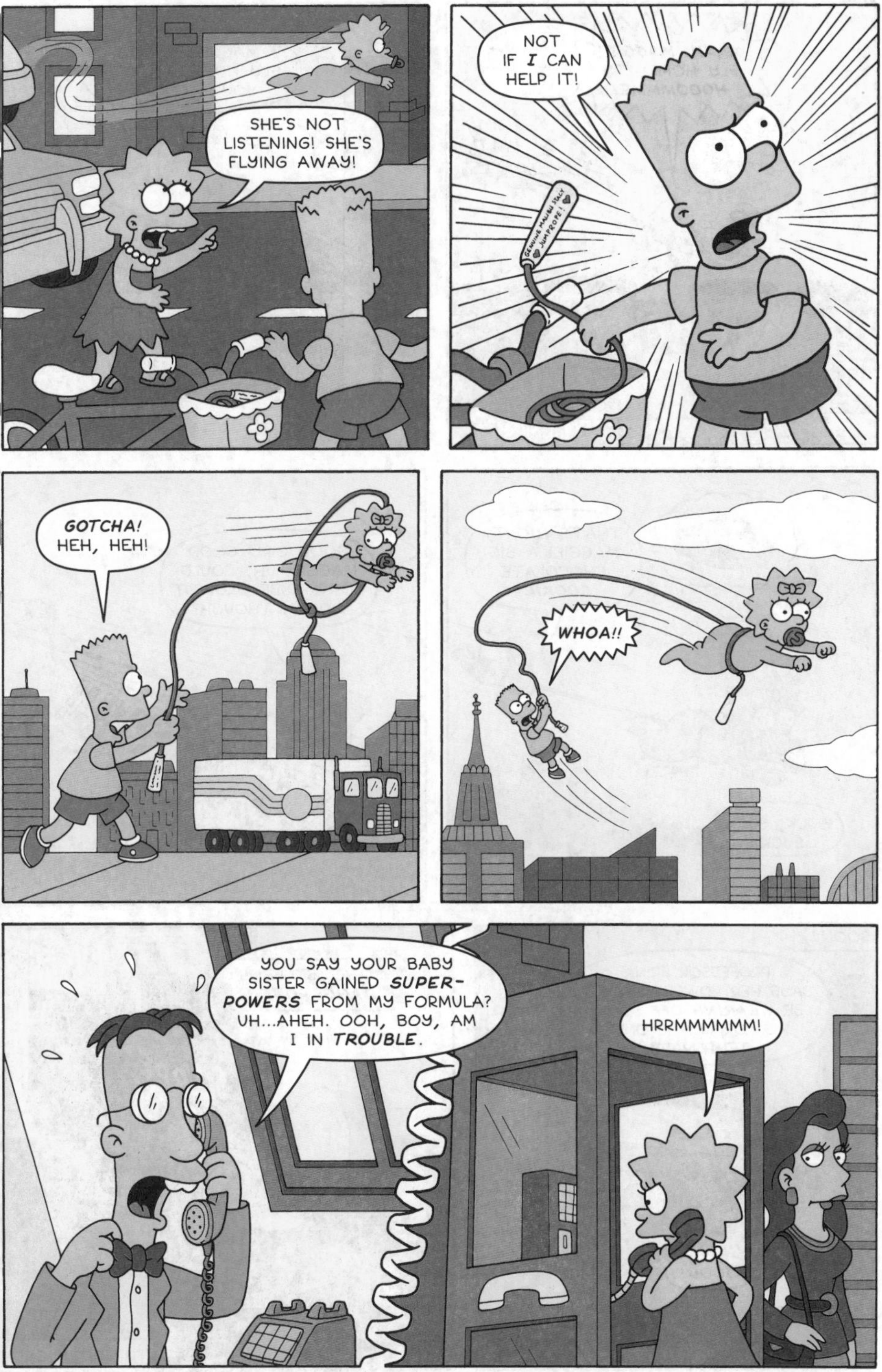
SHE'S NOT LISTENING! SHE'S FLYING AWAY!
NOT IF *I* CAN HELP IT!
GOTCHA! HEH, HEH!
WHOA!!
YOU SAY YOUR BABY SISTER GAINED *SUPER-POWERS* FROM MY FORMULA? UH...AHEH. OOH, BOY, AM I IN *TROUBLE*.
HRRMMMMMM!

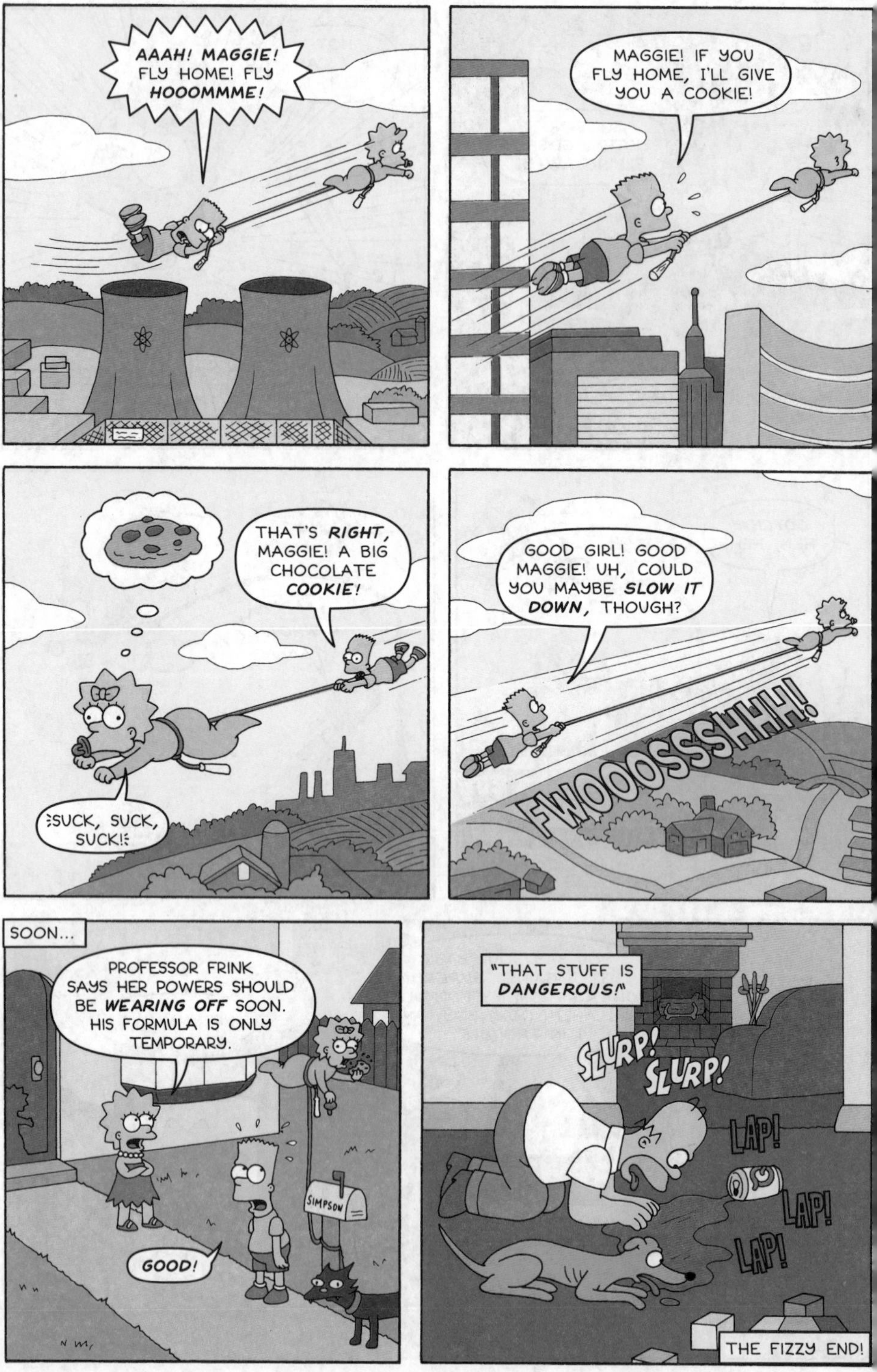
AAAH! MAGGIE! FLY HOME! FLY HOOOMMME!
MAGGIE! IF YOU FLY HOME, I'LL GIVE YOU A COOKIE!
THAT'S RIGHT, MAGGIE! A BIG CHOCOLATE COOKIE!
SUCK, SUCK, SUCK!
GOOD GIRL! GOOD MAGGIE! UH, COULD YOU MAYBE SLOW IT DOWN, THOUGH?
FWOOOSSSHHH!
SOON...
PROFESSOR FRINK SAYS HER POWERS SHOULD BE WEARING OFF SOON. HIS FORMULA IS ONLY TEMPORARY.
SIMPSON
GOOD!
"THAT STUFF IS DANGEROUS!"
SLURP! SLURP!
LAP!
LAP!
LAP!
THE FIZZY END!

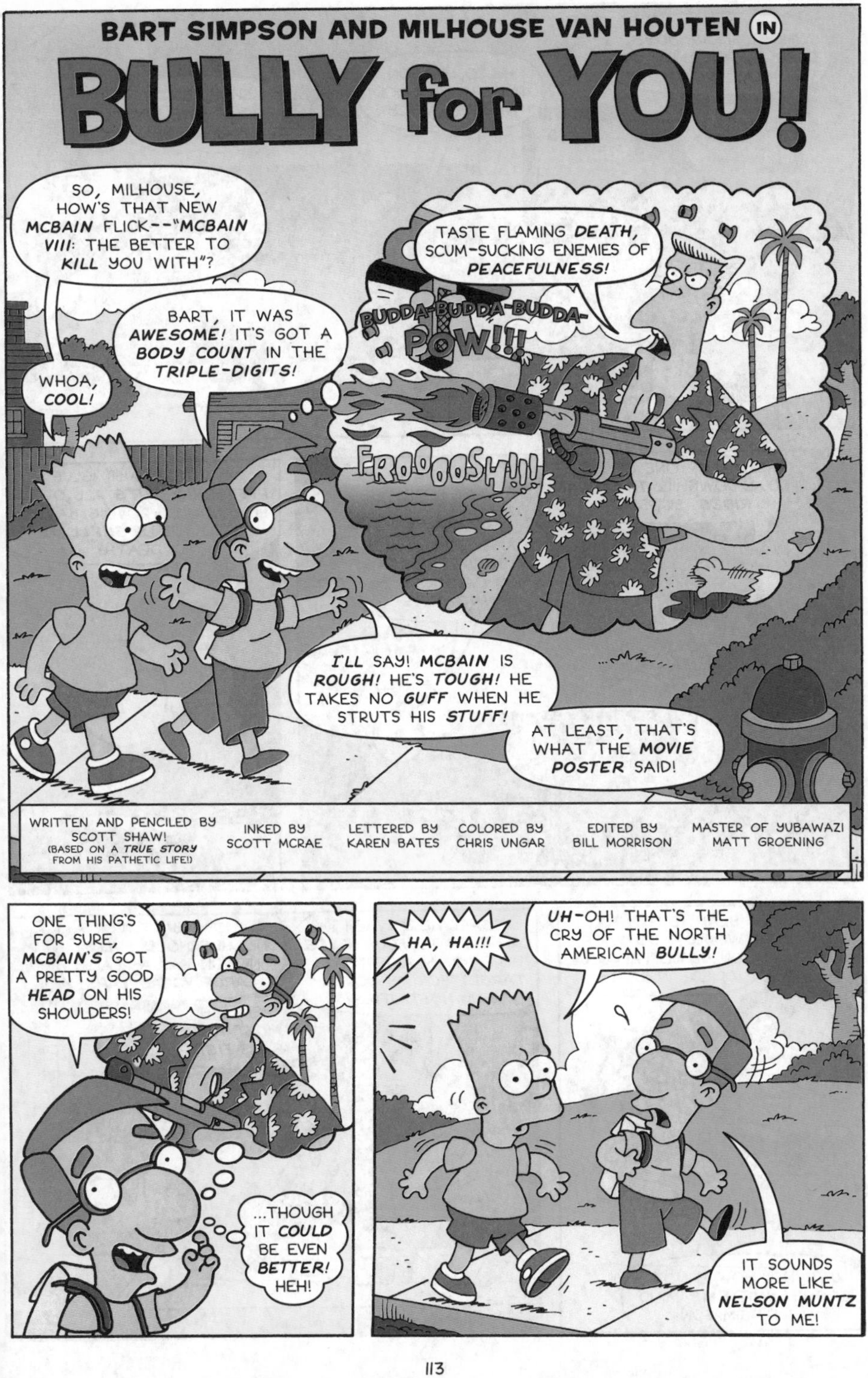
BART SIMPSON AND MILHOUSE VAN HOUTEN IN
BULLY for YOU!
SO, MILHOUSE, HOW'S THAT NEW MCBAIN FLICK--"MCBAIN VIII: THE BETTER TO KILL YOU WITH"?
BART, IT WAS AWESOME! IT'S GOT A BODY COUNT IN THE TRIPLE-DIGITS!
WHOA, COOL!
TASTE FLAMING DEATH, SCUM-SUCKING ENEMIES OF PEACEFULNESS!
BUDDA-BUDDA-BUDDA-
POW!!!
FROOOOOSH!!!
I'LL SAY! MCBAIN IS ROUGH! HE'S TOUGH! HE TAKES NO GUFF WHEN HE STRUTS HIS STUFF!
AT LEAST, THAT'S WHAT THE MOVIE POSTER SAID!
WRITTEN AND PENCILED BY SCOTT SHAW! (BASED ON A TRUE STORY FROM HIS PATHETIC LIFE!)
INKED BY SCOTT MCRAE
LETTERED BY KAREN BATES
COLORED BY CHRIS UNGAR
EDITED BY BILL MORRISON
MASTER OF YUBAWAZI MATT GROENING
ONE THING'S FOR SURE, MCBAIN'S GOT A PRETTY GOOD HEAD ON HIS SHOULDERS!
...THOUGH IT COULD BE EVEN BETTER! HEH!
HA, HA!!!
UH-OH! THAT'S THE CRY OF THE NORTH AMERICAN BULLY!
IT SOUNDS MORE LIKE NELSON MUNTZ TO ME!

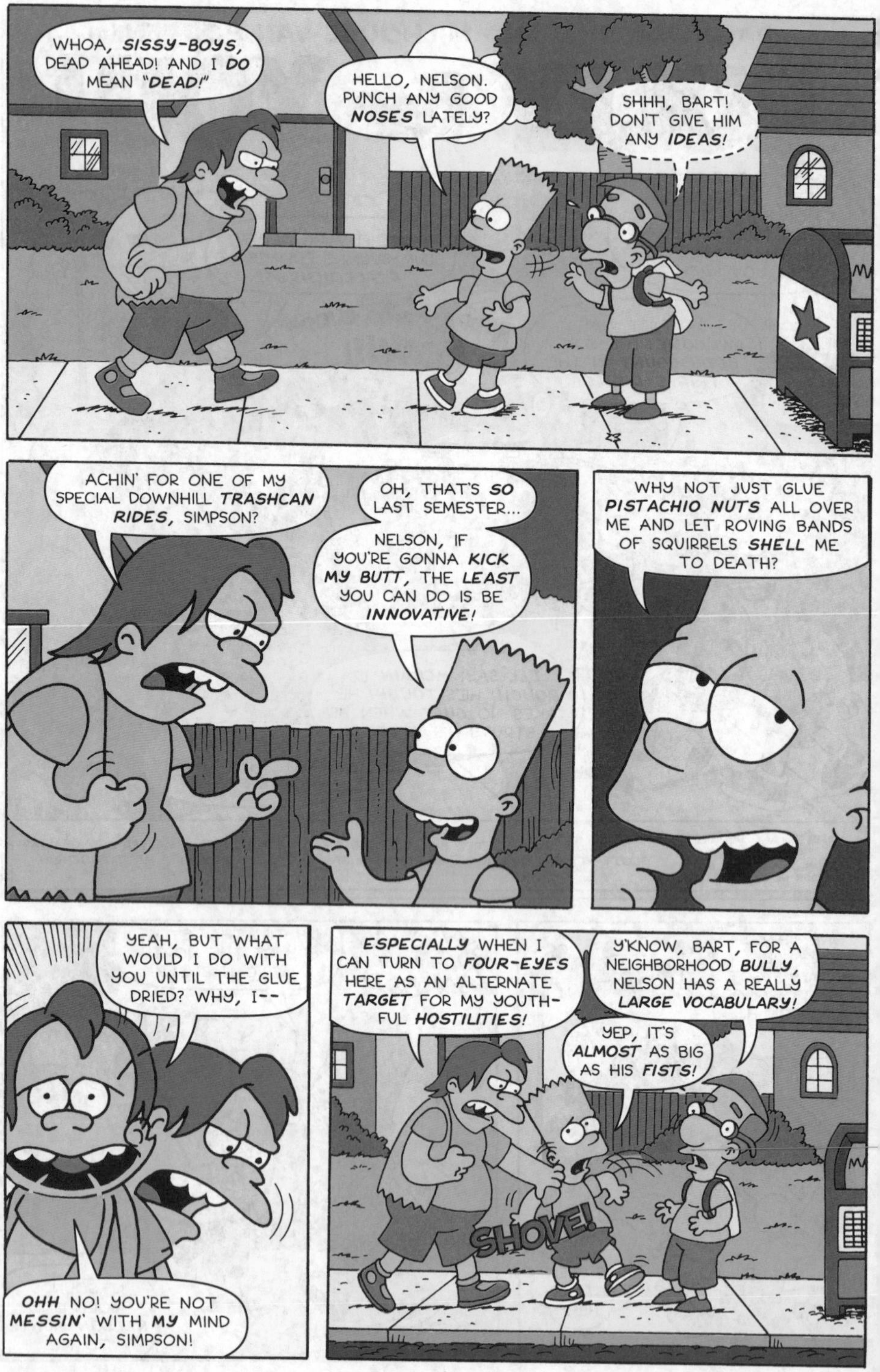
WHOA, SISSY-BOYS, DEAD AHEAD! AND I DO MEAN "DEAD!"
HELLO, NELSON. PUNCH ANY GOOD NOSES LATELY?
SHHH, BART! DON'T GIVE HIM ANY IDEAS!
ACHIN' FOR ONE OF MY SPECIAL DOWNHILL TRASHCAN RIDES, SIMPSON?
OH, THAT'S SO LAST SEMESTER...
NELSON, IF YOU'RE GONNA KICK MY BUTT, THE LEAST YOU CAN DO IS BE INNOVATIVE!
WHY NOT JUST GLUE PISTACHIO NUTS ALL OVER ME AND LET ROVING BANDS OF SQUIRRELS SHELL ME TO DEATH?
YEAH, BUT WHAT WOULD I DO WITH YOU UNTIL THE GLUE DRIED? WHY, I--
OHH NO! YOU'RE NOT MESSIN' WITH MY MIND AGAIN, SIMPSON!
ESPECIALLY WHEN I CAN TURN TO FOUR-EYES HERE AS AN ALTERNATE TARGET FOR MY YOUTHFUL HOSTILITIES!
Y'KNOW, BART, FOR A NEIGHBORHOOD BULLY, NELSON HAS A REALLY LARGE VOCABULARY!
YEP, IT'S ALMOST AS BIG AS HIS FISTS!
SHOVE!

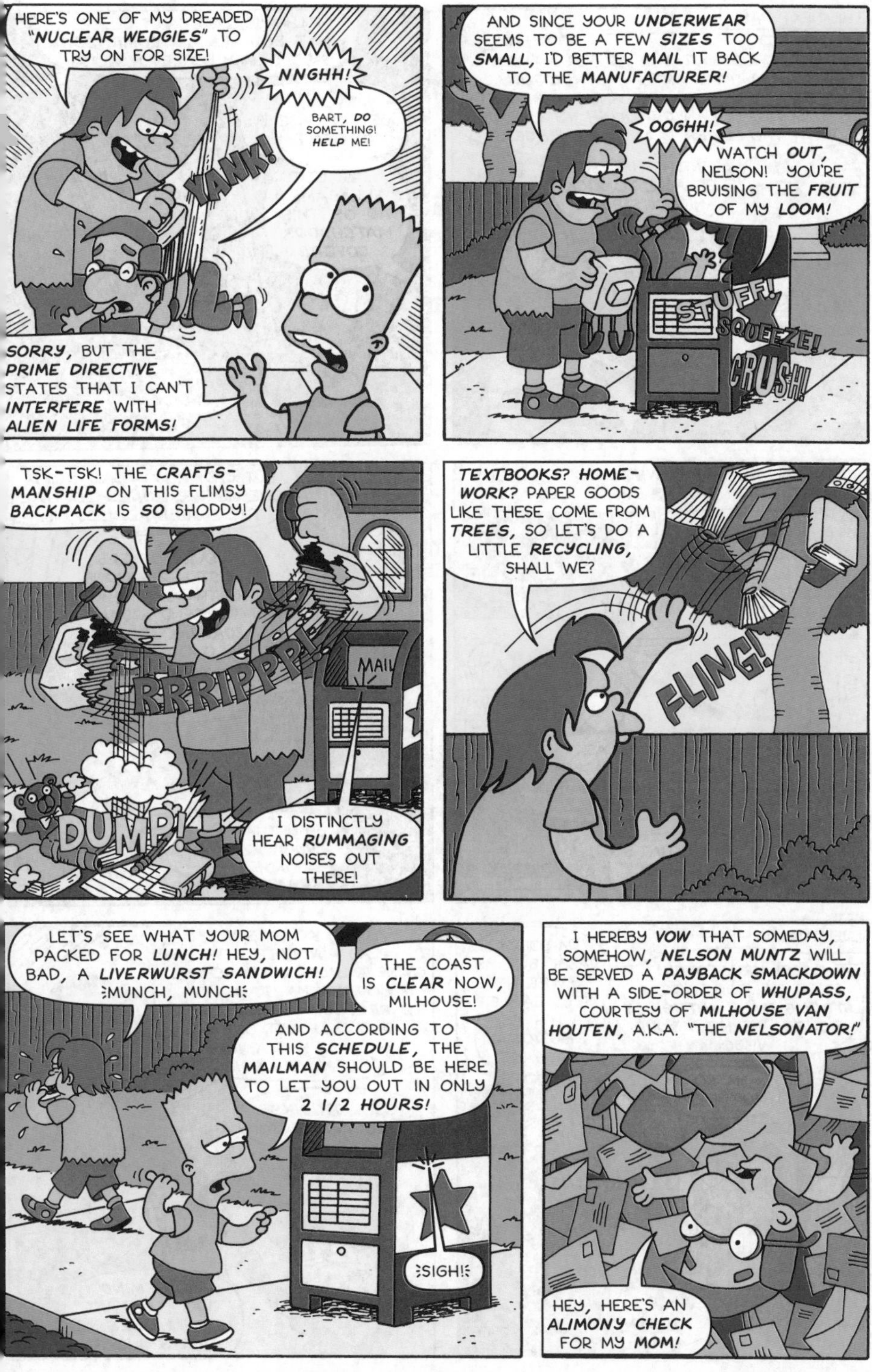
HERE'S ONE OF MY DREADED "NUCLEAR WEDGIES" TO TRY ON FOR SIZE!
NNGHH!
BART, DO SOMETHING! HELP ME!
YANK!
SORRY, BUT THE PRIME DIRECTIVE STATES THAT I CAN'T INTERFERE WITH ALIEN LIFE FORMS!
AND SINCE YOUR UNDERWEAR SEEMS TO BE A FEW SIZES TOO SMALL, I'D BETTER MAIL IT BACK TO THE MANUFACTURER!
OOGHH!
WATCH OUT, NELSON! YOU'RE BRUISING THE FRUIT OF MY LOOM!
STUFF!
SQUEEZE!
CRUSH!
TSK-TSK! THE CRAFTSMANSHIP ON THIS FLIMSY BACKPACK IS SO SHODDY!
RRRIPPPP!
MAIL
DUMP!
I DISTINCTLY HEAR RUMMAGING NOISES OUT THERE!
TEXTBOOKS? HOMEWORK? PAPER GOODS LIKE THESE COME FROM TREES, SO LET'S DO A LITTLE RECYCLING, SHALL WE?
FLING!
LET'S SEE WHAT YOUR MOM PACKED FOR LUNCH! HEY, NOT BAD, A LIVERWURST SANDWICH! MUNCH, MUNCH
THE COAST IS CLEAR NOW, MILHOUSE!
AND ACCORDING TO THIS SCHEDULE, THE MAILMAN SHOULD BE HERE TO LET YOU OUT IN ONLY 2 1/2 HOURS!
SIGH!
I HEREBY VOW THAT SOMEDAY, SOMEHOW, NELSON MUNTZ WILL BE SERVED A PAYBACK SMACKDOWN WITH A SIDE-ORDER OF WHUPASS, COURTESY OF MILHOUSE VAN HOUTEN, A.K.A. "THE NELSONATOR!"
HEY, HERE'S AN ALIMONY CHECK FOR MY MOM!

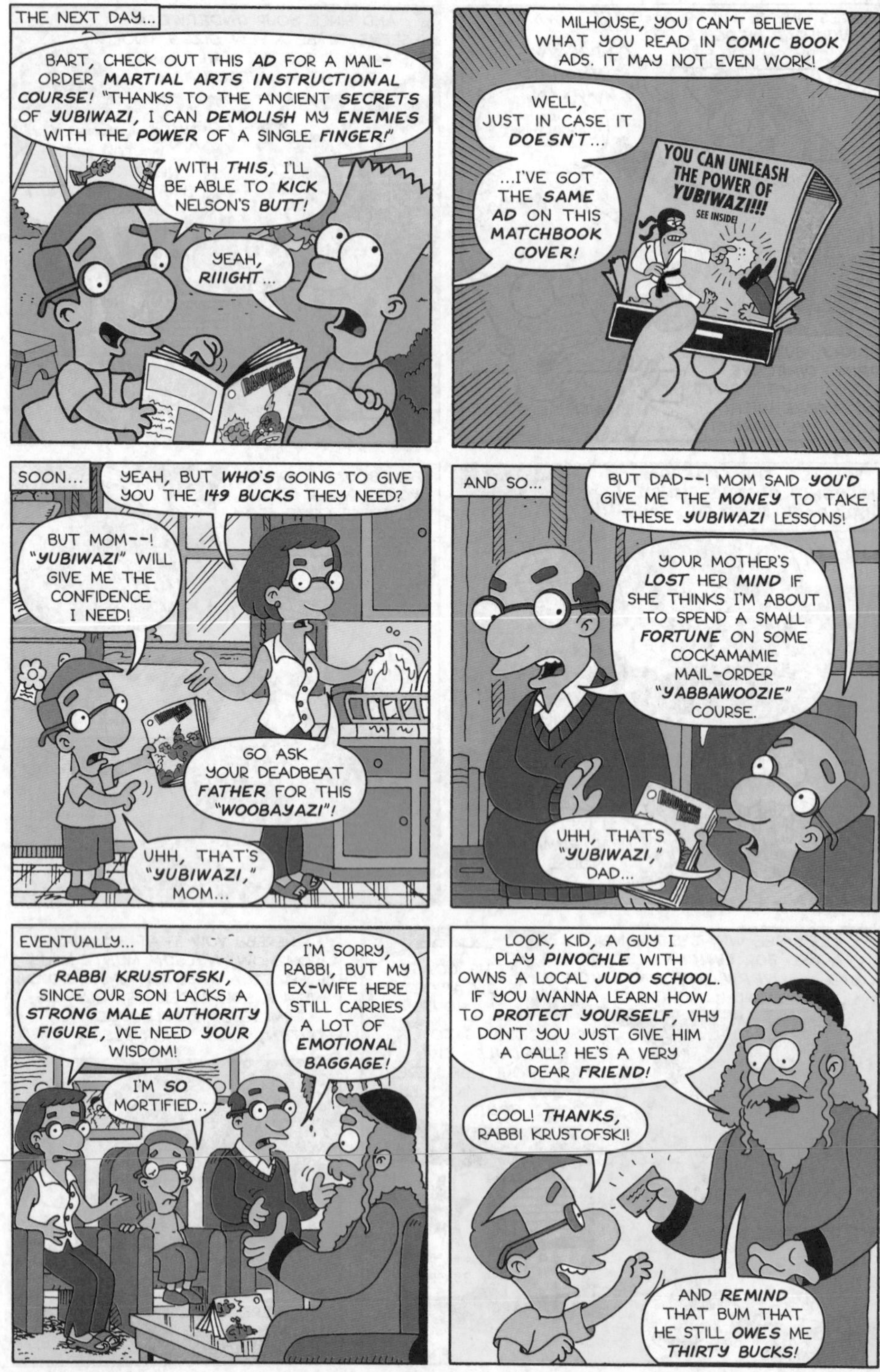
THE NEXT DAY...
BART, CHECK OUT THIS AD FOR A MAIL-ORDER MARTIAL ARTS INSTRUCTIONAL COURSE! "THANKS TO THE ANCIENT SECRETS OF YUBIWAZI, I CAN DEMOLISH MY ENEMIES WITH THE POWER OF A SINGLE FINGER!"
WITH THIS, I'LL BE ABLE TO KICK NELSON'S BUTT!
YEAH, RIIIGHT...
MILHOUSE, YOU CAN'T BELIEVE WHAT YOU READ IN COMIC BOOK ADS. IT MAY NOT EVEN WORK!
WELL, JUST IN CASE IT DOESN'T...
...I'VE GOT THE SAME AD ON THIS MATCHBOOK COVER!
YOU CAN UNLEASH THE POWER OF YUBIWAZI!!!!
SEE INSIDE!
SOON...
YEAH, BUT WHO'S GOING TO GIVE YOU THE 149 BUCKS THEY NEED?
BUT MOM--! "YUBIWAZI" WILL GIVE ME THE CONFIDENCE I NEED!
GO ASK YOUR DEADBEAT FATHER FOR THIS "WOOBAYAZI"!
UHH, THAT'S "YUBIWAZI," MOM...
AND SO...
BUT DAD--! MOM SAID YOU'D GIVE ME THE MONEY TO TAKE THESE YUBIWAZI LESSONS!
YOUR MOTHER'S LOST HER MIND IF SHE THINKS I'M ABOUT TO SPEND A SMALL FORTUNE ON SOME COCKAMAMIE MAIL-ORDER "YABBAWOOZIE" COURSE.
UHH, THAT'S "YUBIWAZI," DAD...
EVENTUALLY...
RABBI KRUSTOFSKI, SINCE OUR SON LACKS A STRONG MALE AUTHORITY FIGURE, WE NEED YOUR WISDOM!
I'M SORRY, RABBI, BUT MY EX-WIFE HERE STILL CARRIES A LOT OF EMOTIONAL BAGGAGE!
I'M SO MORTIFIED..
LOOK, KID, A GUY I PLAY PINOCHLE WITH OWNS A LOCAL JUDO SCHOOL. IF YOU WANNA LEARN HOW TO PROTECT YOURSELF, VHY DON'T YOU JUST GIVE HIM A CALL? HE'S A VERY DEAR FRIEND!
COOL! THANKS, RABBI KRUSTOFSKI!
AND REMIND THAT BUM THAT HE STILL OWES ME THIRTY BUCKS!

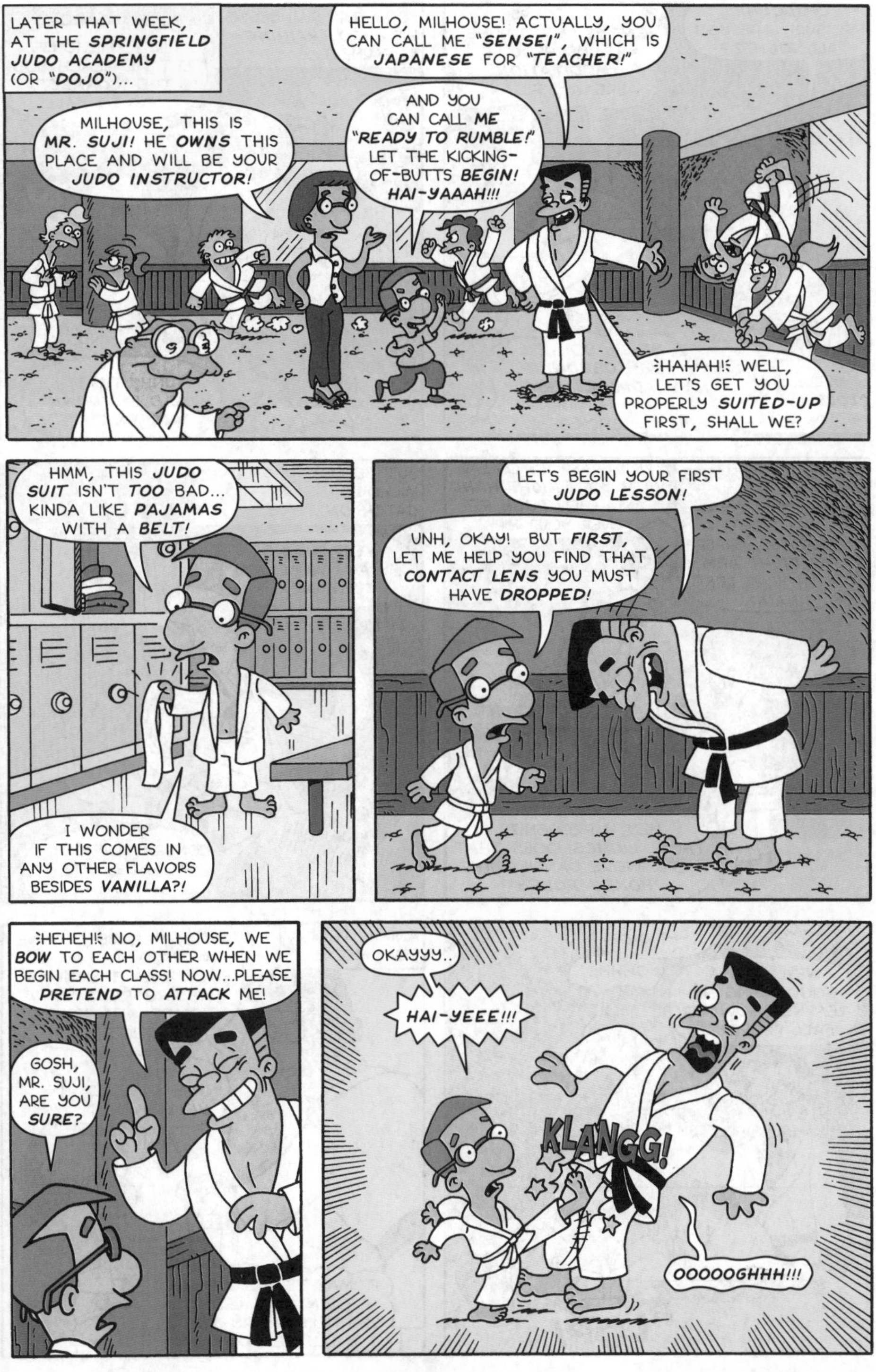
LATER THAT WEEK, AT THE SPRINGFIELD JUDO ACADEMY (OR "DOJO")...
HELLO, MILHOUSE! ACTUALLY, YOU CAN CALL ME "SENSEI", WHICH IS JAPANESE FOR "TEACHER!"
MILHOUSE, THIS IS MR. SUJI! HE OWNS THIS PLACE AND WILL BE YOUR JUDO INSTRUCTOR!
AND YOU CAN CALL ME "READY TO RUMBLE!" LET THE KICKING-OF-BUTTS BEGIN! HAI-YAAAH!!!
HAHAH! WELL, LET'S GET YOU PROPERLY SUITED-UP FIRST, SHALL WE?
HMM, THIS JUDO SUIT ISN'T TOO BAD... KINDA LIKE PAJAMAS WITH A BELT!
I WONDER IF THIS COMES IN ANY OTHER FLAVORS BESIDES VANILLA?!
LET'S BEGIN YOUR FIRST JUDO LESSON!
UNH, OKAY! BUT FIRST, LET ME HELP YOU FIND THAT CONTACT LENS YOU MUST HAVE DROPPED!
HEHEH! NO, MILHOUSE, WE BOW TO EACH OTHER WHEN WE BEGIN EACH CLASS! NOW...PLEASE PRETEND TO ATTACK ME!
GOSH, MR. SUJI, ARE YOU SURE?
OKAYYY..
HAI-YEEE!!!
KLANGG!
OOOOOGHHH!!!

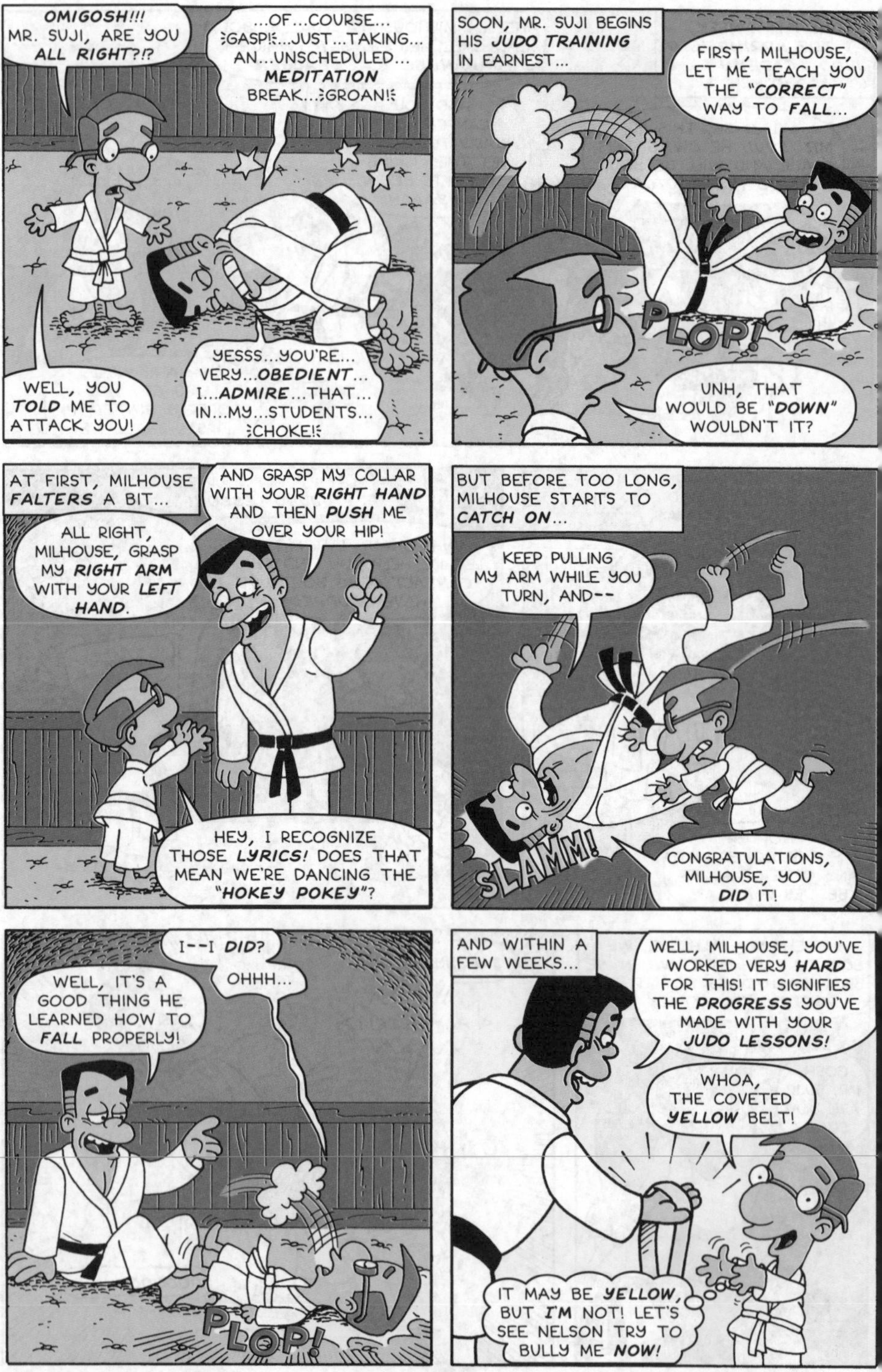
OMIGOSH!!! MR. SUJI, ARE YOU ALL RIGHT?!?
...OF...COURSE... ⁝GASP!⁝...JUST...TAKING... AN...UNSCHEDULED... MEDITATION BREAK...⁝GROAN!⁝
WELL, YOU TOLD ME TO ATTACK YOU!
YESSS...YOU'RE... VERY...OBEDIENT... I...ADMIRE...THAT... IN...MY...STUDENTS... ⁝CHOKE!⁝
SOON, MR. SUJI BEGINS HIS JUDO TRAINING IN EARNEST...
FIRST, MILHOUSE, LET ME TEACH YOU THE "CORRECT" WAY TO FALL...
PLOP!
UNH, THAT WOULD BE "DOWN" WOULDN'T IT?
AT FIRST, MILHOUSE FALTERS A BIT...
ALL RIGHT, MILHOUSE, GRASP MY RIGHT ARM WITH YOUR LEFT HAND.
AND GRASP MY COLLAR WITH YOUR RIGHT HAND AND THEN PUSH ME OVER YOUR HIP!
HEY, I RECOGNIZE THOSE LYRICS! DOES THAT MEAN WE'RE DANCING THE "HOKEY POKEY"?
BUT BEFORE TOO LONG, MILHOUSE STARTS TO CATCH ON...
KEEP PULLING MY ARM WHILE YOU TURN, AND--
SLAMM!
CONGRATULATIONS, MILHOUSE, YOU DID IT!
I--I DID?
OHHH...
WELL, IT'S A GOOD THING HE LEARNED HOW TO FALL PROPERLY!
PLOP!
AND WITHIN A FEW WEEKS...
WELL, MILHOUSE, YOU'VE WORKED VERY HARD FOR THIS! IT SIGNIFIES THE PROGRESS YOU'VE MADE WITH YOUR JUDO LESSONS!
WHOA, THE COVETED YELLOW BELT!
IT MAY BE YELLOW, BUT I'M NOT! LET'S SEE NELSON TRY TO BULLY ME NOW!

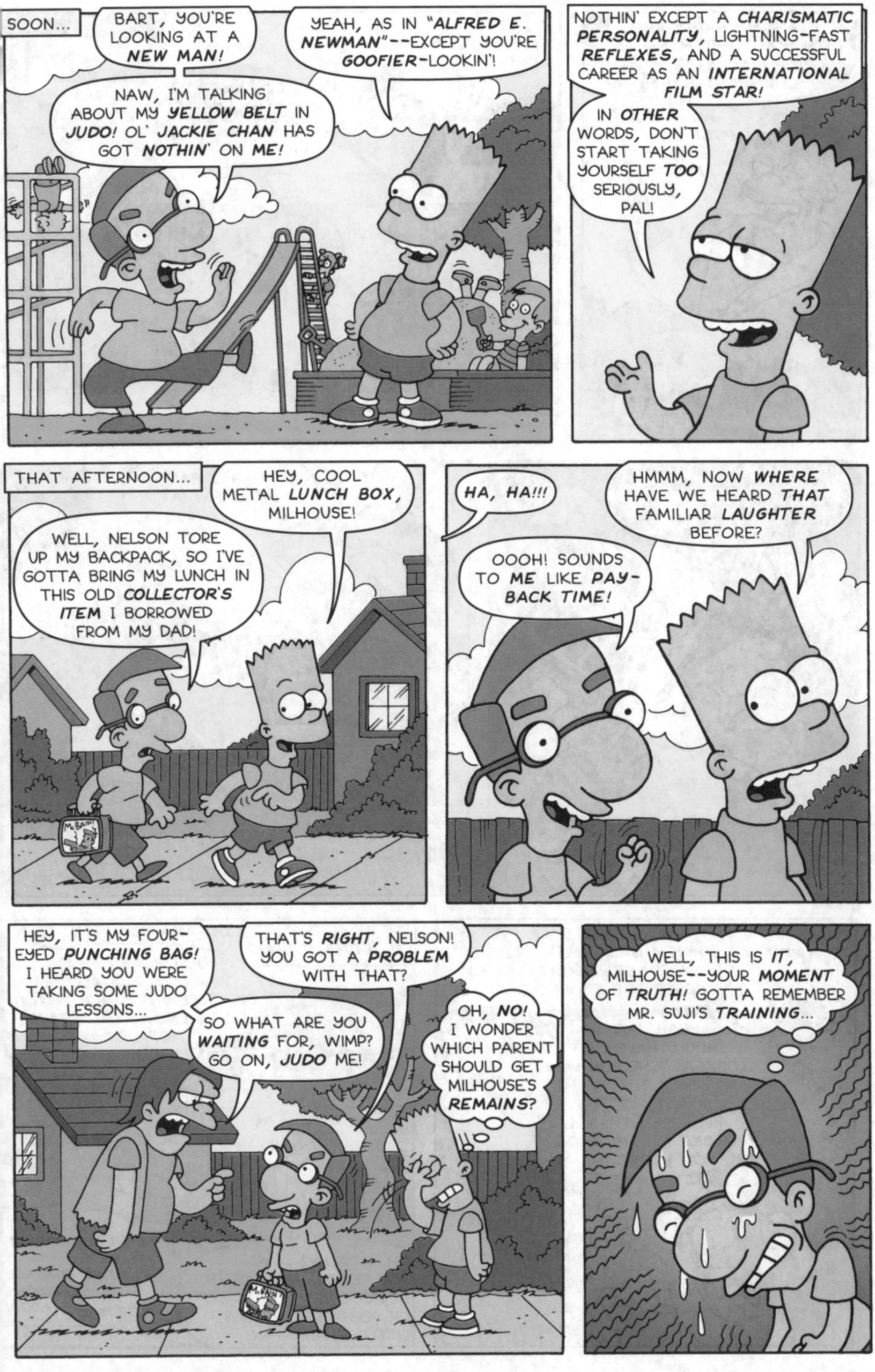
SOON...
BART, YOU'RE LOOKING AT A NEW MAN!
YEAH, AS IN "ALFRED E. NEWMAN"--EXCEPT YOU'RE GOOFIER-LOOKIN'!
NAW, I'M TALKING ABOUT MY YELLOW BELT IN JUDO! OL' JACKIE CHAN HAS GOT NOTHIN' ON ME!
NOTHIN' EXCEPT A CHARISMATIC PERSONALITY, LIGHTNING-FAST REFLEXES, AND A SUCCESSFUL CAREER AS AN INTERNATIONAL FILM STAR!
IN OTHER WORDS, DON'T START TAKING YOURSELF TOO SERIOUSLY, PAL!
THAT AFTERNOON...
HEY, COOL METAL LUNCH BOX, MILHOUSE!
WELL, NELSON TORE UP MY BACKPACK, SO I'VE GOTTA BRING MY LUNCH IN THIS OLD COLLECTOR'S ITEM I BORROWED FROM MY DAD!
HA, HA!!!
HMMM, NOW WHERE HAVE WE HEARD THAT FAMILIAR LAUGHTER BEFORE?
OOOH! SOUNDS TO ME LIKE PAY-BACK TIME!
HEY, IT'S MY FOUR-EYED PUNCHING BAG! I HEARD YOU WERE TAKING SOME JUDO LESSONS...
THAT'S RIGHT, NELSON! YOU GOT A PROBLEM WITH THAT?
SO WHAT ARE YOU WAITING FOR, WIMP? GO ON, JUDO ME!
OH, NO! I WONDER WHICH PARENT SHOULD GET MILHOUSE'S REMAINS?
WELL, THIS IS IT, MILHOUSE--YOUR MOMENT OF TRUTH! GOTTA REMEMBER MR. SUJI'S TRAINING...

GRASP MY *RIGHT ARM* WITH YOUR *LEFT HAND* AND GRASP MY COLLAR WITH YOUR *RIGHT HAND,*

AND THEN *PUSH ME OVER* YOUR *HIP!*

WHAT TH' --?

LET'S HOPE YOU'RE *RIGHT,* MR. SUJI...

GRAB!

KRONK!

McBAIN

YEEOWTCH!!!

HEY, NO *FAIR,* MILHOUSE! WHAT A *BULLY!* ∃WAHHH!∃

GEE, MR. SUJI NEVER *SAID* I SHOULD *PUT DOWN* MY *LUNCH BOX!*

∃WAHHHH!∃

WHOA, I *TAKE BACK* EVERY-THING I *SAID,* MILHOUSE! THAT WAS *UNBELIEVABLE!* NELSON WON'T BOTHER US FOR *DAYS!*

YEAH, BUT I SHOULD HAVE JUST *CLOBBERED* NELSON WITH MY LUNCH BOX IN THE *FIRST* PLACE! BESIDES, I THINK I *BROKE* MY *THERMOS* ON HIS *HEAD!*

SHIKKA-SHIKKA

THE NEXT DAY, AT *COCKAMAMIE'S COLLECTIBLE SHOP...*

YOU *HEARD* ME! I WANT TO BUY *ALL* YER OLD *"McBAIN"* LUNCH BOXES! YOU KNOW, THE *HEAVY, METAL* KIND!

OH, *REALLY*? I HAD YOU PEGGED AS MORE OF A *"POOCHIE"* AFICIONADO-- OR PERHAPS A *"HAPPY LITTLE ELVES"* FAN?

IF I CAN JUST *CORNER* THE *MARKET* ON THESE THINGS, I CAN REGAIN *CONTROL* OF THE *NEIGHBOR-HOOD!*

THE END